KINDRED SPIRITS

JEREMY LEWIS

KINDRED SPIRITS

Adrift in Literary London

faber and faber

This edition first published in 2008
by Faber and Faber Ltd
Bloomsbury House, 74–77 Great Russell Street
London WC1B 3DA

A CIP record for this book is available from the British Library

ISBN 978-0-571-24428-7

Contents

To
Jemima and Hattie Lewis,
dearest of daughters and best of friends

Apologia

A few years ago I published a book called *Playing for Time*, in which I used my time as an undergraduate at Trinity College, Dublin, as a kind of washing-line from which to hang an autobiography that took me up to my mid-twenties, and was all to do with the follies and the ineptitude of youth. Suddenly overcome by the presumptuousness of what I had done, I wrote an apologetic foreword in which I said that the only justification for a nonentity writing an autobiography was that it should entertain, and articulate feelings and states of mind that are common to us all; and that, with luck, it should be easier for an unknown to avoid the pomposity, the discretion and the blandness that blight the memoirs of most public figures once they put childhood behind them. For a nonentity to produce a sequel may well seem a case of pushing his luck too far, not least because trying to write about the follies of middle age while still in mid-stream is a rather more hazardous affair than deriding those of one's youth: if I have failed to pull it off, I can only apologise once more, and reassure readers eager to learn no more that, since this second book brings my story up to date, I should be well into my eighties before I get round to Volume Three.

Like travel-writing in the 1960s and early 1970s, autobiography is, in critical terms at least, an unfairly neglected art, and one at which the English excel. Those that I particularly relish – James Lees-Milne's *Another Self*, John Gale's *Clean Young Englishman*, Julian Maclaren-Ross's *Memoirs of the Forties*, Michael Wharton's *The Missing Will* and *The Dubious Codicil*, P. Y. Betts's *People Who Say Goodbye* – tend to assume a self-deprecating tone, and combine comicality with an underlying melancholy, vigorous anecdotes with a corrosive sense of the sad absurdity of things: to them at least – if not to the other heroes of my book – I offer the double-edged compliment of pallid emulation.

I would like to thank the following for their help and encouragement: Mike Fishwick of HarperCollins, the most patient, enthusiastic and long-suffering of editors; Robert Lacey of HarperCollins, who more than justified his reputation as an unusually sympathetic and meticulous editor; my agent, Gillon Aitken, whose suggested titles for the book – *The Fishwick Papers* and *The Callil Palimpsest* – were reluctantly overruled; James Douglas Henry and Carol Smith, both of whom read the typescript at various stages and urged me on in the face of authorial despondency; my wife, Petra, who read it in proof and proved, as always, the shrewdest and most severe of critics; and Alan Ross, who first published various pieces from the book in the *London Magazine*, and kindly asked to see more. 'Maria Pasqua' and a shortened version of the section on Mr Chaudhuri first appeared in *The Oldie*, and the *envoi* in *The Tablet*. Extracts from *The Letters of Evelyn Waugh*, edited by Mark Amory, are reprinted by kind permission of Weidenfeld & Nicolson Ltd and Peters, Fraser & Dunlop Ltd.

JML

Dreaming of Arcadia

ONE DAY is much like another for the desk-bound office worker: life ebbs away, almost imperceptibly, in a blur of meetings and memos and gossip, of coffee-drinking and conferences and sticky summer afternoons when a post-prandial slumber becomes almost *de rigueur,* and our passage from our thirties into our forties and beyond is accompanied, and given definition, by the complicated movement of pieces of paper from one place to another. For a quarter of a century I worked in the most congenial and convivial of trades, constantly bemoaning my lot and a salary which – not unreasonably, I now feel – kept pace with that of the average prep-school master, yet relishing the company of the raffish, the literate and the indiscreet; and the last ten years I spent with a small but well-regarded firm, which has since been absorbed into an American conglomerate and transplanted to a modern office block, all open-plan and winking VDUs, but was, when I went there in the late 1970s, the epitome of an old-fashioned literary publisher. Our offices were off the bottom of St Martin's Lane, immediately opposite the Post Office: the floors were covered with blue lino, the telephones were Bakelite and the furniture Utility, the rattle of elderly upright typewriters was punctuated, from time to time, by terrible howls from the opera house next door, where sopranos were practising their scales, and the place was staffed by loyal, long-serving spinsters in cardigans and sandals, and – for much of the firm's history at least – amiable and highly civilised men with large private incomes, who considered publishing a better field than most in which to display their talents.

Towards the end of our time in those old offices – before we moved, briefly, into the late-eighteenth-century grandeur of a house in Bedford Square – I occupied a grey-painted, wood-panelled office in the front of the building, high up on the third floor; and from its windows, on somnolent afternoons, I would gaze down into the street below, with its cargo of grimy, leather-clad motorbike messengers and lunatic, red-faced men waving bottles and roaring abuse at hurrying passers-by, or into the windows of the office opposite, where men in their shirt-sleeves and neatly-turned-out girls in black pencil skirts were hard at work opening or closing filing cabinets, or standing about in little groups, or drinking coffee out of polystyrene cups, or gazing absently back in my direction until, suddenly aware of being watched, they hurried importantly away. In between gazing and snoozing, gossiping and counting the hours until it was time to sneak out to the pub for lunch or (better still) to plod back home again, I would busy myself, pleasantly enough, with the various routines of a publishing editor's day – correcting proofs, editing a typescript, writing a blurb, puzzling over the small print in a contract, trying to make sense of an estimate or a computer print-out of sales, soothing an author's ruffled spirits, or indolently reading – while in the background I could hear, like a bagpipe's never-ending drone, the familiar sounds of an office in which, as is so often the case, literacy and liberal views were combined with an autocratic and temperamental style of government: blood-curdling, imperious cries of rage, the slamming of doors, the sob of a retiring underling.

My own attitude towards office life in general, and publishing in particular, was an uneasy, and ignoble, mixture of timidity and detachment: I resented its demands and derided its absurdities and its sporadic self-importance, yet I was never brave enough, or convinced enough, to say what I really thought, to strike a blow for revolution rather than mutter subversion in the wings. I got on well with my authors, especially the more bibulous among them, and did good work for them, as an editor if not as a promoter of their wares; I understood, and knew much about, the complicated workings of a trade that combines, in its ideal state, the intimations of art with the exactitude of commerce; I seemed reasonably popular with my colleagues and, more than most, I relished the parties and the gossip and the indiscretions endemic to that most incestuous of trades: and yet I remained, throughout my career, an observer rather than a participant, unwilling or unable to take the whole business – or, indeed, myself – as seriously as I should, and far too diffident or fearful of rebuff to elbow my way to the front. Years earlier I had, as a large, clumsy and heavily bespectacled schoolboy, rationalised my fear of the physical and my hatred of the team spirit by adopting towards organised games an attitude of derisive superiority and refusing to join in, while at the same time feeling genuinely puzzled by the way in which those set in authority above me – loudly-shouting housemasters in scarves and duffle-coats, or solemn, serious-minded prefects – could work themselves into frenzies of excitement over matters so self-evidently futile as hoofing a lump of leather from one end of a field to the other or thwacking smaller lumps of leather with a stick; and this same combination of the fearful and the over-rational – first implanted, perhaps, by Spam-coloured legs in a scrum, the owners of which were grunting and farting about me and twisting the ears off my head for no very worthwhile reason, or the withering cries of 'For God's sake, Lewis' as I trailed unhappily back to the pavilion, last man in, bowled out for nought – permeated and blighted my life as a working man. I flung myself into the social life of the office, outlasting all but the hardiest at publishing parties and stealing back late in the afternoon from yet another extended lunch, to be greeted by a palimpsest of yellow stickers on my typewriter informing me that the boss had been looking for me since 2.15, and where had I been all this time; I did my work as well as I could, and often enjoyed what I did; and yet I remained on the touchline, refusing responsibility and for ever holding back – in much the same way as, thirty years before, banished from the rugger field on grounds of unpardonable incompetence, I had shivered among the spectators, none of whom reached above my shoulder, my melancholy bass booming unhappily among their excited trebles as the game surged to and fro before us. My heart bled for the sobbing underling or the baffled new arrival, not simply from sympathy for the underdog, though that had its part to play, but because – despite thinning locks and failing sight and an Audenesque network of wrinkles and an uneasy tightening of the trousers and even a place on the board, for what it was worth – I continued to think of myself as a servant rather than a master, as someone who had to be told what to do and, while grumbling with the rest at the folly or the harshness of what 'they' had decreed, was more than happy to leave it that way. Like a grizzled schoolboy, I longed for the boss to go on holiday, or for the firm to be laid low by one of those bouts of 'flu or diarrhoea that sporadically sweep through such places; had I arrived at work one day to discover that the office had burned down in the night, my immediate reactions would have been of jubilation and relief.

Institutional life of any kind, like the games I so dreaded at school, depends on the suspension of belief: we learn to feign – and yet not entirely feign, for our livelihood depends upon it – excitement and delight and rage and indignation and despair, if for a moment only; our features harden and grow strained as we approach the office in the morning and soften and relax as we leave it in the evening, and once installed behind our desks we persuade ourselves, and others, that the weekly sales figures or a particular point in a contract or the urgency of publishing a novel which no one will remember in five years' time or persistent incompetence on the part of an amiable but scatterbrained member of staff are matters of supreme and over-riding importance (as indeed they are). Here too I let my colleagues down, finding it hard to suppress or conceal the views of civilian life. Lacking, to an alarming degree, any trace of the killer instinct or the competitive urge, I found it hard to work up the necessary, if transient, emotions of fury or aggression when faced with the activities of a rival or a predator. I fidgeted through meetings, yawning and glancing at my watch; I was competent at the minutiae of the trade, at estimates and contracts and knocking a book into shape, but proved a poor dissembler, unable – as the best publishers always can – to see all our geese as swans, and to persuade others to think the same. I took refuge in a kind of cynical buffoonery, a world-weary raising of eyebrows at the folly of mankind; and, whenever I could, I sought oblivion in those jovial, interminable lunches with friends whose company I relished and whose views seemed to match my own. Nor was my behaviour at home any more creditable or mature. I had married, in my mid-twenties, a girl who had been at university with me, with the eyes of a Tartar horseman, hair like a badger, and a face and a nature too kind, too trusting and too dear for the world in which we find ourselves; we had two loud and dashing daughters, both of them eloquent, stylish and funny, and both encouraged by me in incurable frivolity; we lived, happily enough, in a small, half-decorated suburban house near Richmond Park (I found it hard to admit to East Sheen), crammed with books and pictures and cats and pieces of paper, with a long, overgrown garden like a hazy cavern of green, and a white wooden verandah on which, on summer evenings, we would sit and drink and talk to our friends while the days and the years and the months stole, almost unnoticed, away. All this made for a congenial if impecunious life, in which far too little thought was given – certainly by me – to such grave matters as pension schemes and insurance policies and the provision for rainy days: at home, as in the office, I shied away from the graver realities of life, leaving Petra to grapple with the bills and juggle our finances and worry about how and whether we would ever be able to afford a new car, while I salved my conscience by tackling a mound of ironing – a job I anyway enjoyed – or, equally agreeably, peeling the vegetables for that evening's supper (deciding what we should eat, and doing the necessary shopping, were not on my agenda: Petra was expected to combine these with a full-time job). To my shame I had – still have – more than a touch of the Harold Skimpole about me. I somehow assumed, on slender evidence, that my refusal to accept responsibility or to deal with the more tedious aspects of life was an endearing attribute of the impractical literary man, whose thoughts were hovering on a higher plane (the fact that my own literary activities were more in my head than on paper seemed neither here nor there); I revelled in infantilism, making much of a belief, assiduously promoted, that all the most interesting and entertaining men I knew were, in their various ways, irremediably childish, and that it

8   *Kindred Spirits*

was this that set them apart from those grey, responsible, prematurely aged figures – keen games-players to a man, no doubt, and avid upholders of team spirit – who assumed their duties with ponderous gravity, wore their middle age like a shroud, and spent more time than I felt quite decent discussing their retirement plans, with special reference to the proximity of golf clubs. And since I remained, for all my haggard looks and creaking joints, incurably infantile when it came to such matters as farts or lavatories or performing tribal dances, clad in nothing save my socks, while the rest of the family was trying to watch television ('Oh Dad, do be *quiet!*'), my refusal to confront or to do battle with the demands and the responsibilities of life threatened to become a full-scale retreat. And although, on good days, I thought myself luckier than many, and liked to affect a lofty condescension to friends who had abandoned the ideals and the enthusiasms of youth for safe, dark-suited jobs and explained, with an embarrassed, apologetic laugh, that they hadn't much time for reading nowadays apart from the occasional Wilbur Smith on the flight to Australia or Robert Ludlum beside the pool in Barbados – since authors like these seemed far harder to read than Dickens or Trollope there may have been more to this than met the eye – I spent much more time than I might have wished being undermined by feelings of terrible inadequacy. I felt inadequate because I knew I earned several thousand pounds a year less than my dark-suited friends' twenty-five-year-old personal assistants, and because I longed to go to Australia and knew I never would, and because I could take my family (or, more accurately, be taken by them) no nearer the Caribbean than Cornwall or the Isle of Wight; I felt inadequate when I went to dinner parties in North London and the conversation eddied and surged above my head and I remembered, all too well, why, thirty years earlier, I had been shown the door by a distressingly large number of Oxford and Cambridge tutors for admissions; I felt inadequate (and irresponsible, too) when men in ribbed jerseys and the up-to-date equivalents of cavalry-twill trousers banged their pipes against the grate and, puffing ruminatively, discussed those ever more imminent pension schemes and retirement plans; I felt inadequate when

my daughters' friends went trekking in Peru or paid homage in
Tibetan monasteries or lent a hand in the Philippines, and I tried
(in vain) to endow my own timid forays as an undergraduate with
retrospective dash and glamour; I felt inadequate when I caught
sight of myself in a mirror, or climbed behind the steering-wheel of
our car with other people on board, or took to the dance floor, or
was expected to kick a football back into play while strolling in the
park; and I felt quintessentially inadequate when, early one
summer, we set out for Holland from the Pool of London on board
a bottle-green converted trawler, and Petra's cousin – the mildest
and most unalarming of sea-dogs – asked me to take the helm as we
threaded our way down the Thames and headed for the open sea.
He needed to go below, he said, to study some charts and plot our
course: would I be a good chap, and remember to keep to the right
(or was it the left? One of the two, for sure, but – instantly panic-
stricken – I had no idea which as we headed straight towards a tug
dragging behind it primrose-painted barges crammed with industrial waste). Within minutes I had succeeded in palming the job off
on our skipper's self-assured son of thirteen, and hurried importantly below, where I felt more inadequate than ever as grave,
manly figures clustered about the charts and compasses and took
readings of various kinds and traded valuable information about
positions and destinations over the intercom with a crackling voice
on the shore. How I envied and admired my fellow-crew members
as they sprang nimbly about the deck, and tossed ropes to grinning
Dutchmen on the quay, and decided, with no evidence of dithering, where and how we should park for the night, while I tried to
look both keen and unobtrusive, one finger carefully keeping the
place in my book. How eagerly I leapt ashore, and how briskly I led
the way once on dry land, as if anxious to redeem my inadequacies
on board.

Seemingly impervious to more mundane concerns, staggering
somehow from one day to the next, middle-aged men with a touch
of the Peter Pan about them may seem, on a good day, enviably free
spirits; and hiding one's head in the sand and hovering in the wings
are both compatible with a degree of happiness. We had less money

than most of the people we knew, but consoled ourselves with familiar aphorisms about its tenuous relationship to true happiness; we loved one another's company, and enjoyed doing much the same things; we spent our holidays sheltering from the rain in Cornwall or on the Isle of Wight, but told ourselves that, in an age of mass travel, when men with lager-bellies could be spotted in Thailand and clerks in ventless gangsters' suits could be overheard in the pub in the lunch-hour discussing holidays in Barbados or the Seychelles, it was probably just as well to stay at home; our house was untidy and decrepit and half-done, but was generally thought to be 'cosy' and 'homely' and 'full of character'; we delighted in the company of our friends, and continued to add to their numbers; like a spoilt child, I grumbled incessantly about my job and the horrors of having to go to work, yet I was far luckier than many in that what I did was, for all its disadvantages, an extension of the interests I had always had, while the company I kept – authors, agents, journalists, fellow-publishers – were usually kindred spirits. And yet, as I hurried all too quickly from my early- to my mid-forties, my vision of the world switched, alarmingly, from colour to black and white. I became even more restless and uncommitted at work, yawning unashamedly at meetings and pausing more frequently than ever to rinse out my mouth and splash water on my face as I stealthily padded upstairs after another three- or four-hour lunch, taking care to avoid the censorious gaze of Perrier-drinkers half my age who had spent the lunch hour behind their desks with a sandwich, their gaze firmly fixed on their VDUs; and my feelings of general dissatisfaction began to wash over into domestic life as well. In my thirties I had been a zealous advocate of domesticity in general, and of suburban life in particular, defending both keenly against the derision of snobs and socialists alike, and pining for the company of clerks and commuters when temporarily transplanted from the serried anonymity of south-west London to the high-minded smugness of North Oxford; yet now I found myself distressingly intolerant of gardens and cats and tins of emulsion and men hurrying for trains and the cluck of domestic chat. I longed to trade in the soporific whirr of the lawnmower for the disco at the office party, suburban leg-room for a broom-cupboard in South Ken, the familiar existence of a middle-aged family man for a bleary resurrection of undergraduate life or a belated stab at the *vie de Bohème*. My attempts at Bohemian life were tentative and inconsistent: I would happily reel home in the small hours after some publishing carousal – my dinner a cinder, my family fearing the worst – but grumbled terribly behind the scenes if my daughters brought friends home or stayed out after eleven, harried my family to bed as soon as the nine o'clock news was over, and spent a good deal of time and energy switching off television sets in mid-show, turning down the music, worrying about keeping the neighbours awake and generally behaving like an old-fashioned domestic tyrant with not a drop of Bohemian blood in his veins.

All this, of course, is familiar to the point of banality: the sad, ignoble sight of middle age pretending to be other than it is, trying to reanimate or cling to the pallid tatters of youth; the terrible awareness that time is running out, that the future is finite, and that every day takes one further from that bright, luminous threshold on which everything seemed possible and time would have no end. Like the rest of us, I liked to think that, somehow, I was different, that I could be immune to the passing of time as well as to the rude intrusions of the real world; and yet with every day that passed I became more uneasily aware that, in the eyes of the young at least, I seemed elderly and dull and slow and out-of-touch, and that retaining one's hair and one's waistline and even one's *joie de vivre* to a more enviable degree than some was merely to postpone or disguise the moment of truth.

On those days when I wasn't having my regular Tuesday lunch in the Marquis of Granby with Dennis Enright and Les the office packer, or straying further afield with one of those whose company I particularly relished – Alan Ross or Richard West or Carol Smith or Digby Durrant or Hilary Laurie or Howard and Ros Jacobson or a short, waxen-featured girl in a purple hat, whose sullen pout and black eyes and boundless appetite for draught Guinness made me feel, for no good reason, that I was a doggy kind of fellow, reliving the days of my youth – I would, from time to time, wander over the road to the National Gallery to look at the paintings by Claude Lorrain. Claude's classical scenes, with their half-naked figures gravely dancing or idling in the foreground, their lush and somnolent vegetation, their crags and armies and ruined castles, their boats bobbing in the bay beyond, and their snow-capped mountains running along the horizon, were paintings of a kind that, thirty years earlier, I would have hurried impatiently by; but now I found infinitely tantalising their intimations of Arcadia, of a timeless, untroubled world in which the young never grew any older, but woke every morning under a cloudless sky of early summer, luminous with promise and expectation, and devoted tranquil, velvet evenings to feasting and drinking and talking on the grass. When, at weekends, I strode across Richmond Park, with its lakes and vistas and carefully positioned woods and trees, I found myself in a Claudian landscape of my own, an Arcadia in the suburbs; I loved it with a passion, but my restlessness remained.

Although I had never learned a word of Greek, and remembered barely enough of my Latin to unravel the inscription on a tombstone, Claude's evocations of Arcadia sent me in spirit at least to the Mediterranean world and, in particular, to Greece, where a quarter of a century before I had plodded in ox-like adoration behind ffenella, bowed down by the weight of our rucksacks, the sweat plastering my shirt to my chest and my specs forever sliding down my nose; and to those authors who celebrated the convivial pleasures of friendship and company, of eating and drinking under skies of a different hue to that which I glimpsed, from time to time, from my window in William IV Street. Nearly thirty years before, as a trainee messenger boy, I had escaped from the dim reality of life in an advertising agency into the lurid yet womb-like world of Dickens; now I sought refuge in the sad nostalgia of Cyril Connolly's *The Unquiet Grave,* in Lawrence Durrell's accounts of raffish, carefree life on Rhodes and Corfu, in Kevin Andrews and Dilys Powell and Gerald Durrell and, above all, in the magical prose of Patrick Leigh Fermor. In both his life and his writing Leigh Fermor seemed the romantic figure of our age, and one who could well have been among the more adventurous and articulate inhabitants of Arcadia. His two-year tramp, when little more than a schoolboy, from Rotterdam to Constantinople, trudging through snowbound Nazi Germany, carousing in nightclubs in Budapest, spinning out long, indolent summer days in Austro-Hungarian palaces or Transylvanian castles; his wartime exploits in German-occupied Crete, culminating in the kidnapping of General Kriepe; the legendary house he had built in the Mani, with its Claude-like setting of sea and rocks and cypress trees and greenery; his Byzantine evocations of climbing Mount Taygetus or sleeping out in a Maniot tower: all these were heady enough, but made headier still by the passionate precision and convoluted grace of his writing. In an age of utilitarian prose, when the subordinate clause was viewed askance and the colon had almost been pensioned off, his strong, rolling sentences, like those of Hugh Trevor-Roper, Isaiah Berlin and Nirad Chaudhuri, harked back to the bolder, more expansive style of Thackeray and Stevenson. But what I loved most was the way in which he evoked, not least in his account of his pre-war hike across Europe, written when he was in his sixties and seventies, exactly how it felt to be young and hopeful and exuberant, when everything lay in the future and the skies of summer seemed (if only in retrospect) as bright and as blue as those that Claude had painted in Tivoli or on the Neapolitan coast; and, on mornings when I had missed my train to Waterloo and had time to kill before the next, I would escape into pre-war Romania or the bear-haunted Carpathians, feeling, in some curious way, as though I were re-living my own timid and unadventurous youth in the pages of my hero.

Slumped and somnolent behind my desk after an interlude with Claude, I would sometimes look up and find a red-faced, blue-eyed satyr leaning against the side of the door, watching me with the kind of intensity normally reserved for a specimen on a microscopic plate or a subject under surveillance. Charles Sprawson was one of my closest friends from university; as the freest of free spirits, who had sampled and rejected the perils of office life in favour of that of a freelance picture-dealer, he liked nothing better, when in London, than to insinuate himself unannounced into offices in which his friends were working, pad silently up to their lairs and watch them for as long as he could while they yawned or picked their noses or made compromising phone calls or bustled about their business or merely gazed vacantly out of the window, waiting for the day to end. Spotting this grinning voyeur in one's doorway was a disconcerting business, but – as far as I was concerned, though others disagreed – a very welcome one. Irrespective of the weather or the occasion, he would be dressed in an open-necked shirt, a dark-blue sleeveless pullover, thick-ribbed corduroy trousers and gym shoes. An avid attender of literary parties, whether invited or not, he refused to adapt his clothing for even the grandest occasion. Early on in his career as a literary party-goer I told him – as a deliberate act of provocation – that I was going to what would almost certainly be a rather formal party given by John Murray for Patrick Leigh Fermor in their gold and white eighteenth-century offices in Albemarle Street, replete with mementoes of Byron and Roman-looking busts with laurel wreaths about their brows; I knew at once, from a slight twisting of the lip and a ripple that ran across his face, that he would be there. No sooner had I sighted him on the far side of the room, deep in conversation with an elderly lady, than a corduroy-swathed arm shot out and took me by the wrist. 'Tell me, dear boy,' said Jock Murray, clad in his familiar uniform of bow tie and scarlet braces, his rubbery, comical features lit up with avuncular interest, his eyebrows an interrogative arch: 'Who is that most distinguished-looking man who has just come in? Can it possibly be — ?' – here he mentioned the editor of a literary magazine which specialised in publishing extracts from forthcoming books by well-known authors. Although, years later, he went on to write a book about swimming which became something of a cult both here and in the States, Charles's literary output was, as yet, restricted to a piece about von Cramm, the pre-war German tennis player, which Alan Ross and I had persuaded him to write for the *London Magazine,* but – suddenly dreading his imminent expulsion – I told Jock that he was a writer of very great importance, though sadly underrated; and seconds later I saw our host – who was, in any case, the kindest and most hospitable of men – advancing on the rude intruder, both arms outstretched before him and calling out the warmest of greetings ('My dear boy, how *nice* to see you here ...').

A friend of both Petra's and mine, Charles had for years swum silently in and out of our lives like a disconcerting, blue-eyed shark. A sportsman, a classicist and an authority on low life in Hamburg, Paris and Amsterdam, he had, after leaving Trinity, Dublin, taught classics at a university in Saudi Arabia, where he was arrested by the Desert Patrol for dancing alone among the sand-dunes to 'La Bamba' on a portable gramophone, and upstaged a bandaged and goggled stuntman by strolling up, a towel on his arm, and casually diving ninety feet into a waterhole – a regular occurrence as far as Charles was concerned, but a circus feat for the stuntman, who was left hopping with rage on the edge of the cliff while his erstwhile admirers drifted derisively away. Back in England with his wife and daughters, Charles worked briefly as a swimming-pool attendant before becoming an art dealer – initially, and unhappily, with an established firm of dealers, and then as a freelance operator. His labours, as far as I could gather, were nerve-racking but sporadic: he would spend days on end in their elegant house in Gloucestershire, reading a history of torture or *The Enormous Bed* by Henry Jones PhD, or swimming with his daughters, or playing squash, or disconcerting middle-aged company directors or respectable solicitors whom he remembered as schoolboy athletes by ringing them out of the blue, after forty years free from such persecution, and asking them not only about their continuing prowess (if any) as wicket-keepers or racquets-players, but about the state of their marriages and their sexual proclivities; and then, quite suddenly, he would hurry away to Guernsey or Southern California or the Isle of Man, sell a couple of pictures for a good deal more than I would earn in a year, and return to Gloucestershire to resume his more absorbing activities. Many of his clients were tax exiles, eager to invest in works of art: he was fearless in their pursuit, scaling an eight-foot wall in the hope of interesting in a nineteenth-century landscape a well-known golfer (caught lounging by his pool, and unamused to find this rubicund figure strolling towards him, a canvas under his arm), and gaining access to the London home of an Arab sheikh by swinging, like Tarzan, from a tree onto a first-floor balcony. More often than not his dashing and unconventional approach paid off, and many of his clients became, in due course, his friends as well.

Every now and then Charles would turn up in London *en route* for the Channel Islands, the boot of his battered Ford estate replete with the discarded sleeping bags and gigantic sheets of cardboard in which he kept his paintings while in transit, together with a pungent mulch of old socks, unwashed shirts, tennis racquets, copies of the *London Magazine* and unopened bank statements. He parked this explosive mixture all over London, mounted on kerbs and defying double yellow lines; after which he would, once his business was done, loom up unannounced in the doorways of his office-bound friends and watch them with a sardonic grin as they filled in the long hours between nine and six. If, by some lucky chance, he materialised before lunch, we would set off at a brisk pace to a Greek restaurant opposite Centre Point where – over two or three bottles of retsina – we would discuss those subjects of perennial if parochial fascination: the past, now rapidly receding, and the follies of our friends. Although I would never have been brave enough to lead the life he did, Charles's company and his unusual adventures – after polishing off the Hellespont in the company of his eldest daughter he had recently, in emulation of Byron, swum the Tagus, only to be arrested as a drug smuggler two-thirds of the way across – had a predictably unsettling effect, and I would stump back to the office feeling more restless and dissatisfied than ever.

Eight years after I had joined the firm, it abandoned the lino and tongue-and-groove of William IV Street for the eighteenth-century elegance of Bedford Square, for gilt plasterwork and a marble fireplace or two and views (for some at least) through tall, room-high windows over the railings and plane trees of the square. My lunches grew still longer and more erratic, for round the corner were the Greek restaurants of Charlotte Street, reeking of charcoal and retsina, and the Fitzrovian pubs in which I spent more time than I should drinking draught Guinness with the girl in the purple hat. By now I was one of the longest-serving members of the firm, a repository of office lore and ancient wisdom. I gave sage advice about copyright and contracts and libel and editorial matters; I knew better than most who had been the agent for a particular author, or who had published what and when; but the kind of books I enjoyed publishing – the adventures of an SOE man in wartime Albania, or the tribulations of a lavatory-cleaner, or the diary of a Russian princess stranded in Berlin during the war, or an account of life aboard HMS *Mercury,* the training ship run by C. B. Fry's termagant wife, who inspected her charges' pyjama bottoms every morning for 'evidence of beastliness' – looked increasingly out of place on the list, and, despite some enthusiastic reviews, they seldom sold more than a handful of copies. With every day that passed I became more of an irrelevance, a curmudgeonly presence exuding dispiriting waves of boredom and disapproval. Such a state of affairs could not last for ever, and eventually it was suggested – for the third time in my career as an office-worker – that perhaps the time had come for a parting of the ways. As on the two previous occasions, I greeted the news with delight and relief, warmly agreeing with all they had to say and hurrying to put my critics at their ease. Since our mutual irritation was mitigated – I hope – by affection on both sides, I was given six months in which to work out my time and set my affairs in order. Far from bending my mind to the future I devoted my period of grace to more frenzied carousing and party-going than ever, downing pint after pint of Guinness in the lunch hours with the girl in the purple hat, cracking bottles of wine in the office after work while the cleaners hoovered and dusted all about us, creeping home on the last bus after yet another Christmas party. And then, quite suddenly, my office life was over. The life I had dreamed of lay before me; like Charles, I would be my own master from now on, free to wander through Arcadia whenever I wished; and the future stretched out like an empty room, featureless and unfamiliar.

CHAPTER ONE

Carbonated Lightning

READERS WHO STRUGGLED THROUGH to the last few pages of *Playing for Time* may remember that it ended with my taking the junior job in the publicity department of a firm of publishers in St James's Place, where I soon distinguished myself by projecting back to front a rare film about the burial of a Moscow dissident – the mourners plucking the coffin from the snowy ground, hoisting it onto their shoulders and stepping sharply backwards into the distance – and by being taken in by my friend Tom, a City man with time on his hands, who had rung up impersonating Alexander Solzhenitsyn and asked me in guttural tones whether we would be interested in publishing his most recent revelations about life in the Gulag.

These excitements over and done with, I began to settle down to the everyday life of an ignorant, and all too disposable, member of the department. In those days publishers still had money to spare – or to waste – on press advertisements, and a good deal of my time was given over to the composition of these. Whereas the jolly Jilly Cooper was allowed, as the senior copywriter, to tackle the 'difficult' ads in the *Bookseller, Smith's Trade News* and the Sunday papers, I was restricted to the provincial press and (since the firm had a long and profitable tradition of publishing religious tracts for the layman) to important weeklies like the *Church Times* and the *Universe*. No great literary invention was required, since the ads invariably consisted of a shopping list of the latest books, giving their price, their size ('crown octavo') and a suitably inflammatory quote, doctored if need be ('Stunning' – *Birmingham Post*). Once I had assembled all this useful information, I sat down with what looked like a sheet of graph paper, some tracing paper and a loose-leafed book in which one could find every typeface known to man, or the Monotype Corporation, laid out in descending order of size like an optician's testing sheet. I knew, as yet, nothing whatsoever about design or typography or printing, but since the firm's ads all looked exactly the same it wasn't too hard to grope my way slowly along, hoping – sometimes in vain – that I could somehow cram it all in within the six-inch double column, or whatever size I was working to. It was, I soon discovered, restful and therapeutic work of the kind I particularly enjoy, like peeling potatoes or cleaning shoes. My labours completed, I would then take the piece of graph paper to the publicity manager for her approval, and if all seemed to be in order it would be sent off to a typesetter near King's Cross to be set up in hot metal in the size and typeface indicated in my layout. A day or so later a proof would appear on my desk, looking a good deal blacker and bolder than my tentative scribblings. A block would then be made of the corrected version, and despatched to the *Glasgow Herald* or the *Methodist Recorder*. My last responsibility was to take a ruler to the ad as it appeared, and work out exactly how much of the six inches was occupied by each of the books on the list: every title had its advertising allowance, and the cost of each appearance was scrupulously logged.

When I was not engaged in compiling and designing these advertisements, I filled in the long hours ticking off review lists – deciding which newspapers, magazines, radio and television pro-grammes and influential people should be sent copies of the books that were due to be published in the next six weeks or so. To help me on my way I was put in charge of a bulky loose-leaf folder in which were listed the names and, where known, the addresses of the leading experts in, and likely reviewers of, a huge range of subjects from owls and ungulates (the firm had a much-admired natural history list) to mediaeval history or industrial relations since the war. Twice a week I would scour through all the review pages, adding new names to the lists and noting who reviewed what kind of book for which particular paper. For as long as I could remem-ber I had, almost instinctively, made a mental note of who was published by whom; this kind of superficial knowledge is essential equipment for the general publisher, who must, by his very nature, be something of a jack-of-all-trades, apparently familiar with the latest developments and up-and-coming authors in a huge variety of subjects while at the same time seeming reasonably well-informed about such diverse but crucial matters as copyright and libel law, printing and book production, bookselling, contracts and the basic principles of business.

All this, though, lay in the future, and much of it would remain for ever beyond my ken: in the meantime I learned something of the gossip of the trade – the vital juice that keeps the wheels in motion – from an army of purple-featured men with broken veins in their noses whose job it was to persuade publishers' publicity departments to advertise their books in their magazines or newspapers. Lunch in a pub was the high point of the day for these convivial spirits, each one of whom seemed to drink more than the last; and over the pints of bitter and the sausages on sticks I discovered, at fourth or fifth hand, about the heroes and the villains of the trade – about Tom Maschler, the hawk-featured, open-necked whizz-kid who had rekindled Jonathan Cape's reputation as the most stylish and energetic of literary publishers, or Tony Godwin, who was revolutionising Penguin with his lurid full-colour covers (and later died of asthma in New York), or George Weidenfeld and André Deutsch and all those other alarming-sounding Central Europeans who were elbowing aside an older generation – Hamish Hamilton, Stanley Unwin, Rupert Hart-Davis, even Sir Allen Lane – as the dominant figures in British publishing. All this I soaked up with the ardour of a convert, feeling very much a man of the world as my bottle-nosed companion bent forward and tapped me on the knee before confiding in me some red-hot item of gossip received only hours before from some other publicity department ('for your ears only, old son'); after which he would stretch back in his seat with a satisfied sigh, the pale autumnal light glinting off the filigree work on his regimental blazer and a drop or two of beer poised on the bristles of his friendly ginger moustache. From time to time these kindly souls would invite me out for an even longer lunch to meet a grandee of the trade – a publicity director from a rival firm, perhaps, or even a book-trade columnist, the best-known of whom, Eric Hiscock, was a dapper figure in his eighties, a veteran of the First World War with flowing white locks, a Wellingtonian nose, hollow eyes and a sucked-in mouth suggestive of false teeth: he lived – or so I was told – off champagne in a flat in Park Lane, had worked under Arnold Bennett on the *Evening Standard's* books pages and deputed for Ian Fleming as Atticus on the *Sunday Times,* and was assiduously courted by publishers, since it was well known that a favourable puff in his column in *Smith's Trade News* could perform wonders in the shops. Best of all were the meetings of the Publishers' Publicity Circle, held in a Spanish-tiled restaurant between Regent Street and Piccadilly and attended by publishers' publicity people, literary editors, gossip columnists, radio and television folk and even the occasional author: I felt, quite rightly, the lowest of the low, but as the faces about me grew ever ruddier and more bedizened with sweat, and the baying and clinking of glasses grew ever more discordant, I knew, with a warm glow of appreciation, that this was a world in which I felt very much at home.

I had joined the firm in October, and as the festive season approached an end-of-term hilarity set in. Lunches became still longer and more frequent; I smuggled out set after set of Harold Nicolson's *Diaries* as presents for my friends; we decorated our six-inch doubles in the *Scotsman* and the *Western Mail* with sprigs of holly and dainty ribbons; bottles and hampers and packs of playing cards were pressed upon us by grateful space salesmen, filtering down even to my level; the streets around were loud with the sound of revelry blasting from pub doors, while the odd secretary, unable to take any more, was noisily sick in a corner, a small circle of friends gathered protectively about her to shield her from the common gaze. The firm's Christmas party, held in the Connaught Rooms, was an altogether more wholesome affair. A former Wimbledon player and an enthusiastic cricketer, our Chairman, 'Billy' Collins, soon to become Sir William, was a devil for games, and expected to win; and no sooner had we been gathered together –

making stiff, uneasy inter-departmental conversation under our paper hats and vainly sucking what appeared to be an alcohol-free fruit cup – than we were marshalled into teams for games of pass-the-parcel and musical chairs. As I watched our leader – by then a dignified man of nearly seventy – springing about the room and waving his arms above his head, his eyes blazing with unnatural excitement, I felt once again those ancient tremors of terror and inadequacy prompted by even the most infantile of games, and by the merest whiff of the competitive spirit. Nor, I suspect, was I alone in this. One of our editorial directors was a smooth Middle European with immaculate iron-grey hair, invariably clad in a pale grey chalkstripe suit, maroon socks and what seemed at the time to be enviably louche suede slip-on shoes: I saw a look of horror cross his face as we were lined up in teams, and then he was seen no more. After a few feeble stabs at passing the parcel or leap-frogging over the back of an equally embarrassed colleague, I sought refuge in the lavatory, and later in the bar, where kindred spirits were found mopping their brows and looking furtive and defiant; emerging only when a hearty roar, and a wave of enthusiastic clapping, announced that the games had been concluded – members of the Chairman's family having triumphed in every department – and that it was time for us to file into the dining-room, still clad in our paper hats, to tuck into prawn cocktails and the office party equivalent of standard Christmas fare.

Six months later we would be subjected to the annual summer party, held in a country club on the river near Marlow. Once again, the Chairman was in his element, hurrying eagerly in white shirt and flannels from the tennis court to the cricket field while the rest of us watched from a reverent distance or, like recalcitrant school children, skulked in the bushes reading forbidden books (all books were forbidden on this particular occasion, including those published by the firm). My particular crony in the publicity department, a Cambridge Blue, forgot himself when his turn came to bat against the Chairman's demon bowling, sending the ball flashing to the boundary with disrespectful ease, disturbing the snoozers and smokers and causing the Chairman's brows, black at the best of times, to grow ever more thunderous as he stalked angrily back to the firing-position, rubbing the ball on his thighs as he went.

All this was pleasant enough and – as it turned out – useful training for the future; but, with a typical graduate's arrogance and impatience, I felt it was a bit beneath me. Had I spent all those years reading Stubbs's Charters in Latin or unravelling the intricacies of mediaeval Ireland ('Was early Irish society tribal? Discuss') merely in order to provide copy for a cardboard cut-out of a rabbit in trousers reading a book, or discuss my holiday plans with middle-aged men in mackintoshes with bottle noses and watery, red-rimmed eyes? As a former editor of not one but two university magazines, surely I should, by now, be at the Chairman's right hand, advising him on what books he should accept or reject – some of those he published looked decidedly 'iffy' to me – and exchanging learned but light-hearted repartee with the more distinguished authors on our list? Years later I found myself irritated by graduate applicants who expressed views similar to those of my youth, and took an unkind delight in pointing out that an Oxford degree in English was of less immediate use than a spell in a local bookshop or a knowledge of typography, that an ability to type would cut more ice than a textual analysis of *Sir Gawaine and the Greene Knight,* and – unkindest cut of all – that none of the best publishers (Jonathan Cape, Allen Lane, Tom Maschler and Tony Godwin sprang to mind) had been near a university; but those above me were too kind or, more probably, too uninterested, to point such things out to me. In that particular firm, though, it was a lesson easily learned: Collins was well known in the trade for its intensely commercial approach to the books it published, whether popular fiction or memoirs or Bibles or road atlases, and whereas in more literary firms the corduroy-clad editors might occasionally condescend to speak to a rep or a bookseller, stifling a yawn as they did so, here the salesmen – hard-featured, red-faced Scotsmen in crisp white shirts and neatly pressed grey suits – reigned supreme, while the editors were looked down on as so many chinless wonders, etiolated ineffectuals whose role was secondary to those of the mighty sales and publicity machines.

The philistine in me – never far from the surface, and easily aroused – found this hard-headed approach to the book trade rather appealing, both for its realism and as an antidote to the pretentious, the fey and the self-regarding. The Chairman himself, whom I greatly admired from a distance, combined – far more successfully than most of his contemporaries – the necessary elements of the hustler and the showman with the more discreet and urbane attributes of the worldly gentleman publisher. Born in the year of Queen Victoria's death, he was a tall, broad-shouldered, fit-looking man; his huge, leonine head, always thrust eagerly forward, was topped by a mane of white hair, and his coal-black eyebrows shot away from his forehead like bolts of carbonated lightning. He remained, in his late sixties, an extremely good-looking man, and his large, regular features were illuminated by a kind of restless, avaricious grin. He wore immaculate tweed suits in Lovat green or Prince of Wales check, and his shoes were highly polished; in winter he sported an enormous mustard-coloured ulster, which made him look like a debonair laird inspecting his estates. This seemed entirely appropriate: the family firm, which had been in business since the middle of the last century, was still based in Glasgow, the home of the printing works, the bindery and much of the less glamorous but immensely profitable areas of publishing – Bibles, dictionaries, text-books, road maps and the like.

By now the Chairman had run his company for some thirty years. Although Collins was one of the biggest – and certainly one of the most successful – publishing houses in the country, the London end at least was still run on highly personal and autocratic lines, in much the same way as André Deutsch or Victor Gollancz ran their respective firms: Billy Collins was, perhaps, the last of the benevolent despots able to keep tabs on every aspect of a firm that size, for we would before long be entering an era when even the most independent-minded publishers were liable to find themselves absorbed into giant conglomerates, and accountants and professional managers would attempt to sweep all before them. The Chairman seemed, from what little I saw of him, to be a man of

formidable will, dominating the proceedings through strength of
character and his overpowering physical presence: impatient and
peremptory with the slow or the circuitous, he was for ever on the
move, hustling and chivvying and barking out orders, his eyes
flickering restlessly about the room, his charm and his ruthlessness
always at the ready. Like all the best publishers, he was obsessive
and monomaniacal, eating, drinking and sleeping the interests of
his firm. An avid traveller, he spent a good deal of time swooping
down on the firm's branches or agencies around the world, berat-
ing unsuspecting booksellers in Auckland or Cape Town should
they be caught out carrying insufficient stock of the firm's titles,
and making a point of re-arranging those they had on display so
that his own publications were well to the fore, face out, while his
rivals' were banished to the background. A stickler for detail, he
insisted on passing and approving even the most modest advertise-
ment in the most obscure provincial paper, and one of my more
alarming duties was to descend to his office on the first floor – a
bow-windowed and panelled eighteenth-century room which
looked like the inside of a cigar-box – and tender a sheaf of proofs
for acceptance or rejection. I was too small fry to incur his wrath
(or, indeed, his approval), but literary editors who failed to review
particular titles were sometimes subjected to terrible bullying over
the telephone; the literary editor of the *Evening Standard,* or so it
was rumoured, had been battered for weeks on end over his failure
to review a standard work on the trout. Although the firm published
some first-rate books, particularly in the field of history, natural
and man-made, Billy Collins was not, I think, a particularly literary
man – he was best-known in the trade for Elsa the lioness, a
lucrative by-product of one of his African tours, and for old-
fashioned adventure stories in which men with firm jaws and
widow's peaks outwitted Hitler's navy single-handed. He was a dull
public speaker, yet when he rose to address the reps at the six-
monthly sales conferences he could play them like a revivalist
preacher or a mob orator of unusual power. These meetings had
about them a touch of a Nuremberg rally, with blown-up photographs of red deer or the bank-managerish features of a popular

theologian taking the place of fluttering swastika flags, and spindly gold court chairs the rough-cast concrete of Albert Speer's Olympic Stadium.

All this took place in a jaunty, nautical-looking eighteenth-century house at the far end of St James's Place. The reception hall had the same cigar-box flavour to it as the Chairman's study on the floor above: the floorboards creaked like those of a country hotel, chintz-covered sofas and armchairs awaited the arrival of important visitors, a vase of flowers blossomed on the receptionist's desk, the bookshelves were discreetly lined with the latest publications, and a full-length portrait of the Chairman's father, hand on hip and roguishly puffing a cigarette, stared down on the proceedings; only the ungainly brown packages left out to be collected by printers' reps or television companies, or the incongruous arrival of a leather-clad, heavily-visored motorbike messenger, clumping ponderously over the carpet like a grimy, gauntleted mediaeval knight, gave any indication that this was a place of work rather than a private house. As one moved away from the reception area and up a fine circular staircase – encountering *en route* Lady Collins, who carried a peke under one arm and edited the religious list – the distant chatter of typewriters or the sight of a fresh-faced girl in sensible skirt and shoes, fair hair held back with a black velvet band, hurrying anxiously past with a pad and a pencil in one hand suggested that somewhere some work was being done; and once behind the scenes all pretence that this was other than a highly efficient and hard-working place of business was rapidly abandoned.

Publishers' publicity departments are good places in which to learn something about the nuts and bolts of what is, for all its amateurish airs, a complicated and difficult trade, since the new arrival is brought into contact with almost every aspect of the business. All too well aware that I was too diffident and too self-effacing to advance my own interests, I quickly realised that I would have to rely on knowledge and understanding rather than bravado and force of personality; so, like an outsize version of a school swot, I set about learning as much as I could on the side – reading books on printing and libel and copyright, fighting my way through impenetrable articles in the trade papers about wholesalers' discounts or bookselling in New Zealand, eagerly ambushing the production director while he was washing his hands or buttoning up his flies so that he could explain exactly what was meant by a 'right-reading positive, emulsion side up' or cornering the sales manager on his way out to lunch to quiz him about book club discounts or the meaning of 'see safe'.

This kept me busy and on my toes, and yet – much as I relished the company of my colleagues, and over-awed as I was by the charismatic Chairman and his retinue of Old Etonian editors – I remained restless and dissatisfied. One day in Ward's Irish House – a cavernous, dripping cellar under Piccadilly Circus where I retreated as often as I could to tuck into boiled bacon and cabbage washed down with pints of stout, and to indulge my nostalgia for Ireland in general and Trinity in particular – Jilly Cooper told me, from the vantage point of long experience, that I shouldn't be so impatient, that the first six months of work were always the worst, and that time thereafter would hurry by all too speedily. Only on the second of these adages did this wise woman prove unreliable, and shortly after receiving her sage advice I found myself, after seven months on the job, getting ready to make my first move.

One afternoon as I sat gossiping with my room-mate – who sat, as he always did in moments of contemplation, with a leg cocked over the arm of his swivel chair, one hand playing with his pencil while the other ran spider-like over the surface of his face in search of an errant pimple – the phone on my desk let out a disruptive squawk and I was told to report to the Chairman's office at once. My heart began to pound, and I was overcome by feelings of panic. I had never been summoned to the presence before; one of my six-inch doubles must have been printed upside-down, or perhaps I had failed to omit a vital 'not' while selecting my laudatory quote ('not the book we have waited for so long'). Either way, it could only mean dismissal and disgrace. My publishing career had ended before it had even begun, and I slunk downstairs with the air of a man on the way to his execution.

Much to my surprise, the Chairman greeted me cordially, even going so far as to remember my name; and far from waving in my face a copy of the offending ad covered with angry scrawls in red, he offered me a seat before introducing me to a large, benevolent-looking man of about his own age who was seated by the window. Apart from being tall and tweeded, my new employer – for so he turned out to be – was, in almost every respect, the antithesis of the Chairman. Whereas the Chairman's face and body were lithe and lean, tapering down from a wide forehead and broad shoulders to a firm chin and twinkling ankles, Jocelyn ('Jock') Gibb was endearingly pear-shaped in the manner of Mr Turveydrop or Louis Philippe, and whereas the Chairman's face was white and drawn, the newcomer's was of a reddish hue, tipped with wisps of ginger hair, with large, watery eyes, a pendulous lower lip and the slightly hang-dog look of a kindly bloodhound. He had narrow shoulders, large red hands and a bulging waistcoat – suggesting that, unlike the Chairman, he was no longer an active force on the tennis court or the games field. He was, I was told, the managing director of Geoffrey Bles, a small publishing house in Bloomsbury which the Chairman had bought a year or two earlier (he had done so, I later learned, in order to get his hands on two best-selling authors of popular theology); and I was being sent to work for him as his publicity manager. Relieved beyond speech that this was all I had been summoned for, I scuttled gratefully away to mop my brow and impart the news to my cronies in the attic where we worked; a new and – as it turned out – remarkably uneventful episode in my career had begun.

A week or so later I reported for duty with my new employers in Doughty Street. A few houses up the road was Dickens's house, and a door or two along – in offices later occupied by the *Spectator* – was a very different kind of publisher, Anthony Blond, whose florid front room, as I peered enviously in over the area railings, had the look of a Pompeian brothel, painted in shades of aubergine and avocado. Much preferring, as I always have, to walk to work wherever possible, I set out in the general direction of Bloomsbury from our family flat in a striped red and yellow block of flats near Westminster Cathedral. It was a damp and misty morning as I made my way along the north side of Lincoln's Inn, through Great Turnstile, across Holborn and up Bedford Row, and as I trudged past the black-featured terraces of Doughty Street the weather seemed to grow still darker and more sombre. I felt as though I was stepping back into the foggy pages of *Bleak House, en route* to Mrs Jellyby's lodging house, perhaps; an impression that grew still stronger as I stopped outside the blue-painted door of an early-nineteenth-century house on the right-hand side of the street, looked up and down to make sure I had the right number, straightened my tie and shot my cuffs, and made my way inside.

I found myself in a long and dingy hall, painted – like an old-fashioned prep school corridor – in grubby turquoise gloss up to shoulder level, and a murky cream above: a scheme of decoration that was to become very familiar to me in a later incarnation. Dim, tobacco-coloured light filtered in through a grimy window on the half-landing, through which I could see the bare branches of a plane tree dripping with early-morning dew. One side of the corridor was lined with those familiar brown-paper parcels containing books that had recently been delivered from the binders. Each carried a white label informing the onlooker that the parcel contained so many copies of a particular book; most of them, I noticed, were by the two popular theologians upon whom our livelihoods depended. From a dark, cave-like room at the far end of the corridor, beyond the stairs, I could hear the sound of whistling and an occasional thump. To my left, in what might once have been a dining-room, was a small partitioned-off reception, containing two maroon armchairs and an assortment of elderly publications on Russian spiritualism and the meaning of prayer; the dust-covers were of a plain, unlaminated grey, with maroon lettering to match the two armchairs. In one corner, with a light shining yellowly through it, was a sliding panel made of frosted glass. Apart from the whistling and the thumping, there seemed no sign of life whatsoever: so, feeling unusually bold, I rapped on the glass, at the same time calling out 'Excuse me – is anyone there?' in the tremulous tones of one who suspects that he may well, in fact, be talking to empty air, and slid the panel open.

I stuck my head through, and found myself peering into a snug and brightly-lit room, so warm that my specs immediately misted over and I had to withdraw, like a tortoise into its shell, and rub them clear before I could take in any more, or make myself known to whoever was inside. That done, I bent low once more and re-inserted my head. A gas fire was plopping and hissing in a grate, surrounded by maroon tiles and a mantelpiece painted cobalt blue; to the left of the sliding panel stood an antique wooden switch-board, a tangle of flexes and brass levers; and in front of the fire, her slippered feet protected from the brown lino on the floor by a brightly-coloured woollen mat, a cup of milky coffee within easy reach, sat a stout, contented-seeming middle-aged lady, busily knitting what looked like a shawl or a scarf. When I said who I was, she came bustling round, introduced herself as Joyce and, pointing up the stairs, indicated where I could find my new employer; after which she padded happily back to her lair, picked up her knitting and continued as before.

Obedient as always, I worked my way up the stairs, pausing on the half-landing to inspect the garden – black walls, black earth, shiny black leaves swept into a corner, a few waif-like black plants peeping through the grime – and to admire an elegant white metal gazebo in the garden of Blond & Briggs. Two doors confronted me on the first-floor landing. From behind one of them I could hear the low murmur of voices, and the clack of a pre-war typewriter: I assumed this must be a secretarial office, so I boldly knocked on the other door, waited for the hearty cry of 'Come in!' and pushed my way inside. I found myself in a grey-painted room overlooking Doughty Street, with a thick Turkey carpet, a glass-fronted book-case along one wall, laden with further volumes on Russian spirit-ualism and the meaning of prayer, a waffle-iron gas fire spluttering in the grate and, above the marble mantelpiece, a large Victorian oil painting of some cows asleep in a field. As I came in my new employer rose from behind his desk to greet me, seizing my hand in an iron grip. He was wearing a well-cut moss-coloured tweed suit with highly polished orange brogues; instead of the familiar scatter of proofs and catalogues and letters waiting to be answered, his desk appeared to be covered with farming magazines and packets of cattle feed. After a few jocular remarks he took me by the elbow and steered me out of his study to meet my fellow-workers.

Devoted, long-serving and wretchedly badly-paid unmarried ladies – many still living at home with demanding or evil-natured nonagenarian parents – used to provide literary publishing with its non-commissioned officers and its collective memory, and Geoffrey Bles boasted a full contingent of these kindly, self-effacing figures. Patient, scrupulous editors, usually better-read and a good deal more literate than those who gave the orders, clad in well-worn cardigans and thick stockings and monastic-looking sandals, they tended – at least in more demanding firms, if not in Geoffrey Bles – to work all evening and over every weekend, lugging sack-loads of proofs and typescripts between their parental homes and the office and receiving meagre thanks beyond the dubious compliment – since they were known to be reliable, loyal and desperately willing – of having more work dumped on them as soon as they showed any sign of flagging. A team of such ladies had been housed in the basement, a Stygian region redolent of damp and beetles and the storing of coal; and as we descended the cellar steps they rose from the murk to shake my hand with sad, self-deprecating smiles before sinking down again. Very different to this twilight region was the room at the back of the building from which I had heard, on my arrival, the sound of whistling and the occasional thump. It was a tall, ginger-coloured wooden chamber, not unlike a sauna or a prep-school changing-room, with a grimy skylight in the roof, a work counter covered with knives and scissors and sheets of cardboard and balls of string, and solid wooden racks set out in aisles on which the books were stored in their brown-paper parcels. Made livelier still by the blast of a portable radio, this sprightly spot – the packing-room and trade counter – was manned by two middle-aged men in brown cotton overalls with pencil stubs behind their ears. In the old days, before London rates and rents became prohibitive, and while publishing remained an agreeably small-scale business, publishers would keep a proportion of their stock on the premises in order to meet urgent London orders from book-sellers; my new employers were among the few who retained this admirable practice, reminiscent of *Pendennis* and Paternoster Row and the days when publishers still saw themselves as tradesmen, and their business as essentially a branch of bookselling. As I examined the books laid out like mummies on the wooden shelves – parables of the Christian life and commentaries on the Gospels by benign-looking rural deans, inoffensive thrillers set in the Home Counties involving poisoned tea cups and maiden aunts, a best-selling guide to vegetable-growing, the brown collotype illustra-tions of which showed working men of forty years before, clad in collarless striped shirts with studs at the neck, pinstriped waistcoats and corduroy trousers tied below the knee, digging trenches in allotments or holding up for display gnarled and out-of-focus root vegetables – I felt that although there was nothing here I could bear to read, this was, in its subfusc way, publishing as it ought to be.

Joshing pleasantries exchanged, we moved back upstairs – pass-ing, as we did so, Joyce's somnolent lair, from which I heard once more the gentle click of knitting needles and the soothing plop of the gas fire. I was introduced to a languid, fair-haired youth in desert boots who was, I gathered, the sales manager, and who fell back in his chair with a gasp, quite exhausted by his labours, after rising to shake my hand; to the managing director's secretary, a peevish-looking girl with string-coloured hair who sighed a good deal and raised her eyes to heaven, making it plain that she felt herself destined for somewhat better things; and to the accountant, a jovial, black-browed Armenian who supervised an attic-ful of stout, simpering ladies, each of whom was busy entering details of royalties or earnings and disbursements in equally stout, leather-bound ledgers, using wooden school pens with brass nibs – dipped into pots of blue or red ink – with which to inscribe the pounds, shillings and pence in the relevant columns. Later, when I got to know these ladies, I would sometimes ask them to explain these baffling columns of copperplate: I was stupefied by the mental arithmetic involved – how was it possible to work out a 12½ per cent royalty on a book costing 27/6, or a discount of thirty-three-and-a-third off a published price of five guineas? – and suspect that although decimalisation and the arrival of the pocket calculator made publishers' lives immeasurably easier, the abolition of the old coinage, like the pensioning off of the Authorised Version, probably had a disastrous effect on the brain power of the nation. Last of all, I shook hands with the production director, whose name – together with those of the Chairman and my pear-shaped new employer – was printed on the firm's notepaper. A Pooterish clerk with a thin black moustache and neatly-parted grey hair in which one could see the furrow-marks of the comb, he wore a black serge suit, a white shirt and a sombre Rotarian tie, trading these in on his return home (or so I liked to think) for a maroon cardigan and a pair of Pirelli slippers before lighting a companionable pipe and discussing the day's events. He commuted in from Beckenham every morning with bowler hat and furled umbrella, spent his days dealing neatly and efficiently with equally old-fashioned and well-mannered typesetters, printers, binders and paper-merchants, ate at his desk the sandwiches his wife had wrapped in greaseproof paper before he hurried for the train, left on the dot of a quarter to six, and knew perfectly well that, though nominally the deputy managing director, he could never expect to consort with his fellow-directors out of office hours, or on anything like equal terms.

My office on the second floor was next to that of the production director, except that whereas he looked out across the blackened garden to the upper storeys of the bronze and zigzagged building that housed the *Sunday Times,* my view was westwards over the slate-grey roofs and orange chimney pots of Bloomsbury. It was a large, bare room with flocked fleur-de-lys wallpaper of the kind then popular in pubs and Indian restaurants and a maroon and cream swirly carpet more appropriate to a comfortable boarding house than to publishers of popular theology. One corner of the room was taken by a hand-operated roneo machine and the other by a large and well-worn armchair, with blackened patches of grease on the arm-rests and on the spot where the heads of numberless space salesmen and snoozing publicity managers had gratefully rested. My desk was sited sideways-on between the two sash windows; immediately opposite it was a glass-fronted bookcase containing the works of Nikolai Berdyaev, the Russian mystic, and a blue-covered copy of Vicki Baum's *Grand Hotel,* one of the firm's few claims to literary fame. After showing me to my quarters, at the same time urging me to make myself at home and to ask for anything I needed, my kindly guide drifted away to his room to read a page or two of the *Farmers Weekly* and inspect the samples of cattle feed, running the pellets appreciatively through his thick red hands; and as he picked his way heavily downstairs he called out a jocular greeting to his fellow-director, eliciting a measured and respectful response appropriate to the occasion. Left to my own devices, and with no evidence of work needing to be done, I was overcome by gloom and despair. Outside it was as dark as ever, and rain was beginning to spatter against the window-panes; everything about me looked dingy and dispirited; a great silence reigned, broken only by the tick of the clock on the half-landing below and, from the production director's lair, the discreet rustle of paper and an occasional dainty cough ('ahem!'). Overcome by unexpected sentiments of banishment and loss, I pined for the exuberance and the gossip and the bustle of St James's Place, for the Chairman's hectoring presence or Jilly Cooper's golden hair trailing into her typewriter keys as, her arms crossed, her eyes closed and her head peacefully at rest on the carriage, she recovered from a long and cordial lunch.

Settling into a new job is an unnerving business at the best of times, involving much eager springing up from behind one's desk, and the fierce perusal of telephone lists and fire regulations in an attempt to persuade oneself (and others) that one is already hard at work, and a succession of well-meaning, unfamiliar faces grinning round the door ('How are you getting on? I'm next door if there's anything you need to know. And do watch out for the lavatory chain – it may well come off in your hand'). In this particular instance, though, no faces came grinning round the door, and I remained undisturbed as I went about the customary rituals of opening and closing desk drawers, peering into cupboards and testing out the telephone.

All this occupied me for the next hour or so. Anxious, by now, for some variety and for some sign of human activity – perhaps those spectral figures to whom I had recently been introduced had, for reasons best known to themselves, stolen away, leaving me to hold the fort? – I tiptoed fearfully down to the lavatory on the landing, like a late-returning reveller in an out-of-season hotel. Visiting the lavatory is, under normal circumstances, a useful and eagerly-awaited antidote to the tedium of office life, involving chance encounters on the stairs and a welcome change of scenery, but no such luck awaited me this time. The clack of the elderly typewriter had fallen silent, and even the production director's rustles and coughs were no more. I trudged sadly back to my cell and, choosing a book almost at random, settled down in the greasy armchair to read a Lenten address on the subject of humility. After another half-hour or so of tomb-like silence, I was woken from semi-slumber – somehow the Lenten address had failed to engage my attention as much as I'd hoped – by the tinkling of the Bakelite telephone. Staggering to my feet, I snatched the receiver from its cradle and addressed it in tones which, I hoped, exuded professional competence and enthusiasm ('Publicity here!'); after which a reclusive voice – stunned, perhaps, by my magisterial tones – told me that coffee was being served in the managing director's office, and that I was welcome to a cup.

Almost the entire staff – minus the two packers, and Joyce the switchboard operator – had gathered for eleven o'clock coffee in our leader's office, and were standing in front of the fire drinking a pallid, milky mixture, like guests at a cocktail party. This, I soon discovered, was a daily ritual; as was, in the winter months at least, a saucerful of Haliborange pills, which was passed around, like a plate of canapés or a dish of communion wafers, as a thoughtful precaution against 'flu and colds. The conversation, I noticed, had nothing whatsoever to do with publishing, and when I tentatively steered it in that direction – asking in an interested way about forthcoming titles and how they were subscribing – it soon became apparent that I had committed a *faux pas*. This seeming indifference to our *raison d'être* was made plainer still when, our milky coffees drained and the Haliborange pills disposed of, and the secretarial element dismissed, those of us who remained were motioned to armchairs where we sat in respectful silence while Mr Gibb spoke on the telephone at some length to the bailiffs of his two farms in Scotland, issuing detailed instructions about silage and fencing and haystacks, smiling and winking in our direction whenever he felt he had scored a point. The conversation over, the publisher briefed us in gratifying detail about the barley harvest and an outbreak of foot-and-mouth. Although none of his staff had, as yet, met either of the bailiffs or set foot on the two estates, they had become, over the years, unusually well-informed about the problems of farming in Ayrshire, and eagerly looked forward to the morning's bulletin; and as we dispersed to our various rooms I overheard them discussing among themselves in thoughtful tones whether or not a new barn should be built, and whether it mightn't be wiser to switch from oats to rye. Rather to my relief, the publisher beckoned to me to remain behind; pushing aside the packets of cattle feed, he produced from his desk various sheets of paper for me to look after, all in my own good time of course. Clutching my week's labour – a 'New Book Announcement' to be written up and roneoed for the reps, ads in *The Tablet* and the journal of the Royal Horticultural Society, and some copy to accompany a cardboard cut-out of a rhinoceros – I trailed dispiritedly back to my office, ungratefully convinced that I was somehow destined for higher and for better things.

Jock Gibb was, as I soon discovered, the kindest and most amiable of men, though hardly the most forceful or interesting of publishers. For some curious reason – perhaps because of our similar height, or the depth of our voices? – he saw in me a kindred spirit, and whenever I appeared in his office he would push back his chair, link his hands behind his head and expound at length about publishing in the 1930s under the maniacal figure of Walter Hutchinson, and his warm friendship with such giants of the trade as Sir Allen Lane, Robert Lusty and Billy Collins. All this was gratifying enough, but hardly made up for the lack of things to do. As publicity manager, I was left to my own devices, and did all my work unaided: which was just as well, for despite some vigorous winding of the ronco machine and the writing of unread letters to literary editors and the choosing of typefaces for occasional advertisements and even – though this was treading on another's patch – designing the jacket for a book on Austrian cooking, and a complicated title page incorporating a line-drawing of an elephant running through long grass, my labours, however spun out, barely occupied me for more than a couple of days a week. Scarred by my earlier experiences as a trainee advertising man – I had been publicly rebuked for reading *Martin Chuzzlewit* under my desk during the course of an office cricket match, played with rulers and balls of screwed-up paper – I was chary about taking refuge in a book, jumping guiltily at a knock on the door and shielding the offending item from public gaze with a protective loop of my arm; instead I filled in the long hours writing reports for a friendly paperback publisher and tiny 'filler' book reviews for the literary editor of *The Times,* and sending out increasingly desperate letters to other and, I hoped, livelier publishers, begging to be released.

After a month or two, relief of a kind was at hand in the form of the annual Collins sales conference in Glasgow. My tweeded superior became very excited at the prospect, and the flow of anecdotes about long-dead titans of the trade assumed the proportions of a tidal wave. We would be travelling up by train, he told me, together with the Chairman and his entourage of editors, salesmen and publicity hounds. He liked, I am sure, to be spotted in the company of the Chairman, chatting easily as equals and contemporaries; the Chairman seemed perfectly happy to go along with this, like a Roman emperor indulging the governor of a remote and barbaric province – partly out of natural amiability and good manners, and partly because of the two popular theologians, whose books, I observed from the daily sales figures, sold in double or even treble figures every day of the week. I was told, as publicity people always are on such occasions, to gather together all the proofs or artwork of book jackets I could lay my hands on (including my unsuccessful stab at *Austrian Cooking,* with its red-and-white frieze of jolly-looking gingermen), along with such 'display material' as I had prepared for booksellers to prop up in their shops or, more probably, hurl into the nearest waste-paper basket with a disdainful grunt: these included the cut-out rhino, slightly out-of-focus, and blown-up studio portraits of our two bespectacled theologians, gummed onto pieces of board.

The day before we were due to leave I committed a grave and wounding solecism. Like the rest of my colleagues I had, as a by-product of our morning coffee sessions in front of the fire, acquired a detailed knowledge of the two estates in Scotland. I knew how many cattle had been sold, what the sheep were up to, how the re-roofing of the barn was getting on and why the cowman had driven the Land-Rover into a ditch and had had to make his way home on foot; although I had never actually spoken to either of the bailiffs, I knew – without, perhaps, feeling quite as interested as I should – how many children each of them had sired, what kinds of cars they drove, and where they were planning to spend their summer holi-days. So when, with a smile both proud and diffident, my employer suggested that, rather than waste good time consorting with reps and overseas agents, we should, when not on duty, hurry out and visit the two estates, I realised that I was being offered something rare and privileged; and yet I was, to my shame and embarrass-ment, reluctant to accept this golden opportunity. Quite apart from an ancient antipathy to bulls and mud and horses' hooves and opening gates held together with incomprehensible twists of wire and chain, I was desperately keen to spend the best part of a day looking over the Chairman's printing works in Glasgow, which was said to be the biggest in the country. Designing my six-inch doubles had brought me into contact with typesetters and block-makers, but I had never seen round a printing works – let alone one which boasted some fabulous new machine which, or so it seemed, could absorb an author's typescript at one end and disgorge bound copies at the other. In my anxiety to mug up on the nuts and bolts of the trade I had read about the imposition of pages and stereos and the screening of half-tones and binding blocks and headbands and colour separations and the rest, but they all remained, as yet, mere abstractions; a visit to the Glasgow works seemed far too good an opportunity to miss in favour of gumboots and silage and haystacks and the steaming breath of cattle. Feeling guilty and ungrateful and self-serving and even – for the first and last time in my life, perhaps – disagreeably ambitious, I explained my dilemma and told Mr Gibb, as tactfully as I could, that, grateful as I would always be, I would rather visit the printing works. I realised at once that I had done a terrible thing. He looked suddenly hurt and bruised, like a child whose offer of friendship had been rejected; the light went out of his eyes, and he turned sharply away, muttering fiercely about things that needed to be seen to. From then on, I suspect, he regarded me as someone on the make, who took himself too seriously; and although he remained as affable as ever, nothing was quite the same thereafter.

Next evening we gathered on the platform at Euston for the overnight train to Glasgow. I spotted the Chairman at once, striding restlessly up and down the platform in his huge mustard-coloured ulster, his long, Lovat-tweeded legs protruding underneath; my leader hurried to join him, so that they could be seen strolling up and down together, while I made my way to the bar and the company of former colleagues from St James's Place. Once again with kindred spirits, I felt as though I had rejoined, if only for a mile or two, the main line after weeks spent pottering along a disused and overgrown branch line; and as we hurtled north, draining warm, fizzy beer out of paper mugs and trading news and gossip – dashing and full-blooded on their part, self-deprecating and rueful on mine – life seemed to regain some of its flavour and sense of purpose.

The Geoffrey Bles 'presentation' had been slotted in at the very end of the second and final day of the conference, by which time the reps, sated with information about forthcoming books and fed up with being hectored and wheedled and charmed by the speakers on the podium, would be restless and chafing to be off, and listening with only half an ear. No sooner had we booked into the Central Hotel than Mr Gibb – not bestowing on me a backwards glance, so deep did my rejection rankle – headed off in his Land-Rover to the Lowlands and the company of his bailiffs, and I was left to my own devices. I sat at the back of the conference hall, admiring once again the Chairman's Nuremberg-like technique, and the way in which even the most fidgety and world-weary reps – all of whom had removed their jackets in a businesslike manner, revealing drip-dry shirts through which their vests could be seen, and curious navy-blue club ties on which a giant crest (Rotarian? Rugger club?) was sandwiched between two sets of diagonal bars – ceased doodling on their order pads or muttering among themselves whenever he rose to speak. When my plastic chair became too hard to be borne, I wandered about central Glasgow, admiring its handsome, cavernous streets and then, at the appointed time, I reported to the printing works for my initiation into the ways in which the books upon which my modest livelihood depended were actually made. Many of the techniques to which I was introduced, and about which I grilled their operators as though cramming for an exam – block-making, hot-metal setting, stereos and the like – have long since been superseded, but I gazed at them all with the reverence of a traveller who finds himself, at last, in a legendary country. The typesetters and the machine-minders were gnarled Glaswegians in boiler-suits, with rolled-up sleeves exposing muscular forearms, while the sewing and binding machines were supervised by middle-aged women in brown or blue cotton jackets; another contingent of ladies was hard at work nimbly wrapping dustjackets round freshly-bound books as they trundled slowly past on metal rollers, like so many cans of fruit. Every now and then a wooden barrow would rumble past on tiny metal wheels, laden with gold-leafed sheets of the Bible heading for the bindery; they were pushed by tiny, frail-looking girls of fifteen or sixteen, their faces the colour of suet, their legs that unappealing mauve I remembered so well from Ireland, under the supervision of a fresh-faced, chalk-striped young Etonian who strode among these bent and haggard figures like a member of the Master Race.

Late on the afternoon of the final day, immediately after the tea break, our turn came to appear on the podium. It was all that I had feared. A small publisher whose books are carried by a larger one, even if the larger one is its proprietor, always risks being consigned to the bottom of the pile and receiving second-class treatment, since the reps' first loyalties will be to their principal employer; still more so if – as was the case with us – its books are unexciting and its leader undemanding and far from charismatic. Whereas the Chairman had been flanked on either side by hard-featured sales managers and suave, suede-shod editors, my unhappy boss – about whom I suddenly felt hopelessly defensive – had his ineffectual, floppy-haired sales supremo lolling negligently to his left, his eyes occasionally closing as sleep overcame him, while I sat to his right, gazing in an embarrassed way at the tips of my shoes while he stumbled through his set pieces, frequently losing his way and laughing heartily at his own jokes, none of which seemed to pro-voke comparable spasms of merriment from his stony-featured listeners. For two days now the reps had quailed under the Chairman's gaze, sitting rigidly to attention in their seats, emitting dutiful barks of laughter at appropriate moments and scribbling keenly on their order pads: faced by our unalarming trio, they not only felt free to relax, undoing their collar buttons and slipping off their shoes, but made no attempt to disguise their boredom about the latest offerings from lady detective-story writers and moustachioed vegetable-gardeners. My leader's closing words were drowned by the shuffle of papers being stuffed into briefcases and the clacking of locks: not even a revised version of a well-known commentary on the Epistle to the Ephesians could engage their interest, and the floppy-haired salesman's attempt to suggest a subscription target for the Bishop of Lincoln's Lenten address was greeted by a flurry of arms shooting their cuffs so that watches could be consulted and train times compared. I held up my cut-out of an enraged-looking rhino preparing to charge, his red eyes peering angrily out through a cloud of yellow dust, but was aware only of chairs being pushed back and a scrum of turned backs as the reps bent low over their briefcases, cramming plastic macs and foldaway umbrellas on top of a tide of bumph; and by the time Mr Gibb rose to make his concluding peroration, looking more than ever like a kindly, baffled bloodhound, the hall was almost deserted.

CHAPTER TWO

Tartar Sauce

WHILE ALL THIS was going on I was still living in my parents' flat in Victoria, equidistant from Westminster Cathedral and the Army and Navy Stores. On the seventh floor of a gloomy Edwardian block, it was the kind of old-fashioned service flat I remembered from my childhood in Prince of Wales Drive, with a long and grimy corridor, a tiled well descending to crepuscular depths, large rooms with baronial moulded ceilings, a creaking lift unravelling yards of greasy metal rope, and a pasty-looking uniformed porter who spent a good deal of time polishing the brass in the hall and wearing an expression of chirpy deference of the kind displayed by able-bodied seamen – Bryan Forbes or Dickie Attenborough, perhaps – in films set aboard wartime destroyers. My parents spent most of their time in their storm-tossed cottage on the seafront at Seaford, giant waves drumming against the window panes and pebbles rattling down the chimney, and rather than sit at home alone I would pass the evening drinking stout with Derek Mahon in Ward's Irish House, reeling home across St James's Park after the last bus conductors had been sent on their way and the shutters clanged behind us; or – feeling as stiff and as English as ever – listening to Irish music in the pubs in Camden Town, racked by terrible nostalgia; or attending unhappy and sparsely-attended poetry readings at the Poetry Society in Earl's Court, where the audience seemed to be made up of mad women with apple-red faces and shopping-bags crammed on their heads and tramps in greasy mackintoshes sheltering from the rain, with the occasional poetry-lover – recognisable, perhaps, by his dark blue shirt and orange tie, or corduroy suit with Aran sweater – perched uneasily between: or – best of all – I would take myself off to see the girl with the Tartar features and the hair like a badger, who had now moved from Cadogan Square and was living with her sister in a flat in Stratford Road. Her face was the colour of putty: both sisters were extremely short of money, and no sooner had Petra got home from the literary agency where she worked than she left for a night-club in Park Lane where she sat behind a counter taking people's coats and scarves and selling souvenirs to Arabs, before plodding home in the small hours of the morning. Since I am incapable of staying awake after midnight and worry terribly about the necessary hours of sleep, this seemed a louche and unhealthy regime to me. I longed to introduce her to my parents but dreaded it all the same, since I knew that my mother – who was convinced that early nights and sea air were the answer to all life's problems – would take amiss the putty-coloured features and the long hours, and have no compunction about making known her views on the matter.

Before long I had become extremely fond of the girl with the badger-like hair, and when she wasn't working in the night-club I would sit silently in one corner of their kitchen, decked out in my new publishing uniform of soft green corduroy, with green suede shoes to match. I spoke, or so I am told, in sonorous, sporadic bursts, not easily understood; and although they were perfectly happy to have me around as they bustled about the house, neither sister was quite sure why I was there, or whom I had come to see. When the time came for them to go to bed I would take myself off and walk home to Victoria, threading my way – like a taxi-driver – down Beauchamp Place, along Pont Street and down across Eaton Square. I had always been explosively flatulent, and liked to boast that farting was my only real talent: I was far too modest to display my skills unasked in the sitting-room in Stratford Road, but sat squirming in my seat, my buttocks clamped together and a light sweat beading my brow; and no sooner had I closed the front door behind me after bidding a fond good night than I released a series of titanic blasts, which sent me spinning down the pavement in the direction of Marloes Road like a clipper before a brisk south-wester.

All this was very agreeable, but seemed to be leading nowhere. I loved Petra very much, and quite early in the proceedings I asked her whether we shouldn't perhaps get married; she seemed happy enough with the idea, while warning me, quite wrongly, that she would have white hair and false teeth on upper and lower jaws by the time she was thirty-five, and took me down in a Green Line bus one afternoon to meet her mother, who lived in a tiny one-up, one-down at the foot of Brill, north of Oxford; but – as is so often the case – I took the word for the deed and did nothing about it, even to the extent of buying an engagement ring. The days drifted by, and winter turned to spring, and still nothing happened – until my parents suddenly decided that they wanted to spend more time in London, and that it was about time I left home and fended for myself. This was too much to be borne. I had never – have never yet – lived alone or made my own way in the world; the very idea was unthinkable; the only answer was to get married at once, and solve all my problems in one go.

My mother-in-law was a forceful and entertaining lady, much given to shouting 'Mark my words', and one of a team of voluble sisters who had been brought up in Calcutta and descended from an Argentinian named Smith who had made his money in the opium trade. Although she distrusted the Church and abominated the clergy, she had brought up her daughters as Catholics and sent them to be taught by amiable, waxen-featured and mildly snobbish Flemish nuns in Haywards Heath; and now that I had committed myself to marriage – driven on by a prophetic vision of Petra being knocked over by a bus in Victoria Street and lying in the middle of the road with her booted, black-tighted legs waving in the air, like a beetle that had been turned on its back – I set out nervously in the direction of the Brompton Oratory to receive a dash of religious instruction. My interlocutor was a former Guards officer, a tall, rubicund, fine-looking priest who exhaled good living and worldly wisdom; and once a week I went along to the Oratory, where we strolled about the garden chatting of this and that and – or so I like to think – winding up the proceedings with a glass or two of sherry. Since neither family had any money left (and not a great deal to start with), the wedding itself, when it at last materialised, was a modest affair, restricted to immediate family and a few officiating friends, with Ian Whitcomb – my friend with the prehensile fingers and the rolling sea-dog's gait – fumbling in his pocket for the ring, and Charles Sprawson, uninvited, leering like Satan over the Oratory railings. My mother suggested a reception of beer and sandwiches in the Bunch of Grapes, on the other side of the Brompton Road, but was outvoted after a kindly MP had offered us his flat in Great Peter Street for the reception. Our honeymoon had been spent in advance sailing round the Hebrides in a green Edwardian yacht with gleaming brass fittings and mahogany panelling and miniature chandeliers attached to the ceiling, and I had devoted a windswept, waterlogged fortnight to moving slowly about the deck like an arthritic pensioner, one hand clutching a book and the other gripping onto whatever piece of woodwork came to hand, or hauling on ropes in a daze of incomprehension while the spray spattered against my specs, or toppling down with an angry grunt as the boom, swinging sideways, struck me a mighty blow to the head: to make matters worse, life at sea induced a paralysing constipation – which was just as well, since I lived in dread of blocking the nautical lavatory, with its mahogany fittings and beer-pull pump, or of stinking out the cabin for hours on end ('There must be a dead rat on board'). At some stage we found ourselves in Oban where, in a spasm of good-heartedness and relief at being on dry land, I bought Petra a bevel-edged gold ring for five pounds in the Happy Ring House; and now, with the ring retrieved from the depths of Ian's pocket and placed at last on Petra's finger, and the wedding lunch lodged agreeably inside us, we set out in Ian's car in the direction of the first of our many homes, a tiny attic flat in a cul-de-sac in Barnes. A day or two before, Petra's mother had driven us there in her Mini, peering keenly out from behind the steering-wheel, her hands in the ten-to-two position. After crossing Hammersmith Bridge she had, on impulse, turned left instead of right, through a pair of ornamental gates, and we found ourselves driving, very slowly, through a gigantic sewage farm, tucked away behind the Harrods depository. 'This isn't how I remember

Cedars Road, dear,' she protested as we picked our way between two steaming circular vats. Eventually we found our way back to Castelnau, and so towards Barnes Common; and now we were safely ensconced, and a lifetime lay before us.

In the months before I was finally expelled from my parents' flat in Ashley Gardens, I decided – for the first and only time – to play an active part in the community. I joined the local branch of the Labour Party, and spent the occasional evening banging on doors and thrusting sheets of paper into the hands of householders rudely interrupted in the middle of supper or *Z Cars*. I dreaded falling into a political argument with those whom we canvassed, since my own political opinions were absurdly elastic, swinging sharply to the right in the company of *Guardian* readers and veering with equal force to the left when faced by a Tory lady, while at the same time tending to agree with whomever had spoken last and loudest; luckily our victims, many of whom were munching as they opened the door, were far more interested in finishing their meals than in debating politics with a vague-looking individual in a green corduroy suit, and my skills as an advocate of party policy (had I known what it was) were never put to the test.

One evening I decided to go to a ward meeting of the local party, held above a pub. Most of those present were traditional Labour supporters, gnarled, old-fashioned figures in maroon or olive cardigans who looked like the survivors from an Ealing comedy, downing bottles of warm pale ale from the pub below and far more interested in local gossip than in the grand strategic issues which I struggled to master once a week in the pages of the *New Statesman*. That evening, however, a guest speaker was expected, so local affairs would have to give way, for half an hour at least, to thoughts on the world at large. Ian Smith had recently made his Unilateral Declaration of Independence in Southern Rhodesia, and a member of one of the banned African opposition parties was to tell us about the iniquities of 'Smithie' and his regime of bull-necked tobacco-farmers and whip-toting amateur fascists, whose Doris Day look-alike wives (or so we were led to believe) spent their days drinking gin round swimming-pools and rapping out orders to barefoot, middle-aged 'boys'. Spot on the dot of eight o'clock our speaker arrived – too late, alas, to join us in a glass of warm pale ale – and took his place behind a small trestle table at one end of the room. He was a shy, rather studious young man in gold-rimmed glasses, and he reminded me at once of those Nigerian and Ugandan students I remembered so well at university, looking stiff and ill-at-ease in immaculate blazers and paisley-patterned silk scarves and thick new cavalry twill trousers. He spoke about what was going on in his home country with eloquence and passion, and in a thick African accent; but within a very short time I was unhappily aware that he had lost his audience altogether, and that the horny-handed pale ale-drinkers were gazing out of the window or rifling through the contents of their pockets or taking surreptitious glances at the *Evening Standard* or muttering confidentially among themselves. I found myself willing him on as one wills on a faltering tenor or a comedian when nobody laughs, clapping loudly whenever a clap seemed in order, beaming encouragement whenever I caught his eye and – despite a shaming absence of real interest in what he had to say – assuming a look that, or so I hoped, combined grave concern with an intelligent assessment of the problems of Southern Rhodesia. Despite the glazed-looking faces before him, the owners of which were fidgeting in their seats like children kept in after class and, as often as not, making no effort to stifle their yawns, the poor fellow stumbled through to the end and was greeted with a ripple of applause, frenzied on my part and comatose for the rest. Were there any questions after that most interesting speech, the chairman wondered? A terrible silence fell, and lasted an eternity; after which our chairman rose to his feet, thanked our guest, shook him warmly by the hand and – far from suggesting that, if he could bear it, he was welcome to sit through the rest of the proceedings and join us afterwards in a glass or two of warm pale ale – steered him firmly to the door that led down to the street below. 'I'm sorry,' he said as he came back into the room, rubbing his hands on the seat of his trousers, 'I don't know about you, but I can't abide being spoken to by a nigger.' This seemed to

go down well, in that no one actively dissented (I was far too feeble
to have done so); and with that unpleasantness behind us we got on
with the real business of the meeting in an altogether happier frame
of mind.

This gave me just the excuse I needed to abandon political life,
providing a priggish smokescreen that concealed boredom, ambiv-
alence and a terrible indifference; and I happily reverted to my
more familiar role as a passenger and an observer. My politics
remained a mess of conflicting emotions: snobbishness and a delight in the English upper-middle classes (taken in moderation) and
a fear of the masses warring with an innate sympathy, in the office
at least, with the rank-and-file and the underdog, and a deep
resentment of that seemingly inevitable transmogrification, like
water turning to ice, that occurred when people I admired as
individuals became part of an oppressive and pompous Establishment, whether of the left or the right. And because of the world I
moved in I came to particularly dislike self-righteous *bien pensants*:
and most of all those, not uncommon in a well-meaning trade like
publishing, who preached the liberal virtues but hectored and
bullied their fellow-workers, many of whom were in no position to
answer back, and combined a theoretical devotion to free speech
with an almost Stalinist addiction to the rewriting of recent history,
and the suppression of conflicting points of view.

One of the many crosses a wife has to bear is listening to her
husband moaning about his job (and vice versa, of course): and
hardly had we unpacked our suitcases in Cedars Road, SW15 –
carefully wrapping Petra's tiny Mary Quant wedding-dress in
layers of tissue paper, which are swathed about it still – before a
lifetime's grumbling began. Life in Doughty Street – or so I
informed my soulmate – was tedious and uninspiring and unlikely
to improve or to lead on to better things: worse, I felt – and here I
was overcome by waves of lachrymose self-pity – that I was no
longer particularly popular. Mr Gibb, though as genial and as
affable as ever, had never quite recovered from my disdaining his
herd of cattle for the Glasgow printing works, and something of his

disaffection seemed to have spilled over onto the spinster ladies. Doughty Street's sober citizens tended to regard the inhabitants of St James's Place as arrogant and flashy, and I was uneasily aware that I was considered, by the spinsters in particular, a tiresome youth who had far too high an opinion of himself and thought he knew all the answers. Twenty-five years on, my sympathies are all with the spinsters. The firm was, for them, a way of life, and one that might – with luck – see them through from the bright, exuberant expectations of their early twenties via the repetitive, weary wastes of middle age to retirement and oblivion; they understood and appreciated its workings and the foibles of its managing director far better than I ever would; no doubt they resented the knowing airs and patronising attitudes of someone who was merely passing through and making use of the place. For the first time in my working life I became *persona non grata* with some of my colleagues. The black-eyed Armenian in accounts still nudged me in the ribs like a genial carrion crow, wringing his hands as he spoke; the production director remained as polite and reserved as ever, and still seemed happy to take time off to explain the different weights and varieties of paper, or the meaning of 'overs' or 'run-on prices'; Joyce on the switchboard continued perfectly affable, the click of her needles audible over the wires as she announced the name of one's caller or put one through to one's destination: but the womenfolk in the firm – the editors in their dank and spider-infested basement, the boss's irritable, cold-eyed secretary – had decided to freeze me out, and a very distressing feeling it was.

All this made me more eager than ever to leave. I went on typing *curricula vitae* – all too short, and sadly unimpressive – and desperate accompanying letters to every publisher I had heard of; but many remained unanswered, and not a single interview was suggested. Could it be that the spinsters had spread the word among a network of fellow-spinsters, and that I was condemned for ever to wind the handle of the Doughty Street roneo machine and design advertisements for collections of Easter sermons, and jackets for books about *torte* and *wienerschnitzel*? But then, much to my surprise, I had a phone call from a publisher whom I admired far more than most and who – in terms of reputation and the books he published – seemed the antithesis of all I had experienced during the past year or so. André Deutsch asked me if I would like to drop by after work one evening and suggested a couple of alternative times, one of which I accepted in a kind of sonorous gasp, writing down the time and the address in my otherwise empty diary in a hand that trembled with excitement. Over the next few days I was convulsed with dread and longing. Deutsch was the kind of literary list I longed to work for, small and lively and just that bit more dashing than comparable but longer-established firms; but he had a formidable reputation within the trade, and I felt quite sure that such a mercurial and demanding figure, the publisher of Norman Mailer and Philip Roth and Brian Moore and V.S. Naipaul and John Updike and Jean Rhys, would find me irremediably bovine and sluggish and out-of-touch.

On the appointed evening I went along to Mr Deutsch's offices in Great Russell Street, opposite the headquarters of the TUC. I rang the night bell, was let in by a buzzer, and found myself once again in a narrow, rather grubby passageway, with a door at one end, two bicycles propped against one wall, and that familiar litter of brown-paper parcels. To my left was a sliding panel made of frosted glass. I tapped on this, and it was opened by a fair-haired, fresh-faced girl with a black velvet band, a row of pearls, a turtle-necked sweater and matching cardigan and, I was fairly certain – for only her head and shoulders were visible through the hatch – a black and white check tweed skirt, thick tights and black slip-on shoes with a gold chain across the instep. When I explained that I had an appointment with Mr Deutsch she frowned and looked at me askance: he had left early and, as far as she knew, he wouldn't be back. All this was very puzzling: but bafflement turned to panic and then despair when she rang upstairs to his secretary to be told that he had been expecting me the evening before. I let out a terrible cry of 'Oh Christ!', slapped my hand to my forehead and unleashed a stream of futile apologies; and as I staggered out into the gloaming – it was a pink, late autumn evening, and the starlings were wheeling and swooping overhead, like particles of ash, readying themselves for flight – I knew that I had through plain ineptitude fouled up the one great chance of my career.

Next morning I was busy typing an apologetic letter to Mr Deutsch, which I planned to drop off in my lunch hour, when his secretary rang to say that he, and not I, was responsible for getting our dates wrong, and could we try again that evening? Two days later, after an interview that was less unnerving than expected, he wrote and offered me a job as a junior editor. I have always been a coward about opening unwelcome or decisive letters, carrying them around for days in my pocket like unexploded bombs: I took this particular letter with me to work – I knew from the franking whom it had come from – resolving to open it as soon as I arrived in the office, and then after coffee and Haliborange pills and the agricultural bulletin, and then after lunch, and then as soon as I'd finished my work for the day. Back home in Cedars Road, I smuggled it into the darkest corner of the bedroom and, averting my gaze, tore open the envelope, blindly unfolded the letter and then – peeking at it sideways, as if from a great height – absorbed its unexpected contents. Within seconds life had utterly changed, and I longed for Petra's return so that I could give her the good news. I would no longer be an ineffectual publicity hound, but would be working as an editor for one of the nimblest and classiest publishers in London; my salary seemed as modest as ever – hovering unashamedly around the eight hundred mark – but at least I would be free of the antique melancholy that seemed to swathe the Doughty Street office, in much the same way as the mist and the darkness had swathed it on the day of my arrival. But before I could make the news known to my friends – barely able to suppress my excitement on the telephone, and feeling a very dashing kind of fellow – an unhappy ritual had to be endured, and one that I dreaded quite as much as, if not more than, my interview with my future employer.

For brazen and self-confident souls, well aware of their own worth and with their eyes firmly fixed on the distant horizon, giving in one's notice is, presumably, a functional, hard-headed business, exciting no strong emotions on either side; but for feebler employees it can be something of an ordeal, involving unwelcome waves of guilt,

embarrassment and fear. Whereas the deserted party may well feel
only indifference or relief, the deserter's jubilation and heightened
self-esteem are often blighted by feelings of ingratitude, of seeming
– all too improbably – a ruthless go-getter who has spurned the
familiar and the everyday in favour of something better; and so it
was when, having postponed the awful moment by walking three
times round the block and re-tidying my desk and visiting the
cracked and marbled lavatory mirror in search of a fresh outcrop of
blackheads, I eventually oozed into Mr Gibb's office – the fire
burning as brightly as ever, the *Farmers Weekly* open before him on
the desk, a fresh packet of cattle feed standing to one side – and
blurted out my news. He looked, as I had dreaded, more hurt than
affronted, flinching back in his chair and blinking and looking more
than ever like a benevolent bloodhound. But no one *ever* left, he
said (which was true). Was I unhappy in my work? Was there
anything he could do to persuade me to think again? Was I really
well advised – and here he lowered his voice to a confidential
mutter and, striding across from behind his desk, took me in
confidence by the upper arm – to work for a *Central European*? Such
questions only add to one's embarrassment, forcing the deserter to
spell out his motives for departure. He was too kind to press me any
further: no doubt he knew perfectly well that my mind was made
up, and would have been amazed if I'd taken him up on his offer.
He sat me down, gave me much avuncular advice about how to get
on in the world of publishing (with special reference to his close
friends Sir Allen Lane, Robert Lusty and Billy Collins), and wished
me the best of luck, Central Europeans notwithstanding; and I
crept away to break the news to my other colleagues, aflame with
admiration and affection.

Three weeks later, on a Friday afternoon, I said my last farewells
to Doughty Street: to Joyce on the switchboard, still knitting – or so
it seemed – the same interminable shroud I had spotted on my
arrival almost exactly a year before; to the spinsters in the basement, grown warmer and more friendly now that I was safely on my
way; to the production director in his black serge suit, whom I
encountered hurrying down the stairs, briefcase and bowler in

hand, *en route* for the 6.15 to Beckenham and a weekend pottering in the garden; to the Armenian accountant, who nudged me in the ribs and winked in the direction of his harem of stout middle-aged ladies, busy screwing the tops on their inkpots and folding their ledgers away; to the languid, floppy-haired sales manager, who was asleep behind his desk; to the brown-coated whistlers and thumpers in the packing room, one of whom thrust upon me a lavishly illustrated *Good Housekeeping* cookery book which, he explained with a wink and a leer, had 'fallen off the back of a lorry' and would make a good present 'for your missus'. Last of all, I raced upstairs to say goodbye to my kindly if ineffectual mentor, who clasped me firmly by the hand and, after some rummaging in drawers, presented me with a copy, hot from the press, of this year's Lenten address. Clutching this in one hand and my briefcase in the other, I raced down the stairs, into the street, and north towards Euston, where the boat train was waiting to take us to Belfast and the empty golden strands of Donegal.

Publishing is a small and introverted profession, in which people move around from firm to firm, nudging their salaries and their status forward a little every time; and one tends, over a lifetime, to come across former colleagues in all kinds of incarnations, at parties or at dinner or merely as a subject of gossip or in the pages of the trade papers. Nearly a quarter of a century later I have yet to come across, or even hear news of, any of my colleagues from Doughty Street – causing me to wonder at times whether it had ever really existed except in my imagination. Somehow or other I gathered that, not many years after I had sprinted off to catch the Belfast train, Mr Gibb had finally retired to one of his two Scottish estates, and then that he had died; that the Chairman had closed down the Doughty Street offices and sold the firm to a younger publisher after removing the two popular theologians; and that after a few more years of sporadic activity it had vanished altogether, lingering on as a dim, forgotten name on the spines and title pages of yellowing, dusty volumes, and in the memories, fast fading, of those who had worked there once.

CHAPTER THREE

'Deutschland über Alles'

MY NEW EMPLOYER was a small, dapper Hungarian with a square, imperial head, a long, humorous mouth, a shrewd but generally benevolent gaze, and a broad forehead topped by a quiff of grey hair. A natty dresser, he favoured well-pressed suits, often in pale corduroy, and pink or diamond-pattern shirts, under which one sometimes spotted the glint of a medallion on a thin gold chain. He still spoke with an engagingly Hungarian accent: 'dear boy' was his usual mode of address to men, while 'love' was bestowed irrespective of sex. He had been born in Budapest in 1917: his father was a Jewish dentist, while his mother was, allegedly, of French, Turkish and Hungarian stock. From an early age he had nursed a flatteringly romantic view of England and the English; debarred from attending a university, he worked in his uncle's tyre factory and trained as a photographer before arriving in England only months before the war broke out.

After a spell as a bird-scarer in Shropshire, which he once described as the most congenial job he ever did, since it was undemanding and left him plenty of time for reading, he was working as a floor manager in the Grosvenor House Hotel when, in December 1941, Hungary entered the war on the side of the Axis and he found himself interned – initially in the parrot house in Manchester Zoo, and later on the Isle of Man. Among his fellow-internees was Arthur Koestler's cousin, a dubious Hungarian publisher called Ferenc Aldor; and when, in due course, Deutsch was released, Aldor asked him if he would like to look after his business in exchange for £8 a week, and the use of his mistress and his flat in Mayfair. This gave Deutsch an entrée into publishing, from which he moved to the more respectable if soporific firm of Nicholson & Watson, where he busied himself learning about every aspect of the trade from typesetting to selling subsidiary rights. To supplement his income he wrote occasional book reviews for the left-wing weekly *Tribune*, of which George Orwell was then the literary editor. Orwell was having difficulties finding a publisher for *Animal Farm* – Victor Gollancz, Jonathan Cape and T. S. Eliot at Faber were among those who had turned it down for fear of affronting the Russians – and Deutsch was amazed and frustrated when his bosses at Nicholson & Watson refused it as well. Orwell then suggested that Deutsch should set up on his own and publish *Animal Farm* as his first book: in an uncharacteristic failure of nerve Deutsch turned down a chance to make his fortune and his reputation, but the whole incident sharpened his resolve to be his own master as soon as he possibly could.

Eventually Deutsch managed to scrape together £3000 from his own savings and from his friends – these included a literary-minded handbag manufacturer – and set up on his own. According to the conventional wisdom of the time, £15,000 was the minimum needed to set up a publishing house from scratch, and the shortfall made the young publisher all the more aware of the need to watch the pennies: later in life Deutsch was renowned throughout the trade for his parsimony, and made no bones about his enthusiasm for switching out lights, recycling envelopes and installing low-wattage electric lightbulbs in the lavatories to help keep the firm afloat. Trading under the unthreatening name of Allan Wingate – it was thought that 'Deutsch' might be counter-productive so soon after the war had ended – the new firm got off to a flying start with *Operation Cicero*, the story of a butler in the wartime British Embassy in Ankara who turned out to have been a German spy, gravely eavesdropping as he bent low in his morning coat and sponge-bag trousers and then hurrying down to the pantry to flash the news back to his masters in Berlin; but it was with the publication of Norman Mailer's *The Naked and the Dead* in 1949 that Deutsch produced his first and most spectacular best-seller. Denounced in the *Sunday Times* as something that should not be left around to contaminate 'unsuspecting womenfolk', it went on to sell 150,000 copies in hardback, but this brought serious problems in its wake. Publishing is a capital-intensive business – even the most modest advance to an author may take several years to be earned back, and printers' and papermakers' bills will almost certainly have to be settled long before the booksellers shell out for the copies they have bought – and Deutsch had to take on new shareholders and new directors to raise the money with which to finance a series of reprints, losing control of his firm in the process. Deutsch remained, throughout his working life, the choosiest (and so the most realistic) of literary publishers, only taking on those books he believed in, and steering clear of those titles or areas of publishing which might make a fortune for somebody else, but lay outside his own area of expertise. His new directors wanted to publish books of a rather different kind, leading to a period of stalemate; Deutsch's eventual departure from the firm he had founded made him resolve never to sell out again, and never to be so over-stretched financially as to lose control of his business.

In 1952 he started all over again, trading under his own name this time; and soon he had established a reputation as one of the liveliest general publishers in London, publishing worthwhile and interesting books without the benefit of a large backlist. Like all the best publishers, he combined the instincts of a street trader with a love of good writing; he had no idea of the meaning of 'cash flow' and did all his calculations in his head while on the telephone, scribbling sums in an illegible hand on the back of an envelope or the margin of a typescript, but he knew better than any how to sustain that fine balance between the demands of art and commerce that is the mark of the outstanding publisher. Some time in the early fifties he bought up the list of Derek Verschoyle, a dubious, gin-sodden graduate of Trinity College, Dublin, who had been the literary editor of the *Spectator* and an undercover agent – at one stage in his career he seems to have busied himself attaching limpet mines to boats in Trieste harbour – and ended his days editing *The Grower,* a magazine devoted to vegetables, and whose authors at Derek Verschoyle Ltd included Roy Fuller, Alan Ross,

Lawrence Durrell, Patrick Leigh Fermor and Julian Maclaren-Ross.

In all this Deutsch was helped and complemented by his two founding partners, whose roles were reflected in the firm's colophon of a bow within a circle with three arrows laid across it, one of them slightly forward from the others. Diana Athill was a modest, fresh-faced Englishwoman of about his own age, who – by the time I arrived there some eighteen years later – wore her grey hair in a bun, beavered quietly in the background editing the likes of Jean Rhys and V. S. Naipaul, and was the author of a remarkably frank slice of autobiography, *Instead of a Letter*, some pages of which were devoted to the early days of the firm; while Nicolas Bentley, the third arrow, was a dapper, immaculate figure with hawklike features, bushy eyebrows and an impeccable widow's peak, who was best-known for his elegant, economical cartoons and drawings for such works as T. S. Eliot's *Practical Cats* and Hilaire Belloc's *Cautionary Verses*, but also doubled up as a crime novelist and military historian. André – as I would soon be allowed to call him – provided the entrepreneurial energy, the single-minded dedication and the zest for wheeling-and-dealing and striking a bargain without which a firm like his would expire in a haze of lofty thoughts and fine intentions; Diana supplied the patience and the sympathy and the literacy and the attention to detail of the ideal old-fashioned editor; Nick had the contacts and the sense of perspective of a man of the world who had grown up among writers and artists and Edwardian public figures – his father had been a close friend of Chesterton and Belloc – and he greeted the hyperbole and the rhetoric and the over-stimulation that are an essential if transitory ingredient of all successful publishing with an amused, world-weary sigh and a sardonic elevation of the bushy eyebrows in the direction of the widow's peak.

It all sounded both daunting and exciting; but in the meantime, as Petra and I strode side-by-side along a crescent of strand in Donegal, the sand the colour of custard, the sea an Aegean blue, the mountains shimmering mauve in the background, and Doughty Street a dot receding rapidly into the background, life seemed an

altogether more hopeful affair than it had on that despairing evening when I had turned up in Great Russell Street for the chance of
a lifetime, only to learn that the bird had fled.

A week or so later I reported for duty for the first time as a
publisher's editor, albeit of the humblest variety. By now we had
left Cedars Road, SW15, and were living in the ground floor flat of
a house in Maida Vale in which – or so I learned a good many years
later – the young Victor Gollancz had grown up. I was as keen on
walking to work as ever, and even when living in Barnes I had made
a point of walking from Waterloo to Doughty Street and back every
day, and I decided to set out early so as to give myself plenty of time
to pick my way from Elgin Avenue to Great Russell Street, via
Hamilton Terrace, Lord's, Regent's Park and those solid Gals-
worthian streets that lie between the Euston Road and Oxford
Street. Just as I was turning the corner into the gate by the park a
dashing-looking sports car drew up and my employer stuck his
head out, rather puzzled to find his new editor strolling absent-
mindedly along so far from his place of work. I explained what I
was up to and waved away his offer of a lift, hoping after he had
sped away that this didn't suggest a lack of keenness on my part;
later I learned that although he lived in South Kensington, he often
took a circuitous route to work in order to have breakfast with his
mother in St John's Wood.

The office occupied a small, smoke-blackened early-nineteenth-
century house, recognisable from the pavement by an enamelled
inn sign swinging above the door and incorporating the bow and its
three symbolic arrows. A door or two down the road was a vege-
tarian Indian restaurant, the whiffs of which filtered through the
building, lending a curryish flavour to memo pads and filing
cabinets. The house next door was let to a firm of rat-catchers and
insect exterminators; one of their vans, painted a pestilential
mustard and featuring, on its side panels, a scarlet rat sniffing the
air and a couple of cockroaches waving their antennae, was invariably parked outside, mounted high on the kerb to avoid the stream
of traffic hurtling its way from the Tottenham Court Road to the

British Museum and points east. Great Russell Street was, as I soon discovered, a lively sort of street, with much to lull or distract the office worker – trade unionists chanting and waving placards outside the TUC's headquarters two or three times a week, clogging the pavements with the adult equivalent of school crocodiles, bussed in from all over the country; studious, unhappy-looking Indians and Nigerians, wrapped up against the cold, their noses and fingers an unwholesome mauve, hastening towards the Reading Room, their briefcases bulging with important papers about hydro-electric dams or the legacies of imperialism; pastel-garmented American tourists wearing cotton trilbies wrapped in polythene, anxiously consulting an *A to Z* in the rain; and, best of all, a recurrent group of street musicians, picking their way in Indian file along the gutter, their leader an unshaven, gaberdine-mackintoshed Sidney Bechet, whooping and screeling on a soprano saxophone. And although in the years since then publishers have been scattered all over London, driven out by soaring rents to resettle, unhappily, in Hammersmith and Pimlico, Bloomsbury was still the centre of the trade: in our near vicinity were Cape and Hamish Hamilton and Michael Joseph and Allen & Unwin and Thames & Hudson, and friendly rivals could be spotted heading purposefully down the street for lunch or pacing to and fro in their shirt-sleeves in their first-floor offices, like figures from a literary Punch and Judy show.

Inside the office was – as most publishing houses were in the days before open-plan and VDU terminals had blighted their antique mystery – a pleasing mixture of elegance and chaos, in which gilt mirrors and paintings by familiar names jostled for space with cardboard boxes and office machinery and tottering piles of bumph. The same fair-haired girl was on duty in reception as I pushed open the door and sidled in past the bikes and the brown-paper parcels; but this time she knew who I was, told me that 'AD' would like to see me at once, and buzzed up to say that I'd arrived. I made my way up a rectangular wooden staircase in the middle of the building, lit from above by a skylight, and found my new employer on the landing, waiting to greet me for the second time that day. For a moment or two I sat with him in his office, taking my first look at the lair of an unabashed literary publisher. Whereas the Chairman's office, with its bare panelled walls, could have been a country-house study or a rather masculine London drawing-room, and wouldn't have looked amiss in an old-fashioned City bank, while Doughty Street had shades of a hunting parson, André Deutsch's office left one in no doubt about the business of its occupant; and I found the mere sight of it congenial and reassuring. It was a deep, sombre, cave-like room that seemed to burrow its way back into the body of the building, growing ever more cavernous and ill-lit as one moved away from the two large sash windows that overlooked Great Russell Street. The walls were covered in tobacco-coloured hessian, and above a white marble mantelpiece was a large, three-panelled gold mirror in which one could, if so inclined, examine oneself for signs of an incipient double chin or a receding hairline while waiting for Mr Deutsch – who was unable to resist a phone call and, once hooked, found it harder still to extricate himself – to stop talking to a fellow-publisher in New York or an author or a persistent literary agent or an unforthcoming literary editor. There were books everywhere one looked: old books, new books, proofs, typescripts, books from rival or American publishers, paperback editions; books arranged alphabetically by author in bulging shelves along one wall, random or unruly books precariously piled on chairs, on the desk, on the floor and on the mantelpiece. Mr Deutsch himself sat, with his back to the window, behind a leather-topped desk the size of a snooker table, every inch of which was covered with paper – with letters, proofs, catalogues, reviews cut out for him to inspect, advertisements, contracts that needed to be signed, parking tickets, theatre tickets, invitations, magazines, trade journals, sample pages from the printer, jacket roughs, urgent memos scrawled on the backs of envelopes or pages of discarded typescript, libel readings and editorial reports. In one corner stood a bottle of whisky, a survivor from the night before; uneasily balanced amidst all this was a steaming cup of black coffee, a biscuit perched in its saucer. Years later I went for an interview with his arch-rival and old friend, a fellow exile from Danubia and an internationally-minded publisher of great distinction, and found, much to my dismay, that his desk seemed as bare and as orderly as that of a hairdresser's receptionist; the rival was a far more flamboyant and better-known figure, certainly to the world at large, but if their desks were anything to go by, André Deutsch had the greater distinction of remaining a practising publisher, still dirtying his hands with the everyday minutiae of his calling.

Never the man to waste a moment if a deal could be done or a phone call intercepted, Mr Deutsch instructed his secretary to take me round the building, introduce me to my new colleagues, and show me to my desk; and so I began, yet again, that familiar, baffling routine of grinning and shaking hands and explaining who I was and where I'd come from, before moving on to the next unknown face and unremembered name. The offices were small, cramped and densely populated: editors and designers and secretaries had been squeezed into what had once been larders or coal-holes or garden sheds, and even the tiniest cupboard, when opened, seemed to contain some affable figure, clad in jeans and an open-necked shirt, hammering out a blurb on an elderly upright typewriter or puzzling over a set of proofs.

My own office, for the time being at least, was in part of a partitioned-off former bedroom in the front of the house, almost immediately over Mr Deutsch's head. I was not to stay there long for, as I soon discovered, 'AD' took a keen and restless interest in moving people's offices, including desks and filing cabinets, from one floor to another, and from the front of the building to the back. He was reluctant to spend money hiring professional removals men on such unproductive labour, and since I was the largest member of staff I found myself spending more time than I had anticipated humping office furniture – other people's as well as my own – from one room to another. In this important work I was sometimes joined by André's right-hand man and deputy managing director, a pale, willowy figure not much older than myself who had acquired an encyclopaedic knowledge of publishing since joining the firm from Oxford, and had one hand permanently plunged in his trouser pocket, jiggling and rearranging various parts of his anatomy. On one occasion we spent the best part of a morning nudging a heavily-laden filing cabinet from the second floor to the basement. My fellow-porter, who looked ashen and red-eyed at the best of times, with a hollow chest, stooped shoulders and a persistent smoker's wheeze – he smoked in the National Service mode, the cigarette held between the thumb and first two fingers, the smouldering end facing into the palm – was constantly interrupted by his secretary asking him to take a call from New York or talk to a literary agent or see 'AD' on a matter of urgent business; at which he would set down his end of the filing cabinet with a grunt of irritation and hurry away, leaving me balancing the cabinet halfway down the stairs, sometimes for as long as twenty minutes. We were about to manoeuvre down the last narrow flight of stairs into the basement when, much to my alarm, he vanished altogether, and, peering round the khaki cabinet I saw him lying prone on the haircord carpet. He had turned the colour of a dishcloth, his eyes had rolled up into his head, and his lips were flecked with foam. Carefully setting down my end of the cabinet, I sped away in search of water and a helping hand; a minute or two later he came to, and we continued our journey undisturbed.

At Geoffrey Bles I had found myself with nothing to do on my first day, and for many days thereafter, but in Great Russell Street, much to my relief, I was plunged in mid-stream at once. One of the most basic jobs in any publishing house – usually reserved for junior editors or outside readers who come in once or twice a week – is sifting through and sampling what is known as the 'slush pile': that tidal wave of novels and memoirs and diatribes about the pyramids or intergalactic travel and conspiracy theories and poems from the school of Ella Wheeler Wilcox that flood in by every post and flood out again as soon as someone has found the time to take a look at them, writing a short report on each in case the author pops up later claiming that no one had taken the trouble to read his book. It is, almost invariably, dispiriting and unproductive work, though an essential part of the publishing process: most of the offerings are irremediably bad, and instantly recognisable as such, though there is nothing more pleasing or rewarding than those rare, almost numinous moments – occurring once in every five years, perhaps – when something publishable shines out among the dross like gold in a panhandler's sieve. Because most of the works on offer are so bad, and because time is short and the slush pile never-ending, a cursory glance is usually more than enough, the sampler taking care to remove any hairs he may come across and to correct the order of pages deliberately shuffled by the sender, who may otherwise write an angry if triumphant letter after the book has been sent winging on its way, a rejection slip clipped to its cover, claiming (rightly) that his masterpiece hadn't been read from cover to cover since the hair was still in place and the pages out of order; but on that first day, ablaze with idealism and as yet unsullied by self-protective cynicism, I sat solemnly down behind the yard-high mound of typescripts I had inherited from my predecessor, and started to work my way through them, making careful notes as I went so that I could, in every case, write the kind of careful and constructive letter their senders begged for in their covering notes. Two such letters were written and sent, but by lunchtime I was beginning to pall, and a further eighteen inches of typescript had arrived by the second post; by the end of the day all my scruples had melted away, and I found myself sampling a page here and there, doling out the rejection slips like confetti, falling gratefully on stout, self-evidently hopeless cases that could be summed up in a second and, once despatched, made a satisfying hole in the mound, and bitterly resenting those infuriating offerings that hovered on the borderline, not bad enough for immediate expulsion, adequate enough to keep one dithering and – in the last resort – not good enough to merit publication. All publishers, thank God, are fallible, and, as embattled authors love to point out, a flurry of rejection slips is occasionally followed by a spell on the bestseller lists or literary acclaim, but, like all editors, I soon came to recognise dependable warning signs: the impeccably-typed offering bound in hand-tooled leather, the roneoed, single-spaced tract announcing a revolution in man's thinking (these tended to be grubby as well, with worrying brown stains here and there and occasional evidence of missiles blown from the nose and dried on the page in unwelcome grey granules), the epic poem written in capital letters on torn-off sheets of closely-lined paper from a school exercise book, the faded carbon copy of everyday life in the 1930s, replete with those touching, give-away turns of phrase that herald a hopeless case ('I'll never forget the day' or 'What a character Jack was!' or 'How we all laughed!'). And yet, for all my soon-discovered hardness of heart, I found looking after the slush pile both sad and humbling. I liked to think of myself as the kind of person who was bound to write something one day, yet I had produced nothing on which to base this assumption beyond the occasional book review and a few rather whimsical poems which had struggled into print in obscure magazines and which I had once recited in a crowded pub in a tremulous rumble. Three-quarters of the books on the slush pile were full-length novels; all over the country men and women were doing what I could never do, brewing up plots and inventing characters and making people walk and talk and go about their business, however ineptly (part of their business was, inevitably, making love very noisily and at great length, and the pages pulsed and steamed with enormous, perfectly-shaped bosoms and rigid nipples and throbbing members and buttons being torn off dresses and brassieres hurled aside); and when I thought of how much work, and how much of themselves, the authors had put into even the most absurd and incompetent of these offerings, which we sent on their way with a mixture of derision and resentment, I felt a terrible sense of pathos and shame. Some things, it seemed, were better not thought about too closely: a certain steeling of the heart was needed to survive, or at least to get through one's work without being overcome by a sense of sad futility.

Such was my initiation into the mysteries of the editorial life, and more was to follow on my second day. While hidden behind the slush pile, I had heard much talk in the corridor outside of a particular novel that was due to be discussed at the weekly editorial lunch, at which – or so I was told – we were supposed to come up with bright ideas for books to be written or authors pursued, as well as airing our views on manuscripts and synopses that had been submitted to us by literary agents or American publishers, working out offers for those we wanted to publish, and reporting back on the progress of such negotiations, as well as on the general gossip of the trade. These meetings were, as I soon discovered, awaited with a certain dread by my colleagues, who spent a good part of the morning beforehand shuffling and reshuffling their papers, gathering up their ammunition, and making detailed shopping lists of exactly what they wanted to say and when: like most human dynamos, André was impatient of waffle and circumlocution, had a limited attention span, and displayed a disconcerting genius for asking the awkward, crucial question that no one else had thought of, so throwing an entire argument into disarray. The meetings were held round an elegant dining-room table at the cavernous end of André's office; the editors tended to shelter together at the extremity of the cave – a door at the far end providing some kind of bolt-hole – while André presided from the opposite end, his pallid, chain-smoking deputy seated at his right hand and the telephone on his desk a mere carpet's-breadth away. Between André and the huddle of editors were various functionaries who were called upon from time to time to give their views: the sales manager, pressed to reveal how many copies Smith's might take of such and such a book; the publicity manager, conjuring out of the air possible television interviews or profiles in the Sunday papers; the rights manager, speculating keenly about the sale of second serial rights; the production manager, there to advise about possible problems with printers or binders or block-makers, but seizing the opportunity to grumble about editorial lateness in getting typescripts into production and the likelihood of publication dates being missed and postponed, while the editor concerned stared redly at the ground, gritting his teeth and waiting for the storm to pass. Diana Athill, quite unfussed by the occasional shafts of lightning that played about the far end of the table, and never greatly involved in the commercial side of the business, provided calm, dispassionate advice and comforted the battered and the bruised; while Nicolas Bentley, a man of few but pointed words, reassuringly togged out in a dapper fawn cardigan with shiny leather buttons, smiled and raised his eyebrows at the wilder flights of fancy or momentary outrage, seeming, as he did so, like a benevolent messenger from the world outside. Typescripts and readers' reports and synopses and American proof copies and lawyers' libel readings and agents' letters and estimates and contracts were spread before us on the table, jostling for space with sticks of French bread and plates of pâté and cheese and bowls of tomatoes and bottles of red wine; and as the meeting wore on the tenor of the occasion – never unpleasant, but often nerve-racking – became steadily more genial and easy-going.

Such goings-on were a far cry from Doughty Street's Haliborange tablets and agricultural anecdotes, and all the more welcome for it. As yet I had nothing to say for myself, relishing that brief breathing-space or honeymoon that goes with the first days in a new job, but rather dreading the moment when I would be called upon to prove my worth; and at some stage in the proceedings, André – anxious to give me something to do, and giving no clue about his or anyone else's view on the matter – suggested that I should temporarily abandon the slush pile and take a look at the talked-about novel instead, since he'd be interested to know what I thought. The typescript was passed reverentially along the table, with instructions to report back to him by the end of the day, since the agent was agitating for a speedy decision. Feeling both honoured and awestruck, I bore it off to my cell in the attic, moved to one side the slush pile – which had grown by three feet over lunch – and began reading right away.

In those days, in up-to-the-moment publishing houses aspiring editors in jeans and corduroy jackets – most of whom had been to public schools and ancient universities, and felt dreadfully ashamed at the 'sheltered' or 'privileged' lives they had led to date – were, from time to time, overcome by an irresistible urge to associate themselves with what they imagined to be the 'real' or working-class world, and kept a keen eye out for novels in which the characters said 'fuck' and 'cunt' and wiped their lips with the backs of their hands after downing a pint of mild-and-bitter, while the writer eschewed grammar as a relic of bourgeois formalism; and this one was very much in that line of country. It described the adventures of a gang of North Country girls in black mini-skirts who spent their days stoking up on LSD and waiting outside stage doors to ambush unsuspecting pop stars, whom they bore off into the bushes for a spot of gasping and puffing of the kind encountered in the slush pile. I thought it ghastly after a couple of pages, and the more I read the cruder and more semi-literate it seemed. Every now and then an expectant, beaming face would thrust itself round my partition door and ask with eager, almost proprietorial zeal, how I was getting on and what I thought of it; and as face after face appeared, all wearing much the same expression, I became unhappily aware that each of them thought the book a masterpiece, and was longing for me to agree. This put me on the spot in the most unnerving way. I wanted above all to be accepted as a kindred spirit by my new colleagues, all of whom seemed so much brighter and sprightlier than the unhappy spinsters I had left behind in Doughty Street, yet were I to say what I really thought I would surely be branded at once as a fogey and a dimwit and even – oh horrors! – a Tory, hopelessly at odds with those with whom I had to work and the whole ethos of the firm. Should I fix an identical grin to my face and pretend – for the sake of a quiet life – that I shared their curious enthusiasm for this drivelling tale of a pop star and his mini-skirted groupies? Perhaps I *was* hopelessly out of touch as the result of over-immersion in Russian mystics and Lenten addresses? In the meantime, I desperately played for time, greeting each fresh enquiry with a non-committal grunt or pleading that – maddeningly – I had been repeatedly interrupted, and hadn't been able to read as much as I'd hoped. Such excuses grew thinner and less plausible as the afternoon wore on, and only a page or two remained to be read: before long the moment of truth would be upon me, when I must either declare myself and start my new career as a dissenter with priggish proclivities, or feign a bogus enthusiasm to curry favour with my colleagues. Some time in the late afternoon – dusk was falling in the street outside, and a few early commuters could be spotted hurrying anxiously along in the direction of the Tube –

the telephone rang and I heard André's clear, inflected voice bidding me downstairs. He was on the phone again by the time I reached his study, leaning back in his swivel chair and barking instructions into a box-shaped receiving device from which, every now and then, a reedy voice could be heard saying 'Yes, AD . . . No, AD . . . but, AD, you said . . . No, AD, of course not . . . right away, AD . . .', while I stood in front of his desk like an overweight, heavily-bespectacled version of the young Royalist in 'And When Did You Last See Your Father?' After some minutes the one-sided conversation with the box came to an end, and leaning even further back in his chair and fixing me with his humorous, heavy-lidded eyes, he said 'Tell me, dear boy, what did you think of –' and here he mentioned the name of the novel that had blighted my afternoon and, almost certainly, ruined my prospects of promotion and a life of easy camaraderie. Faced by that shrewd and beady stare, I knew there was no point in flannel or dissimulation, and taking a deep breath I told him, in the kind of garbled rush reserved for confidings of an intimate kind, that I knew I was the odd man out and I was awfully sorry and I hated to be a pest and cause trouble but I absolutely loathed it and thought it one of the worst novels I'd ever read and couldn't understand how anyone could seriously want to publish such a tidal wave of twaddle . . .

That said, I gazed at the edge of his desk in trepidation, waiting to be told that he had been mistaken in me after all, that he was gravely disappointed to find me taking such a bufferish and wilfully obstructive line towards one of the most remarkable novels of our time; but not a word was said, and when I eventually looked up I saw that, far from being incoherent with rage, his face wore a beatific smile of gratitude and wonder, and that he was gazing up at the ceiling with his hands raised up before him like a footballer who has just scored the winning goal, or a nun who has spotted the Virgin Mary hovering in mid-air. 'My dear, I am so grateful to you,' he said; and seeing my look of puzzlement and relief he went on to explain that he alone had disliked the book, that he had been under tremendous pressure from everyone else to take it on ('Oh André, you're so *stuffy*!'), and that had I liked it he would have had to bow to the inevitable. Now I had, quite unwittingly, made him master in his own house again, and his relief and delight were engagingly apparent.

As far as I was concerned, the news was both good and bad. I was glad in a rather priggish, misanthropic way that we wouldn't be publishing a book I disliked; I was relieved to find that I wasn't alone in my heretical opinions; and none of this can have done me any harm in the eyes of my boss, whose good opinion I was – like everybody else – eager to acquire. But the problem of my being the odd man out was made graver still by the revelation that mine was the casting vote: not only would my reactionary views be known to the world at large, but unkind spirits might easily assume that I had tailored my views in order to ingratiate myself with my new boss, or that, as an evident man of straw, I had been bullied or bludgeoned into acquiescence.

As it turned out, I needn't have worried. By the time my interview with André was over, most of my eager interrogators had gone home; and early next morning André announced that he was going to exercise his prerogative as managing director, and that he had decided, unilaterally, not to publish the book. After he had broken the news there was much muttering and whispering in corridors about André's high-handed and undemocratic ways of going on and the Spirit of '68, through all of which I retained a pious and ignoble silence: later on it was widely and wrongly assumed that the sales director, who was thought to be something of a philistine, had been responsible for persuading André to take a stand, and all the opprobrium that should have been heaped onto my shoulders was diverted onto his. As for the book itself, it did very well for another publisher – so proving for the first of many times that, whatever my editorial virtues, the vital ability to spot a best-seller was not among them. Its success was pointedly and repeatedly referred to at subsequent editorial meetings, but André – who had picked up a good few best-sellers in his day, but knew equally well what he wanted to publish (or not) – remained smilingly unrepentant, and my guilty secret remained intact to this day.

* * *

A year or so later André caused a comparable ripple of outrage to run through the office when he announced that he had voted Conservative in the general election of 1970 which ousted Harold Wilson's Labour government and replaced it with that of Mr Heath. Despite this grave apostasy – whether it was true or not was another matter – his list had always had a radical and leftish tinge, and never more so than in the late 1960s. The editor of the *Sunday Times* and André used to go skiing together, and this had borne fruit in a series of 'Insight' books about, among other subjects, Thalidomide babies and the Philby affair; and the so-called 'events' of 1968 provoked a further flurry of radical publishing, with dimly-remembered names like Bernadette Devlin and Danny Cohn-Bendit joining our list of authors. This was, too, the age of the Black Panthers and Malcolm X, as well as of student revolutionaries and opposition to the Vietnam War, and the firm took a keen interest in a variant of radical publishing which was not only consistent with the leftish slant of the list but with a longer-standing interest in American, West Indian and African writing.

From his earliest days as Allan Wingate, André had been an enthusiastic publisher of American authors; and, like his rivals at Cape and Weidenfeld & Nicolson, he spent a good deal of time in New York talking to American publishers and agents. As publishers always are, he was subject to fashion and the trends of the time. Philip Roth, who had recently defected to a rival firm, had, by an unkind twist of fate, provided his new publishers with a best-seller in the form of *Portnoy's Complaint*, as a result of which New York Jewish novels became the most sought-after items in the market. Every post was heavy laden with novels about Jewish adolescence in Flatbush or Brooklyn Heights, and we spent long hours puzzling over *bar mitzvahs* and *Yom Kippurs* and looking up *schleppers* and *shnorrers* and *meshuggeners* in *The Joys of Yiddish* as we ploughed our way through second-rate Bellows and Malamuds and Roths; in much the same way as, ten years later, following the success of Paul Theroux's *The Great Railway Bazaar*, publishers who had long ago written off the travel book as a thing of the past, rendered redundant by television documentaries and mass travel, hurried out to commission dim, unnecessary adventures, pressing large advances on gratified practitioners whose works had hitherto sold a tiny handful of copies and acclaiming as classics of the genre books which, though honourable and competent, were, as often as not, better left in quiet oblivion.

Our enthusiasm for salt beef and bagels was complemented by a guilty feeling that more should be done for black writers. André himself had taken the eminently practical steps of setting up educational and academic presses in Nigeria and, later, in East Africa, but this somehow lacked the *réclame* of publishing a Panther. Steps would have to be taken, so we commissioned a work by the English equivalent of Malcolm X; I did my bit by editing a book of incomprehensible Zulu poems, blazing with strongly-felt emotions and pleasantly redolent of bare feet stamping rhythmically in clouds of orange dust. Diana, for her part, was, as a subsequent memoir makes plain, personally as well as professionally involved with an American protégé of Malcolm X called Hakim Jamal, who was now living in London. A drug addict and a petty criminal with delusions of divinity, Jamal had lived for a time in Paris, where he had had an affair with the actress Jean Seberg; after which he had become involved with a rich English socialite called Gail Benson, who had dutifully emulated him by trading in her name for something more Islamic. Every now and then Jamal or one of his cronies would come into the office and behave in a way which, had he been a middle-class Englishman, would have led to his being seen off the premises: as it was, my fellow-editor and I – as nicely-brought-up English liberals, eager to seem on the side of the angel and the underdog, and terrified rigid by the very idea of black militancy – laughed ingratiatingly at his impenetrable jokes or gazed whimsically out of the window as he leered horribly at the editorial secretary who shot us imploring looks, longing for him to make his departure but terrified at the idea of offending an author, and a radical author at that.

One weekend, while all this was going on, I found that I had left in the office something I badly needed. Pestering André for a key was out of the question; but Diana was always unalarming, so I rang her at home in Primrose Hill to ask if I could possibly borrow hers. Of course I could, she said, but she was just going out: could I possibly collect it from a house in Ladbroke Grove, perhaps in an hour or so's time? In those days Ladbroke Grove was nothing like as fashionable a part of London as it has since become, and the address Diana had given me turned out to be part of a seedy stuccoed terrace next to the motorway flyover. I got out of the car, wondering what Diana was doing in such an improbable part of the world, climbed the steps of a pillared portico from which the paint was peeling in blisters, and pressed the doorbell. From inside I could hear the pulse of pounding rock; no one answered – not surprisingly, given the pounding rock – so, feeling suitably unnerved, I tried again. Eventually the door was flung open by a black man wearing a tight black shirt, black jeans, wrap-around dark glasses and a woolly hat like a tea-cosy, and wafting after him a sweet-smelling cloud of pot. By now I was certain I must have come to the wrong address – surely Diana must be elsewhere in Notting Hill, attending a meeting of PEN International, or taking tea further along the Bayswater Road at the Royal Society of Literature? – but, having brought the man to the door and disrupted his afternoon, I felt I ought to ask. 'I'm terribly sorry to bother you,' I said, feeling unusually stiff and far from radical, 'but I'm looking for someone called Diana Athill, and I wondered . . .' At this he took me by the arm in the kindest and most unfrightening way and, urging me to make myself at home ('Come in, man, come and join the party'), ushered me into a large ground-floor room. The pounding rock was louder than ever, and the clouds of pot more Wagnerian: but as far as I could see – blinking uneasily across the jerking, gyrating bodies, and wondering what I should do were a joint to be thrust in my hand – there was no sign of Diana. I was just about to back away with more profuse apologies – he must have misheard me, or have had another Diana in mind – when a vaguely familiar-looking woman with long golden hair, clad in a shining yellow dress, came up to me, dangling a key in one hand, and said, in clear upper-class tones, 'Here's the key to the office, Jeremy – let me have it back in the morning, won't you?' It was, of course, Diana, but – to look at at least – a very different Diana from her weekday incarnation with her sensible tweeds, homely grey bun and heavy spectacles. She was as friendly and as easy and as amused-looking as ever, and seemed in no way disconcerted at my coming across her in these unexpected surroundings; but, keen as I was to read about such things in books, I was utterly undone, and backed unhappily out of the room, turning down all invitations to stay, before hurrying nervously back to the car, the key to the office clutched in one heavily sweating hand.

Next morning, rather dreading our encounter, I went into Diana's tiny office to return the key. She was perched behind her desk as usual, toiling patiently through great mounds of proofs and typescripts: her bun was neatly pinned in place and her specs on the end of her nose, and she looked – as she always did – demure and self-effacing and arty in an unthreatening way, like a Petersfield potter or a bookshop-owner in Camden Town. Not a word was said about Ladbroke Grove or the clouds of pot or the pounding rock or the benevolent figure with the tea-cosy on his head. I must, I decided, have imagined it all, or perhaps – being unused to such things – I'd breathed too deeply on the fumes of pot, and had hallucinated within seconds of entering the room; but then, as I turned away I saw, hanging behind the door on a hook, a glittering golden wig.

It's unlikely, in fact, that Hakim Jamal was among the jerking and gyrating bodies – not long afterwards he moved to Jamaica, where Gail Benson was murdered – while the wig, more brown than gold in fact, was a harmless and short-lived fashion of the time. In her book – which was published nearly a quarter of a century later – Diana describes, with unnerving frankness, her infatuation with this half-demented figure, and the curious, intoxicating mixture of idealism and self-deception that prevailed in those years.

I liked Diana at once, admired her talents as an editor and envied the speed and ease with which she could sit down at her typewriter and knock out the blurb for a book: years later, when I had acquired a comparable facility, and came to realise that the blurb has a formal pattern, as tight as a sonnet's, I would watch my successors crumple up ball after ball of typing paper as they fought to master this odd but essential talent, and wonder why they found it so hard. Towards André, on the other hand, my feelings were not so much ambivalent as slightly uneasy. I admired him enormously and liked him instinctively, but our relationship was – quite rightly – that of a very junior employee to his boss, and I was too fearful and too on edge and too tongue-tied to see him as other than a volatile and demanding titan, capable of unleashing a barrage of thunderbolts that whizzed about our heads, dangerously close. Like all the best publishers, and particularly those who have founded their own firms and kept them afloat by native wit, he appeared to have no time for anything beyond the interests of his firm; like all workaholics, he seemed to suffer, and benefit, from a kind of tunnel vision, resulting from a complete absorption in matters of the moment, and a refusal – so hard for more frivolous or trivial spirits to comprehend, let alone emulate – to be distracted from them by irrelevancies or the outside world. Only much later in life, after he had retired, unhappily, from the firm which still bore his name, did I meet him as a friend rather than an employer, and realise – with a terrible feeling of regret at the passing of time and opportunity – how much I liked him as a man as well as admiring him as a publisher. In the meantime, though, he was possessed of that monomaniacal demon without which little of value is ever achieved; and those of us who worked for him – milder, less driven, altogether less effectual – stirred nervously in our seats when we knew he was about, awaiting with childish dread the sudden blast on the phone or the summons to his office. He was never terrifying or tyrannical, and there was nothing in him of the bully or the brute: but the slow and the indecisive and the uncommitted, who never quite know what they think about anything and don't terribly mind either way, are easily unnerved and thrown off balance by the quick and the resolute and the fiercely partisan, exciting impatience or anger or derision as they blunder in their wake. This obsession with the here and now had its comical moments. Over for a week or two from Hungary, and anxious to give his son a treat, André's father once took him to watch a football match at Highbury, only to discover that André had brought with him proofs of the forthcoming catalogue, from which he never looked up; encountered by us at the theatre one evening, he hastened up to me with a cry of 'Dear boy' and a list of things to be done next day, before heading off with Petra's handbag in his hand.

Though famous throughout the trade for switching off lights – sometimes, on winter evenings, plunging a roomful of editors or designers into darkness – André was always generous with time, if not with money: he was – unlike most human dynamos – perfectly happy for his staff to work at home provided they did what needed to be done on time; nor had he ever learned that, from an actuarial point of view, time was money, and that for his employees not to be hard at work was, in effect, so much waste of money. This was most apparent in his addiction to the telephone. Summoned to his office, one would stumble downstairs with a thumping heart – had one forgotten to put the author's name on the title page, or muddled up the captions to the photographs so that a battleship was now described as the author's wife, or scenes from the Western Front as a pre-war holiday in Bognor? – and then, just as both parties were about to open their mouths, the telephone would ring and André would be off, haggling and cajoling and charming and defying. Very often this might go on for some twenty minutes: efforts to escape were thwarted by a sideways waggle of the forefinger – indicating, erroneously, that matters were coming to a head – or a scooping motion of the hand in the direction of a chair: either way, one was left with little to do other than worry about the urgent items languishing on one's desk or gaze abstractedly at one's reflection in the heavy gilt mirror over the mantelpiece or leaf through the pages of the *Bookseller* or pull down books from the shelves or, most rewarding of all, try to read the more confidential-looking papers on André's desk upside-down and without being caught in the act.

André's inability to resist the telephone reached a fine climax during a sales conference at which Laurie Lee – who had recently joined the firm from The Hogarth Press – was due to introduce the second volume of his autobiography, *As I Walked out one Midsummer*

Morning, to the assembled reps and overseas agents. André's sales conferences were, in those days at least, the antithesis of the Chairman's, and as far from a Nuremberg rally as could be imagined. As befitted, perhaps, a more literary firm, the editors rather than the salesmen ruled the roost, droning on at length about the plots of long-forgotten novels and assessing the views of the critics, while the reps snoozed in their chairs, occasionally starting from slumber with an epileptic jerk or a noisy smacking of lips, André fidgeted behind his desk, and the rest of us gazed into space or at the tips of our shoes while our colleagues stumbled through their speeches, laughing a good deal at their own jokes and seldom making much sense. In those days the sales conference was held in André's office; and since Laurie Lee was something of a star turn, whom André was eager to impress, the room was even more crammed than ever as secretaries and production assistants and book-keepers and assorted riff-raff, none of whom would normally attend, piled in to catch sight of this celebrated Bohemian and to hear him play the violin which he had carried with him on his travels in Spain before the Civil War, earning his keep in the process. This was to be the climax of the conference, after which the reps would rush out with their order pads, notching up record subscriptions, and as Laurie Lee threaded his way to the front of the room – wearing a brown corduroy suit and looking suitably louche and poetical – an expectant hush fell. André rose from behind his giant desk, shook his distinguished visitor firmly by the hand, and spoke a few warm words of welcome ('familiar to you all . . . needs no introduction from me . . . an honour and a privilege to have him on our list') before retiring, mole-like, behind his desk.

Laurie Lee then spoke, equally engagingly and in a well-honed Gloucestershire burr, while we all leaned keenly forward in our chairs, looking a good deal more alert than we had earlier in the proceedings and roaring with laughter at appropriate moments. All this time his violin was lying in its battered leather case on André's desk; and after he'd finished his peroration he suggested, to general surprise and delight, that we might like to hear some of the tunes he'd played in Spain nearly forty years before (murmurs of approbation, and more eager craning forward). After some preliminary sawing sounds he launched into some kind of merry jig or sea shanty, and once it became clear that we weren't going to be subjected to, and embarrassed by, a terrible display of rasps and screeches, like knives upon a plate, we settled back with smiles of relief to enjoy the performance. What none of us had reckoned with, however, was André's telephone. Our visitor had just launched into a particularly lyrical passage when the telephone erupted with a fearful ringing of bells. Far from cutting it off at once with a promise to ring back, or diverting the caller to his secretary next door, André – unable to resist, and suddenly oblivious to all about him – began to do deals with the intruder, whose voice, amplified by the wooden box, boomed and thundered about the room, counterpointing André's lighter tenor and the gypsy violin. For a while all three fought for supremacy, while the rest of us – quickly caught up in the telephonic drama, and anxious to know its outcome – fought to disentangle the thread of the conversation from the swoop and trill of the violin; and then, quite suddenly, both violin and telephone were silent, and André, back on his feet again, a satisfied smile playing about his lips, was shaking his author fervently by the hand and winding up the proceedings before escorting him to the back of the room, now rapidly draining of its surplus occupants, where wine and French bread and cheese and pâté had been laid out for lunch.

Every now and then André used to invite a guest – a literary agent or a paperback publisher or a literary editor – to our editorial meeting, and he or she would join us for lunch once the main business of the meeting had been despatched. On one such occasion, after I'd been with the firm for about eighteen months, our guest of honour was a blue-eyed, fresh-faced literary agent who laughed a good deal and had difficulties in pronouncing his 'r's. We had had some dealings of an amiable kind over an author he represented, and over lunch he seemed the quintessence of joviality as he forayed keenly for the camembert or speared a tomato, his shoulders shaking with merriment in the manner perfected by Ted Heath; and a day or two later he rang me at home to say how much he'd enjoyed meeting me, and to ask if I'd be at all interested in starting a new career as a literary agent.

My instinctive – and, as it turned out, entirely correct – reaction was to say 'no'. Life in Great Russell Street was nerve-racking and turbulent at times, but I loved the work, enjoyed the company of my colleagues, and admired André Deutsch himself more than anyone I had worked with before or since; and I knew that although I was a fairly sympathetic and efficient editor, and got on well with my authors when it came to working on their typescripts or sitting in the pub, I had nothing in me of the haggler or the wheeler-dealer, and would almost certainly prove an alarmingly ineffective literary agent. On the other hand, to be courted and flattered is a heady and persuasive brew, of the kind that is seldom offered; I had a vague idea that, when starting out in publishing, it was thought a good thing to advance in a kind of zig-zag, widening one's experience and inching one's salary up the scale in the process; and the prospect of knowing about such elevated, mysterious matters as royalty rates or one-shot rights or reversion of rights clauses or even American copyright made me feel unusually masterful and dynamic, inducing intoxicating visions of my mixing on a man-to-man basis, as an equal and a friend, with the open-necked, tousle-headed whizz-kids who dominated the glamorous firms like Cape and Weidenfeld & Nicolson, with André, perhaps even with the Chairman himself. Strolling absent-mindedly along Henrietta Street debating the pros and cons of going or staying, I bumped into the moustachioed figure of Giles Gordon, then the editorial director of Victor Gollancz, and a whizz-kid from the likeable and approachable end of the spectrum. When I explained my dilemma he became extremely agitated and began to bang his fist up and down on a bollard. Literary agents, he roared, were the scum of the earth and a race of parasites; it would be an act of utter folly to join their ranks, and he would think much the worse of me if I did. A week or so later, after I had decided to accept the offer, I wrote Giles a contrite letter begging forgiveness, and received back a note of official absolution; and not many months later I read that he had left Gollancz to become a highly competent and effective literary agent.

What finally persuaded me to go was an ignoble mixture of poverty and cowardice. Literary publishing has always been – and should be – a marginal trade, in which modest wages are made up for, to some extent, by the interest of the work and congenial company; and smallish literary firms – like Deutsch or Chatto or Victor Gollancz – paid even less than most. Never adept at looking after my own interests, I had, from my earliest days under the Chairman, found myself lagging behind most of the secretaries I knew, and several hundred pounds adrift – or so it would seem from hints and intimations, for we were all far too gentlemanly to discuss such matters openly – of even the most diffident of my colleagues. Fearful of being given the sack on the spot if I made the most modest demand on my own behalf – or, still worse, of being told some unpalatable home truths – I affected a jocular indifference to my material welfare, misleadingly suggestive of non-existent private means and the insouciance that goes with them. During my eighteen months with André I had neither been offered nor asked for a rise of any kind, nor – given my feebleness in these matters – could I see any prospect of a change: it seemed that the only alternative to spending the rest of my life on a three-figure salary was to become a literary agent, still more so since I was being offered a rise of at least £400 – which, if present form was any guide, would be the last of my career. That decided it. I crept out of the office to a phone box behind Bedford Square, from where – my voice a conspiratorial whisper, my heart sinking as I spoke – I told my new employers that I would like to accept their offer; after which I braced myself once again for that fearful, guilt-inducing ritual of giving in one's notice.

Because I was so fond of André and admired him so much, and because I knew I was taking a false step, this proved an even more agonising business than resigning from Geoffrey Bles. This time I procrastinated for two days, telling myself I'd see André after lunch, or as soon as I'd finished editing a particular book, or first thing next morning, and emitting a gasp of relief when, having finally rung through to fix a time, I was told that he had already left or was tied up all afternoon. Eventually, late on the evening of the second day, I found myself standing on the other side of his desk in the pose of the penitent thief, my head hung low and my hands clasped before me as I stammered out the details of my crime. Far from fulminating or damning me as a turncoat and an ingrate, André was the soul of kindly concern, nicely blending congratulations with a rueful regret at my leaving so soon. A moment later he leaned back in his chair, his hands behind his head, and summoned his right-hand man via his alarming telephonic box. This was the same pallid, hollow-chested character – a cigarette for ever dangling from his lower lip, one hand deep in his trousers pocket jiggling and re-arranging unmentionable parts of his being, or excavating the Stygian wastes that lay beyond – with whom I had, on so many occasions, carried desks and filing cabinets from one floor to another; and within seconds he was advancing towards us, his right hand vigorously stirring and rotating under his grey worsted trousers, his face lit up with an engaging, lop-sided grin, his eyes peering out, like those of a Byzantine saint, through black-rimmed oyster-shells of exhaustion and ill health. Perched sideways on one corner of André's desk, his eyes narrowed against the curl of smoke from his cigarette, he confirmed, on André's prompting, that of course they could have matched my new, tycoonish salary; and more flatteringly, that they would have far preferred to lose my fellow-editor, a languid, chalk-striped Oxonian who concealed his likeability and his shyness behind affectations of grandeur and disdain which, far from impressing his master, drove him wild with irritation. Incompetent as ever, I had left it too late for negotiation, for the cunning playing-off of one against the other; and so, very sadly, I prepared to quit what seemed to me – and seems to me still – the most exciting and sympathetic of publishing houses for the alarming and uncongenial life of a literary agent.

CHAPTER FOUR

The Steam-powered Computer

EAGER TO DO my homework before I assumed another incarnation, I borrowed from the Holborn Public Library a book entitled *The Author's Empty Purse*, which described the rise of the literary agent in the late nineteenth century; and from it I learned that the firm for which I would be working was among the oldest in the business, and that it numbered among its clients many of the great names from the first quarter of the century. Not a great deal had happened since its Edwardian heyday – agents are easily seduced into putting their feet up, at least until particular pots of gold go out of copyright – but my predecessor, who had gone back into publishing at Jonathan Cape, had done much to remedy matters by attracting a cluster of glamorous younger names, while my friend with the periwinkle-blue eyes and the weatherbeaten complexion was equally hard at work luring remunerative and newsworthy authors onto his list. For some years now he had run the firm with the senior partner, a benign, bright-eyed man with a beard who was an expert on the minutiae of contracts and copyright but preferred to spend as much time as he could beagling in Dorset. What he really wanted of life was to be a farmer, but persistent hay fever had ruled this out: he hated London and was bored stiff by publishers and their problems, but instead of opting for the life of a quiet country solicitor he had, for no very obvious reason, ended up as a literary agent. As I soon discovered, he was endlessly patient in unravelling the small print of a publisher's contract or spelling out the implications of American copyright registration, whereas his more flamboyant partner was happier hurrying from one deal to the next: I came to like him a great deal, but the miasma of boredom that swathed his office had a generally dispiriting effect. Back home in Dorset, however, he became an entirely different man, keenly sniffing the air as he stepped off the train, discarding his mouldy-smelling grey or Lovat suit for a windcheater and corduroys, briskly rubbing his hands together as we strode out to where the beagles were barking at the leash.

It was my job, as a new agent, to build up my own list of authors from scratch, trawling through magazines and newspapers and publishers' catalogues for bright young writers whose work I could sell as advantageously as possible here and in America; and as I gazed at my empty desk – devoid of everything save a telephone, in and out trays, a couple of ball-point pens, a copy of the brochure sent out to prospective authors, and a good-luck note from my predecessor, pinned to an account (never published) of an Etonian's adventures in Turkestan – I felt that I had come to an awful moment of truth. I wasn't too worried about finding suitable authors, or giving them advice about the kinds of book they might write or how to improve what they'd already written, or even what publishers might suit them best, and I saw no reason why I shouldn't be perfectly competent at the more nannyish aspects of the job, at pouring drinks and mopping up tears and listening to groaning sounds on the telephone and inserting noises of my own that were sympathetic or congratulatory or consoling or en-thusiastic or indignant, depending on the occasion: but all these are things that can be duplicated by a competent publisher's editor, and I knew with a terrible sinking feeling that when it came to the literary agent's *raison d'être* – haggling with and outfacing and outbluffing and being resolute with publishers and editors so as to achieve the best possible deal for a particular book and author – I would prove the frailest of broken reeds; and I dreaded that inevitable moment when, all honeymoons behind me, I was set my first test and failed it.

The agency, in those days, occupied a set of rooms on the fourth and fifth floors of a bogus Georgian office block just off the Theobalds Road and pleasingly near the gardens of Gray's Inn, where I would pace nervously up and down, steeling myself to

make the telephone calls I dreaded to fierce, quick-witted publishers who, I knew, would dispose of my stammered requests in a
matter of seconds and leave me gazing hopelessly at the receiver
dangling in my hand. Except for that belonging to the windswept
character, which was daubed in a violent orange – said to be
soothing by psychiatrists, but liable to bring the rest of us out in a
light sweat as soon as we passed the threshold – the offices were
painted a uniform battleship grey, with a dull matt finish that
showed up every fingermark. Behind the reception area was a
packing-room, in which typescripts and synopses were bound in
distinctive maroon covers before being sent out to publishers and
magazine editors and film companies and the rest; and next to that
was the lair of the office archivist, a shy, civilised man whose
Wellsian moustache, reddish nose, tight high-buttoned jacket,
well-scuffed shoes and impeccable copperplate hand gave him the
look of a clever, slightly dissipated Edwardian clerk. The agents'
offices stretched away along one side of the building, overlooking
some genuine Georgian houses on the other side of the street; the
place was very silent apart from the voice of the windswept one
doing a deal on the phone, and an occasional piercing shriek from
an ebullient, fair-haired woman called Carol Smith, who looked
after the sale of serial rights and soon became my closest friend in
the office.

The archivist's Edwardian looks and the heavy-bottomed glass
inkwell into which he dipped his pen were quite in keeping with a
firm that owed so much to literary life at the turn of the century,
and still made much of its money from authors who had died thirty
or forty years before; and this elderly *Leitmotif* was extended to the
floor above, where the accounts department went about their business. Lodged in the attic, their rooms had sloping roofs and dormer
windows, through which the local pigeons could be spotted strutting importantly up and down the parapet, their chests stuck out
like so many regimental sergeant-majors; the air was loud with
their cooings, while the parapet itself was whitened and encrusted
with their droppings. The chief accountant was a pasty-faced,
black-haired man with wild staring eyes and a curious lump on his

head, like half a hard-boiled egg taped to his scalp, which some-times engaged one's interest while in conversation with him, caus-ing one to lose the thread of what he was saying. I liked him well enough, but he was said to become over-excited, waving his arms about and stamping his foot when crossed and exacting a terrible revenge on his juniors when given inconvenient or unexpected instructions by either of the two partners, both of whom he treated with due reverence. His deputy was a fine, cynical man, with the hook nose and battered features and grizzled locks and high colour of a Captain Marryat sea-dog or a wily countryman: he got on well with his more fractious senior, raising his eyes to heaven at the sound of a foot being stamped or teeth being ground in the room next door while he quietly went on checking publishers' six-monthly royalty statements and transferring the details into gigantic cloth-bound ledgers, or wrote out cheques for those authors to whom money was owing. Although the pocket calculator had yet to be invented, the accounts department was defiantly unmechanised, even to the extent of the simplest calculating machine. The two accountants were in charge of a bevy of yet more middle-aged spinsters who spent their days filling in yet more ledgers with old-fashioned fountain pens in a hot little room under the eaves: kindred spirits, though generally slimmer, to the Armen-ian's harem in the attic in Doughty Street. This particular office was so crammed with yellowing, dusty sheets of paper that there was hardly room enough for the spinsters to move about in. Pre-war ledgers with marbled bindings and fading dates on labels on their spines were stacked on shelves and in teetering mounds on the floor; wire baskets were balanced on sooty files, with a khaki filing cabinet providing the foundations for the tower, and a packet of sandwiches wrapped in greaseproof paper and an ink bottle doing the duties of a finial; the flex of an elderly kettle snaked its way across a cardboard box full of old Bulldog grips and over the small stretch of pale green lino that was still open to the sky, before scaling the side of another tottering cliff, on top of which the kettle itself was uneasily perched. The spinsters, like their masters, spent a good deal of time brewing up, and since the kettle was not of the kind that turned itself off, the room was permanently shrouded in steam, misting up spectacles and causing even the clear-sighted to grope their way about like stranglers in an old-fashioned pea-souper fog. The sight of such confusion induced waves of panic-stricken claustrophobia whenever I ventured in to ask about some payment that should have been made or some money that was due. On one particularly dreadful day I was standing politely by, trying to stifle my impatience while one of the spinsters very slowly moved aside a pile of ledgers in search of the one she wanted, pausing now and then with a pursing of lips to blow the dust aside, when the chief accountant burst in looking more de-ranged than usual, his hair shooting from his scalp, his eyes blazing like coals, and the hard-boiled egg suffused an unfamiliar shade of pink. There was a panic on, he explained – unnecessarily, under the circumstances – since one of the firm's most important authors needed to know at once why a particular sum of money hadn't come through on time: all else must be set aside until the problem had been sorted out. Waving his arms more frenziedly than ever, he removed some papers from a tall, Edwardian office stool; he then climbed onto the stool and, standing on tip-toe, reached out to take from the top shelf the all-important ledger that would tell him all he needed to know. It was then that disas-ter struck. The ledger – which was about five inches thick, with hard board covers and two bronze bolts holding its contents in place – suddenly burst open as he tore through it on top of the stool in search of the crucial piece of information. It opened up like a bird in flight: the front cover knocked the kettle off its perch, sending boiling water streaming down the cliff on which it stood; the back cover caught one of the spinster ladies a glancing blow on the side of the head, causing her to emit a sudden gasp of pain and spill her brimming mug of coffee over the papers she was sifting through on my behalf; while the leaves that had lain between fluttered in spirals to the floor, gratefully drinking their fill of coffee and boiling water. The chief accountant bounded off the stool with a cry of rage and despair and vanished into his office, slamming the door behind him; and little was seen or heard of him for the rest of the day, apart from the occasional moan and the sound of a chest being beaten.

Not long after this moment of high drama the senior partner decided that it was time to modernise the accounts department, and without consulting the chief accountant – whom he knew to be an instinctive Luddite – he went out and bought a computer. Office computers were, as yet, large and primitive affairs that went about their business in a series of fits and starts with much clanking and whirring of wheels and unravelling of rolls of paper peppered with mysterious holes, and occasional jets of steam or alarming puffs of black smoke. Quite how the senior partner, who was the most unmechanical of men, went about choosing a computer, let alone plugging it into the mains, is shrouded in mystery, nor is it known who helped him to manhandle it up five flights of stairs; but one Monday morning the chief accountant and his deputy arrived to find an enormous grey object the size of a coffin clogging up the entrance to the accounts department, and their anger was terrible to behold. The chief accountant was outraged at being asked to abandon the practices of a lifetime in favour of something so self-evidently inefficient by comparison, but being a polite and deferential man he made soothing noises of co-operation to the partners – neither of whom normally set foot in the accounts department, except perhaps to instal the computer – and continued as before. Both accountants were sent on a crash course in computing, throughout which they sat at the back of the class, dozing or doing the crossword, and learned from other disgruntled Luddites how to play the computer equivalent of table tennis, a tame and dim affair that made use of the flashing green lights that were, with the juddering spools, the computer's only memorable feature. For a week or two the sea-dog and the chief accountant amused themselves with bouts of table tennis, but boredom soon set in, and the unhappy interloper was covered over with polythene bags and left to its own devices. Some years later one of my colleagues sold it to the Francis Holland School for a modest sum; but by then it had been overtaken by nifty new models a hundredth its size, none of which made clanking noises or released an occasional puff of black smoke, and no doubt it ended its sad, undervalued existence on a scrapheap reserved for the rejected and unloved.

All this made the accounts department a good deal livelier and more entertaining than the floor below, where the only light relief was afforded by Carol Smith's carefully closing the door behind her before advancing towards me across my office with the exaggerated stealth of a Shakespearian villain, one finger raised to her lips and her eyes bulging with excitement, in order to reveal in a stage whisper from behind a lifted hand some gobbet of gossip about our colleagues or friends in the publishing trade. In the time left over from listening to Carol's gleeful whoops or the rending sound of the chief accountant tearing his hair from its roots, I set about the uneasy business of becoming a literary agent.

Building up a list of authors was a slow but agreeable affair; doing deals and haggling was – as expected – a very different matter. Authors' advances – the most dramatic subject of dispute between publishers and literary agents, and the one that filled me with greatest dread, the small print presenting no great problems – are, in effect, a loan from the publisher, to be set against earnings from that particular book in the form of royalties and the author's share in any subsidiary rights that the publisher may sell. Haggling over terms as a publisher is a relatively straightforward business, in that one can work out how many copies one is likely to sell at what price, producing royalties of such and such, and what the income from subsidiary rights is likely to be; if the publisher – whose instinct will be to pay as little as he can by way of an advance – is then bullied or blackmailed into paying more than he wants, or more than the book is likely to earn, at least he has some idea of the extent to which he has gone adrift. Haggling as an agent struck me as an altogether more nerve-racking business, in that what the author needs to live on, or feels he is entitled to, may well be thousands of pounds in excess of what the publisher's figures suggest he should sensibly pay; and the agent has to combine common sense and realism – not allowing his author to expect the impossible – with the nerve and the dash to ask and hold out for something approaching his author's ideal.

As I had always expected, I was far too timid and far too reasonable to be an effective literary agent. I hadn't the nerve to ask for large sums of money, or threaten to move an author to a rival concern if the money wasn't forthcoming at once, or play one contender off against another; I was easily browbeaten or outwitted by fast-talking whizz-kids in jeans and open-necked shirts, or by tweeded senior publishers, old enough to be my father, who exuded gravitas and ancient wisdom and treated my diffident suggestions with the disdain reserved for a minor irritant or a wasp without its sting; and – most fatally of all, in that it undermined my ability to deal with even the mildest and least alarming of publishers – I found myself far too sympathetic to the publisher's point of view, so much so that by the end of what was (for me at least) an exhausting round of negotiations I felt almost entirely on his side and thought it quite unreasonable for the author to be asking for anything at all. Matters invariably got off to a bad start in that the publisher – quickly assessing the kind of man he was up against – put in an even lower starting price than would otherwise have been the case, and well below the bare minimum which the author and I had in mind (since I was far too embarrassed to discuss anything as crude as sums of money in front of my authors, and they were as gentlemanly back, this figure had been arrived at by some kind of telepathy or communion of spirits). This left me feeling flat and anti-climactic, but worse was to come. Having staked out his ground, the publisher – anxious to keep in with my client – would hurry to assure us both that he absolutely loved the book and that it was the best thing the author had written yet; after which – equally anxious not to raise our spirits too high or plant any seeds of rebellion – he would explain at great length exactly why, much as he would love to, it was absolutely impossible to pay a penny more, given the current state of the trade. Library budgets had been slashed, printing bills were about to go up yet again, the paperback market was wretchedly depressed – here a sob caught in his throat, and I felt a sympathetic tear start from the corner of my eye – the cost of paper was soaring because of a strike in Scandinavia, booksellers were demanding an extra two-and-a-half per cent: by the time I had listened to all this, my throat constricted with grief and my pulses racing at the spectre of imminent bankruptcy, I would have been more than happy to reduce their diminutive advance still further or give the book away for nothing rather than submit my poverty-stricken friend at the end of the line to any more pernicious and debilitating demands. All passion spent, we would agree terms and settle the unalarming side of the business with loud expressions of mutual esteem and professional regard, and much reaching out for diaries and rustling of pages as we settled a day for the celebratory lunch, to be paid for by the publisher of course; and only after I had reported back to my luckless author, and seen the look of baffled disappointment that clouded his brow as he contemplated the mighty gulf that separated dreams and reality, did I realise that once again I had made a hash of things.

I decided that, as before, the only way to make up for my inadequacies was to know more than most about the minutiae of the business: this was the area in which the bearded and beagling partner excelled, guiding me through the 1911 Copyright Act, implications of, and the Berne Convention on copyright, and a long-forgotten legal ruling over whether or not 'one-shot' rights were equivalent to volume rights (they were, but – alas – such knowledge never proved of the slightest practical use). Anxious to understand if not outwit those publishers who prattled so persuasively about printers' bills and the cost of paper, I diverted time that might otherwise have been spent reading Dickens under the desk or gazing out of the window or trading gossip with Carol Smith into finding out about printers' storage charges or the different varieties and weights of paper; in the hope that one day I might find my way back into publishing proper, I fought my way through starchy volumes on libel and pompous, self-important memoirs by retired publishers, redolent of yellowing press-cuttings and long-forgotten best-sellers and waggish repartees on the steps of the Garrick Club; I made a point of meeting every publisher I could in the hope that one of them, one day, would welcome me back to the fold.

All this was to no avail. I remained as affable but incompetent an agent as ever, and an increasingly demoralised one, for although the two partners were far more tolerant and long-suffering than they might have been, trying to do work one dislikes and for which one has no aptitude is a soul-destroying business. Despite the shenanigans upstairs – the flying ledgers and the giant computer resting under its bed of polythene – the firm had an excellent reputation, not least as far as their accounting was concerned, and the two partners were as competent as any in their difficult and necessary trade; but my face didn't fit, and I knew I couldn't last. I took longer and longer lunches, draining pint after pint in The Lamb in Lamb's Conduit Street with my one-time fiancée Suzanne Lowry, then forging ahead as a woman's page editor, or going on enormous exploratory walks around Smithfield and Islington and Bloomsbury and King's Cross, or sitting for hours on end in a candle-lit High Anglican church that reeked of sodomy and incense: I was back where I had been a few hundred yards up the road in Doughty Street, filling in the time and waiting for the end.

Early on in my career as England's most ineffectual literary agent, we were still living in our two-room ground-floor flat in Elgin Avenue. Every now and then Charles Sprawson would drop by, clad as ever in open-necked shirt, corduroy trousers, v-necked sleeveless pullover and freshly-blancoed gym-shoes: after a spell as a swimming-pool attendant, he was now working as an art dealer, and the boot of his car was heavy-laden with nineteenth-century French paintings of moustachioed musketeers in ruffs and baggy pantaloons raising glasses of cherry-coloured wine in courtyards crammed with clucking hens and buxom wenches, or lurid landscapes produced to order by a professional post-impressionist still hard at work in France: the laughing cavaliers ended up – or so I liked to think – on the walls of Berni Inns, whereas the post-impressionist's works were commissioned in bulk for tax exiles in search of a sound investment. Another welcome visitor was our old friend Weale, who had abandoned the raucous and spendthrift ways of his youth and was steadily working his way up the ladder in one of Britain's best-known companies. He would arrive looking unwontedly spruce in a sharp grey suit, white shirt, sober tie and

well-polished black shoes, and as we uncorked a bottle of wine he
would tell us – his eyes blazing with conviction, his fist thumping
the kitchen table – about the importance of commerce and making
one's way in the world, and how the arty trades were all very well
but had little to do with real life. All this was grave and sobering
stuff, and we looked on with awe as Weale opened his case of
samples and expounded at length on what lay inside. He was
dealing at the time in Terylene ties, hundreds of which – in shades
of silver and grey and powder blue – squirmed and wriggled inside
his case like a sackful of snakes. By the time we had drained the
second bottle of wine Weale's own tie was askew, his hair was
ruffled and his dionysiac self was surging to the surface, all talk of
commerce and office hours forgotten. On one occasion Derek
Mahon and I, inflamed by drink and anti-business rhetoric, empt-
ied his briefcase of ties into the basement garden below (this was in
revenge for an earlier incident in which Weale had hurled Mahon's
stock of underpants out of the identical window): the occupants of
the flat were away, so Weale had to be lowered into the garden on a
rope to retrieve his mud-stained samples for display the following
morning.

Before long more permanent residents of the ground-floor flat
materialised in the form of a cat, and then a baby. The cat,
Raymond, was discovered chasing fallen leaves in the street outside
as we left for work one morning. He was still there when we got
back that evening, busily chasing the leaves, and again the following
day. We took him in the day after that, and left him asleep on the
bed, curled up on a pair of my pyjamas: some fifteen years later we
wrapped him up in the same pair of pyjamas and buried him in our
Oxford garden in a drizzle of tears before I hurried off to catch the
London train. An undistinguished-looking tabby, he had a powerful intellect – I liked to boast that he was a graduate of the Rapid
Results College – and was adept in emitting waves of disapproval,
particularly towards those who occupied his chair and found themselves driven out by his concentrated frown. Though bad-tempered
with our friends, he was the soul of bonhomie where other cats were
concerned, and appeared to lack any territorial or proprietorial

urges: my father built him a gangplank so that he could let himself into the garden via the window and the garden wall, and more than once we were woken up in the night by the sound of padding feet and put the light on to find him leading a crocodile of embarrassed-looking cats in the direction of the kitchen and his plate of Jellymeat Whiskas. Nor was he endowed with the killer instinct, much preferring cotton-reels to mice, though one evening he did bring home, rather shame-facedly, the mummified carcase of a budgerigar squashed flat as though it had been trodden on. I found him another kindred spirit, and we loved him with the passion reserved for a first and only child. One terrible winter, he caught a particularly lethal kind of 'flu: the vet looked grave and told us to prepare for the worst, but I rubbed Vick on his chest and Petra took him to work for a week and fed him through a pipette – the important thing, we were told, was to keep up his supply of liquids – and somehow he pulled through.

All this time Petra, now pregnant, was working for a rival literary agency, housed in an elegant, bow-fronted building in Buckingham Street, off the Strand. One morning a colleague of hers rang my office to say that she had had to go into hospital at short notice: could I follow on via Elgin Avenue, where I could pick up whatever she needed? I was eventually tracked down at a publishing jamboree in a tent in Bedford Square, and made my way to the Middlesex clutching a small suitcase and a copy of *Bleak House*, which I was reading out loud at the time; and I spent the next thirty-six hours with Dickens propped against Petra's belly, reading on and on about Mrs Jellyby and Mr Turveydrop and Spontaneous Combustion, while the baby inside made no effort to bestir itself, or exchange the peace of the womb for the tribulations of the world outside. And then, at long last, I was shown a tiny creature with a face like a tangerine and a lick of greasy black hair; and life thereafter was never the same again.

Jemima was the easiest and most benign of babies, smiling broadly as she fouled her trousers and, unlike her more choleric younger sister, never objecting when deposited in alien bedrooms and happily sleeping to the clink of glasses and the baying of laughter round a dining-room table. Two rooms and no garden is no place for a baby, and after a year so so back in my parents' flat in Ashley Gardens – no place for a baby either – we bought a large semi-detached house in East Sheen, with a long garden merging into an allotment beyond and black-and-white tiles in the hall and fresh-faced young families all around and a retired clerk as a neighbour, clad in a checked shirt and a purple cardigan and grey worsted trousers that rose up under his armpits. A year or so earlier, driving through Sheen on the South Circular and peering up side-streets crammed with identical houses, I had turned to Petra and said 'Can you imagine anything more hellish than to live in a place like this?'; yet here we were, in a house of the kind I had been brought up to despise, with a second daughter on her way and the cat asleep on the Aga, and home life at least seemed very good indeed.

Though neither of us relished the sticky fingers and jam-encrusted faces and raucous cries and nonsensical ramblings of babies and small children, much preferring our daughters as they grew ever larger and more entertaining, and abominating the saccharine tones and googity-goo-goo voices adopted by more sentimental parents when addressing their repellent offspring, I proved adept at changing and rinsing out even the most foetid nappies, far defter at buttoning up a babygrow than at negotiating deals on behalf of my authors or bringing in enough commission to cover even my modest salary. By now I had been with the firm for nearly six years, daily awaiting that embarrassed cough and closing of doors and a voice both definite and diffident saying 'I don't think things are quite working out, do you?' or 'I wonder if you're really cut out for this kind of work?' Nothing of that kind had happened as yet, but in the meantime relief was at hand once again in the form of the chief accountant and his nautical-looking lieutenant.

Despite the ledgers and the fountain pens and the steaming kettles and the endless cups of coffee, the firm's accounts department was greatly admired by its rivals for their scrupulous examination of publishers' royalty statements and the errors contained within – this was the sea-dog's especial domain – and the speed with which they processed money due to authors. As a result the two accountants found themselves with a good deal of time on their hands, especially during the lunch hour. Both were keen pub-goers and shared my liking for The Lamb, with occasional sideways lunges to the Princess Louise in Holborn or The Plough in Coptic Street, where rheumy-eyed relics of Fitzrovia could be sighted hawking and spitting through clouds of tobacco smoke, reddening their noses still further as they recalled the dear dead days of David Archer's bookshop and Dylan Thomas cadging a drink and Mac-laren-Ross waving his silver-knobbed stick in the air. About half-way through my stint as a literary agent the Campaign for Real Ale began its assault on fizzy keg bitter, and the two accountants were soon enrolled as eager supporters, sniffing and rolling round in their mouths ferocious treacle-coloured brews from Rutland or the Yorkshire dales, and exchanging notes and tips with other devotees from publishers' accounts departments. These tips, and the quest for still rarer and more turbid-looking ales, kept at exactly the right temperature in dusty oaken barrels, led them to try out new and unfamiliar pubs, far from the familiar round. Soho and Covent Garden were scoured for Theakston's Old Peculiar or Murphy's Cork Stout, then Islington, and the wilds beyond King's Cross; from Fleet Street they pressed, undaunted, into the City, where the last of England's bowler hats could still be spotted moving among the hatless crowds, like shy nocturnal mammals, and over the river to Southwark, where rich pickings could be found; from West-minster it was only a step to Pimlico and Victoria, and so on to the rich heartlands of Chelsea and South Ken. By now the ac-countants' lunch hours had become major expeditions from which they returned late in the afternoon, sweating and exhausted. Morn-ings were spent turning the pages of a Real Ale guide, poring over the *A to Z* and planning the day's campaign with teams from Faber or Seeker & Warburg; in case they were needed by either of the partners in their absence, elaborate instructions were left with the spinsters, all of whom ate dutiful sandwiches over their ledgers, washed down with instant coffee, popping out once or twice a month for a little light shopping before hurrying back by two. In the early days I sometimes joined the accountants on their journeys into the unknown, but I found it hard to drum up that much interest in fine gradations of rustic ales, most of which, though pleasant enough, tasted much the same to me, and I disliked having to waste so much of my lunch hour, long as it was, waiting for the Tube or clambering onto a bus; but I listened to their travellers' tales of pints consumed and crowds of baying clerks and sausages on sticks and repartee between the sea-dog and the royalty manager of Sidgwick & Jackson with a suitable blend of deference and awe. Before long expeditions had been mounted, successfully, as far afield as Hammersmith and Highgate, more often than not on a Friday afternoon, when the end-of-term atmosphere was most conducive to such forays; and those of us who had remained behind would hurry from our offices, consumed with curiosity, as the intrepid travellers returned at half-past four, dusty but triumphant. And then, one boiling summer afternoon, the two of them were overheard roistering in the lift just as the rest of us were getting ready to go home. They had been, they told me in a confidential drone, to a pub in Blackheath which stocked a rare and potent brew from East Anglia which the Faber contingent had sworn by: to get there they had taken a boat from the Embankment at Charing Cross to Greenwich, travelling on by bus and returning by the same slow but agreeable means. This, they both agreed, marked the climax of their lunchtime travelling; from now on they could afford to put their feet up and look back on a lifetime of adventure and achievement. Their wandering days were done, and the pubs of Gray's Inn and Holborn and Bloomsbury, so long neglected and unloved, would receive their patronage once more.

This suited me well enough, since I had had my fill of solitary lunch hours spent gazing glumly into space over a salmon and cucumber roll: but not for much longer it seemed, for the moment of truth – so long and so eagerly awaited – had come at last. As anticipated, there was a good deal of clearing of throats by the two partners and funereal closing of doors, following by the kind, obligatory rituals of severance. Just as I had some fifteen years before, when sacked from my job as a trainee advertising man, I hurried eagerly forward to set them at their ease, agreeing wholeheartedly with all they had to say and urging them in no way to feel bad on my account. The interview over, I sped away to break the good news to Carol Smith, who was on the point of departure herself, and to the two accountants in the attic, whom I eventually made out through a fog-like cloud of steam – one of the spinsters had forgotten to turn off the kettle – comparing beer mats in a corner. I then broke the news to my authors, some of whom – absent-mindedly forgetting how ill I had served them – seemed angrier and more surprised by the news than they should have been. A week or two later I cleared my desk and made my last farewells, and six more aimless years were behind me.

CHAPTER FIVE

Seaview in the Rain

ALL I KNEW about life as a freelance editor was that it was extremely badly paid; that since one usually charged by the hour, it was essential to cram in as many hours as one could per day in order to bring in even the most modest income and not fall hopelessly into arrears with mortgages, insurance policies, telephone bills and all those other wearisome matters which I was more than happy to leave Petra to deal with, perched on the edge of the bed puzzling over our non-existent finances while I read in a deck-chair in the garden or strode across Richmond Park, eagerly interviewing myself in my head as I went; and that whereas office workers earned salaries to sit about drinking coffee and gossiping and snoozing through interminable meetings in which large amounts of paper were passed around the table, and to mow the lawn at weekends and even take their annual holidays, we freelances had to keep going every hour of the day, paying our way with the sweat of our brows in a manner undreamt of by the toilers from nine to five. Not a second must be wasted: I abandoned my life as a literary agent on a Friday evening, and at 6.30 on Saturday morning I sprang anxiously out of bed, made us both a pot of tea, shaved, and was hard at work by seven, knocking into shape a book about the future of British airports. During my last few months as an agent I had begun to take on freelance work, reviewing for the *Sunday Telegraph* and *The Times* as well as editing for publishers, so I started off with an ample supply of work; and before long I settled into a way of life which, though nerve-racking in monetary terms, was far more congenial than most. The girls were only five and one, so Petra was still at home: I was adamant about my hours, refusing to be distracted by windy, sunny days or by mothers who called to pick up children or drop off the remains of a stew if we seemed particularly hard-pressed, but every now and then I would lean against the Aga and, lightly dusting my hands together, announce that I had finished all my work and had nothing left to do. At this Petra would turn ashen with alarm, visions of bailiffs banging on the door and bank managers peering gravely over half-moon spectacles whirling feverishly through her brain; but no sooner had I broken the news than the phone would ring, and the moment of truth would be held at bay once more. And although I missed, as many freelances must, the companionship and the gossip of the office, I never missed the work itself, or the strain it imposes on even the idlest or most apparently imperturbable of office-workers; I liked nothing better, as a freelance, than to visit friends or former colleagues in their offices, to perch on the edge of their desks and read their memos upside-down or listen to their phone calls, to pick up the tittle-tattle and keep in touch yet not to be part of it all, free to drift away home via a walk in the park while they nervously assembled for yet another meeting, the very thought of which may well have given them sleepless nights and a weekend blighted by dread.

If we went away for the weekend I would, automatically, take a typescript or a review copy with me, and lock myself away for part of the time in order to notch up my hours. Nowhere was this more enjoyable than at Sparrows Hanger, a house high up in the woods in Selborne, looking down on the church and the meadow below. Though I loved the suburbs and had no desire to live anywhere else, I still hankered after an earthly paradise; but whereas years earlier, as an unhappy trainee advertising man, I had looked for Arcadia in eighteenth-century pastoral poems, or George Morland's rosy-tinted paintings of fleshy village maidens in Empire gowns gazing over the half-doors of stables at a smith shoeing an equally fleshy carthorse, or in the more saccharine passages of Dickens, in which retired chandlers or deserving schoolmasters passed the evening of their days in bowery tea-room cottages, with lambs to hand and children sporting on the green, I caught glimpses of it now, fleetingly and out of the corner of my eyes, in particular houses that I loved: and nowhere more so than at Sparrows Hanger. Perched among the trees at the end of a winding, unmade-up drive, it was lived in by two of our closest friends and their children; he was a schoolmaster, and the house had formerly belonged to her parents, who had created it from nothing and endowed it not just with charm and elegance and oddity, but with that mysterious, elusive sense – shared – by those few magical houses one encounters in a lifetime – that somewhere, behind some yet-to-be-discovered door, off some shadowy, dusty landing, a timeless, unchanging world of consolation and reassurance lay waiting to reveal itself. The house itself was, in the very best sense, a fake, consisting as it did of an undistinguished Edwardian bungalow with eighteenth-century fittings, and a second floor added at some later date. My friend's father was a lean, aquiline figure, clad in a battered tweed jacket and chestnut-coloured corduroys which – so lean was he – seemed even baggier than usual about the buttocks: he talked a great deal, wittily and well, a cigarette drooping from one hand, and a bottle of Roquemar stood open on the sideboard, for he and his wife – tiny, crooked, unfussed, for ever banging about in the kitchen and producing the most delicious meals – were the most hospitable of couples. He was a poet of the Georgian school, a painter, the author of a life of Gilbert White and a well-known figure in the village; trained as an architect, he had served in the Auxiliary Fire Service during the war, after which – having just enough money to live on – he had retired while still in his twenties and moved from London back to Selborne, where he spent the rest of his life reading and writing and talking to his friends and campaigning (successfully) against plans to open a sewage farm in the fields behind his house and opening bottles of Roquemar and watching Benny Hill and screwing up his eyes against the spiral of smoke that drifted up from the Woodbine as he raised it to his lips. At some stage in the early days of his occupation of Sparrows Hanger an early-eighteenth-century house was demolished in Golden Square (I like to think it was that occupied, a hundred years earlier, by the wicked Ralph Nickleby): doors, fireplaces, panelling and an entire staircase complete with barley-sugar balustrades like tiny echoes of the baldachino at St Peter's were nimbly removed from the wreckage and installed inside the Edwardian bungalow, the outside of which was draped with square lead Queen Anne drainpipes, embossed with some entirely misleading date and also removed from Golden Square. The Edwardian bungalow was transmogrified overnight into an improbable hybrid, in which pointed gables and diamond-pane windows happily co-existed with the more elegant intruders. Held roughly in place with some badly banged-in nails, the panelling in the dining-room and the hall was of the unpainted, cigar-box variety that I remembered from the Chairman's office in St James's Place, while that in the sitting-room, to the right of the hall, was painted in the sombre matt-finished reds and greens of the early eighteenth century. Elsewhere – in the kitchen, the workroom, the dark, cave-like book-room, the window of which looked out onto the Ruskinian rocks and roots and tangled vegetation that formed the backdrop to the shelf on which the bungalow stood – the Edwardian bungalow reasserted itself, with tongue-and-groove painted in white or cypress green gleaming through golden arches of eighteenth-century wood. The floors, on the ground floor at least, were of loose unpolished parquet, covered here and there by an occasional Turkey carpet – a combination I came to know still better when, many years later, I went to work for the publishing house in William IV Street, and found myself relishing once again that elegant, casual combination of rattling, uneven parquet floors, faded Turkey carpets, unpainted wicker-work chairs and nautical tongue-and-groove. The great baroque staircase rose, incongruously, from the middle of the hall to a dark and narrow landing: the bathrooms, at the back of the house, shared the book-room's Ruskinian view of rock and dripping foliage, while the bedrooms – the windows of which were, even more incongruously, of the 1950s metal-frame variety – looked down over the tree-tops across a steep and narrow valley, on the far side of which one could see brown-and-white cows munching in a meadow, the red-and-white flag of St George fluttering from the church tower, and wisps of smoke rising from the roofs of the village. Immediately outside the front door was a small verandah, with a vine trailing along its topmost edge; beyond that was a terrace on which, in summer, we sat and read and ate our meals, taking care not to topple over the side through an Amazonian jungle of trees, while the church clock struck the hours and the voices of children drifted up from the meadows and – as the setting sun touched the treetops with gold and glinted off the dining-room's diamond panes – our hostess suggested, with a look of comical, bogus diffidence, lips pursed and an outstretched hand making a kind of fluted, twisted motion, suggestive of corks being drawn or glasses drained, that perhaps the time had come for a little drink . . .

For over twenty years Sparrows Hanger provided us with an escape from the humdrum and a glimpse of Arcadia, the thought of which could lighten the spirit or provide some kind of consoling perspective as one trudged across London to a meeting one dreaded or an encounter sooner avoided. And it was there that, years later, we met and made friends with one of those rare, heady individuals who, like the house itself, seemed to suggest that some-where, somehow, lay the answer to life, while at the same time endowing what were, to the rest of us, the most banal of operations – pouring a drink, or peeling an orange – with a sense of romance and occasion that has yet to fail him in all our encounters since. James Henry was a large, powerful-looking man with an iron handshake, thick spectacles, a largeish nose that might or might not look inflamed, and a face, not unlike that of W. C. Fields, that looked and seemed so well lived-in that it was impossible to imagine what he looked like as a boy, or even as a man in his thirties. He and his Australian wife, Kate – who was thirty years his junior – had been cutting down trees in the Lyth and were invited up to supper to meet us. James had recently returned from Yugo-slavia, he told us, and he and I drained a bottle of slivovicz he had brought with him as a present: he suggested that within the next week or two we should drive out to Yugoslavia together and pick up a further consignment, along with some equipment he had left there. Such suggestions crop up now and then in the course of a bibulous evening, and one plays with the notion from the comfortable vantage point of knowing that lack of money and the obligations of the office rule out any possibility of their realisation: but James had the ability of making fantasies seem feasible, momentarily reviving – like Leigh Fermor's recreation of his adolescent walk – that sense one has when young of life as an adventure, in which everything is possible and the future stretches out with the luminous promise of a Claudian summer morning. James's own life had been appropriately picaresque: his father was a peripatetic mining engineer, and he had been born in Macedonia, spent his childhood in an as yet unblighted Algarve, and been educated in the bush in Queensland. After the war he had lived for some years in Tangier, making his living by supporting free trade in a small boat around the Mediterranean; his wives had included a well-known novelist, one of the beauties of her age; he had worked as a stockbroker and then as a television reporter, travelling the world in search of his stories. He brought to Sparrows Hanger, and later to suburbia, a louche, hard-living, worldly presence, making us feel simultaneously both callow and sophisticated by his friendship; he combined an aphoristic and occasionally impenetrable worldly wisdom, redolent of *liaisons* and high living and well-managed affairs that never flared out of control, with a practical knowledge of the kind I could never aspire to, of cooking and wine and seamanship and sharpening knives and hacking down trees; early on in our friendship I suspected him – wrongly and unjustly, as it turned out – of inventing or embellishing his adventures and his areas of expertise, but from our first encounter I was won over by his generosity, his romanticism, his enthusiasm and his unremitting interest in those whom he met. As I grew older I found myself endowing – and eager to endow – heroic status on certain of my friends, whether known in the flesh or through the pages of their books, in a way that I never had when young; and James, with his iron handshake and his knowledge of the world and the disruptive sideways glint in his eye as he prepared and poured the first gin and French of the evening – the ice cubes carefully laid at the bottom of the glass, the ingredients precisely measured and then poured to the brim, the twist of lemon shaved from the fruit with the finesse of a Grinling Gibbons, squeezed across the surface, and then left floating as the finished drink was handed over – soon acquired for us both, and for our friends at Sparrows Hanger, the enviable if demanding role assigned to those whose every word and action will be the subject of endless debate.

All this, though, lay in the future; in the meantime we spent our summer holidays, as often as not, on the Isle of Wight, together with our friends from Sparrows Hanger and their children, a holiday-loving black labrador called Polly, our cat Raymond – who early on bagged the best chair in the house for himself, creating such an atmosphere of disapproval when our hostess unwisely occupied it for a time that she was forced to abandon it for a wooden stool instead – a network of prams and pushchairs and bottles and bibs, and a large mound of typescripts which I could work on and so help to pay the bills. We stayed in the Seaview equivalent of the kind of beach house which in Key West – or so one liked to imagine – would be occupied by unshaven men with bloodshot eyes and a drink problem: but instead of a rocking-chair and a rifle and empty bottles of Jack Daniels rolling underfoot, the wooden verandah in front of the house was filled to overflowing with buckets and spades and faded red liloes and fishing nets with bamboo handles and limpet shells and the dried-up bodies of starfish; and since the bungalow had been built in the 1930s, the impression of mild and agreeable gentility was reinforced by leaded windowpanes, a shiny red-tiled fireplace of the kind that appears in the 'Little Grey Rabbit' stories, and the thin black beams and high-handled doors one associates, pleasurably, with farces by Ben Travers.

To relive these holidays now might well prove a form of torment, involving as they did the interminable changing of nappies on boards laid over the bath and the emptying of brimming pots (in my case, out of the bedroom window), and pushing prams along the sea-front at midnight in a desperate bid to persuade some livid, hot-featured jack-in-the-box to stop its screaming and lie down at last, and meal-times blighted by the angry hammering of spoons on the table and hair and faces coated with stew and terrible cries of rage and the sudden thrusting aside of a spoonful of rice pudding, scattering its contents far and wide: but even those of us who find small children – and other people's small children in particular – tedious and repellent are able, at that stage in our lives, to endure the unendurable, and every year we loved and longed for our holiday in Seaview.

In a bad year it rained every day we were there. We swam in the rain and shopped in the rain and dug holes in the sand in the rain and went for long walks in the rain and stood sniffing in the rain, wondering why the smell of sewage was quite so strong this year; in the evenings every chair was draped with sodden clothes steaming in front of the two-barred fire in the Alison Uttley fireplace, sprinkled afresh every now and then as the labrador came storming excitedly in to report on its findings on the beach and shook itself dry with a flailing motion, like a fur-coated watering-can. At moments like this I was filled with feelings of awful bitterness towards whoever it is that organises the English climate, and – quite deliberately, it seemed – sent enormous black clouds bowling in our direction as soon as the clerks had traded in their briefcases for a pair of ill-fitting espadrilles; I vowed that, cost what it may, we would never spend another summer holiday in England, and dreamed ineffectual dreams of royal-blue seas and meals in the sun and vats of ice-cold retsina and afternoons spent dozing in the shade of elderly olive trees on a bed of desiccated goats' messes.

Within half a mile of our storm-lashed beach house lay two entirely different Englands. If one walked, as I often did, towards Ryde one soon found oneself in a world inhabited by pasty-faced men in their twenties with gigantic beer bellies that hung over their belts like polythene bags filled with water and trousers which never quite covered the cleavage of their buttocks, and fat girls with lank black hair in short denim skirts and denim tops and teetering high-heeled shoes stumping angrily along the beach, weighed down by ghetto-blasters the size of a family suitcase, and cross-looking children in mauve and black and lime-coloured track-suits wrenching open packets of onion-flavoured crisps or dashing to the ground a freshly-drained tin of Coke. On one particularly torrential afternoon I took refuge in a windshelter on the front: the glass had been replaced by plywood, and those who cowered within – elderly couples for the most part, the men in fawn cardigans with inlaid panels of bogus suede, their wives clutching huge white handbags that looked to be freighted down with rocks – could treat themselves to an orgy of four-letter words and anatomical drawings, hideously engorged, in which the hairs were represented by dots very similar to those I remembered from Desperate Dan's five o'clock shadow. Such sights filled me with a terrible sense of living at the fag-end of a civilisation, with illiterate, overweight barbarians sweatily pressing at the gates.

Five minutes' walk in the opposite direction, along the sea-front and past an important, shiny-looking yacht club, and all was utterly changed. Seaview proper is a sprucely painted little town, with a steep main street overlooking the concrete towers of Portsmouth and the Napoleonic forts that pepper the Solent, and an abundance of white stucco and bow windows and wrought-iron balconies and curious little aerial greenhouses from which – or so I liked to imagine – retired admirals gazed sternly out to sea to the accompaniment of several large pink gins. Most of the retired admirals one saw striding briskly about in the obligatory uniform of blue-and-white check shirt, navy-blue guernsey, faded tan sailing trousers and blue-and-white 'Ted Heath' sailing shoes were almost certainly ex-ambassadors or City men in seasonal fancy dress: but they played the part to perfection, sporting weatherbeaten looks and gazing keenly about through cool blue eyes and lending a knowledgeable hand with the launching of a dinghy and drawing up lists of competitors in the annual regatta.

Equally conspicuous, and equally in command of the situation, were those in their thirties and forties and their offspring: the men – many of them, no doubt, army officers or stockbrokers, with firm jaws and fair, crinkly hair and loud authoritative voices – wore the identical uniform to their seniors, though the faded tan trousers had sometimes been converted into shorts, while their bare, sunburnt feet were thrust into salt-encrusted red or green nautical moccasins, which they continued to wear while wading out to sea to launch their children in a dinghy, barking instructions as they went in voices horribly reminiscent of incorruptible school prefects or the captains of cricket teams; their wives had straight fair hair and highly polished teeth and the kind of suntan that leaves its possessors with little crows' feet of white at the corners of the eyes; their children – the products of Westminster or Bryanston or Bedales – had a well-fed, almost polished look about them, the girls in candy-striped cotton trousers and navy-blue windcheaters with restrained but exotic slogans on the chest, the boys in parti-coloured Bermuda shorts and more flamboyant slogans, both displaying the confidence of those who know that they will inherit the earth, or at least their particular part of it. For those of us who worried that the English upper-middle classes were a vanishing species, unnerved by recurrent failures and elbowed aside by bogus gents on the make and the burger-and-chips brigade, Seaview in summer was a deeply reassuring sight; and yet, glad as I was to know that they existed, and going about their business in so stylish and so confident a manner, the mere sight of all those men who were born to command and knew all about tying knots and shouting at dogs and firing shotguns and tacking to starboard and changing the wheel on a Volvo, and the sound of their humourless, un-answerable commands drifting over the sand towards us, over the heads of children digging with spades and pensioners snoozing in deckchairs, filled me with a sudden, schoolboy insubordination, and I would find myself, almost unwittingly, striding back in the direction of Ryde and the holiday camp, and the stench of hot dogs and waterlogged onions and the raucous cry of the ghetto-blaster.

The best answer to this perennial English problem was to cut straight through Ryde – an elegant little town, full of Italianate mid-Victorian houses, once peopled by maiden aunts and retired naval officers, but now given over to landladies and the holiday trade – and out the other side, along the coastal path to the wooded inlet of Fishbourne, where the car ferry comes in. In its present form at least, Quarr Abbey dates back to the early years of this century, when a group of French Benedictines – driven out by one of those bouts of anti-clericalism to which the French are traditionally prone – left Solesmes and established themselves on the Isle of Wight. Perched on a promontory overlooking the harbour, Quarr is not only one of the most magical places in England, the inaccessible heart of which remains part of my private Arcadia, but one of the most handsome and original buildings to have been put up in Britain in the last eighty years or so. Built in a narrow pale-pink brick, the abbey church and its surrounding monastic buildings are an odd and pleasing hotch-potch of Flemish-looking stepped gables and tiered dormer windows, mosque-like arches and Moorish battlements, and an almost Irish round tower that raises itself above the trees like an admonitory finger. Nothing is more soothing, for the unbeliever as well as for the faithful, than to listen to the monks singing vespers while the evening sun streams in through the open door, or to watch them moving about their business at the far end of the enormous empty church, bathed in amber light like the figures in a Rembrandt painting, while the clouds of incense waft slowly down the aisle towards one. Yet the great church is riven with cracks, some as wide as one's finger; and every year the monks look older and fewer and whiter and more bent, and the rows of black stalls more glaringly empty, and the great Gregorian chants – identical, perhaps, to those that had wafted over the water at Beaulieu in the pages of Conan Doyle's *The White Company* – swell ever more softly and sadly on the ear.

Although – or perhaps because – I have, more than once, been brought low by a pair of eyes staring up from under the brim of a hat at a publishing party, I much prefer the predatory, ever-mutating scrimmage of a drinks party after work to the sedate but exhausting tedium of a formal dinner party. My sinews stiffen as I enter a room full of half-familiar faces, take a drink from a tray, and plunge greedily into a vortex of roaring voices and eyes flickering over shoulders at the waves of new arrivals and never-completed conversations broken off by a face held up for a kiss or an arm snaking out from the group alongside; yet although I like nothing better than interminable meals in the company of friends, I am too restless and inconsequential to relish the dinner party at which one is supposed to meet new faces, and find myself writhing stiffly in my chair and scratching about for things to say and wondering why everyone else seems so alarmingly well informed, and waiting, a grin glued to my face, for that fateful moment, suggestive of another hour's suffering at least, when a voice from the far end of the table asks 'Who's for coffee? Proper coffee or decaff? Or would you prefer some kind of herbal tea?'

The best parties of all are those professional affairs where shop is talked and gossip is at its most intense, though such events are best avoided by outsiders, who may well end up feeling as though they have strayed into a game of pass-the-parcel as they are hurriedly shunted from one gossip-monger to another, each of whom – once the intruder has been identified as such – will, within seconds of starting a conversation, look desperately over the shuntee's shoulder in search of some other party-goer on whom the burden can be unloaded; if that fails, the party-lover – desperate to learn who has been sacked or who is sleeping with whom – will glance ostentatiously at his watch, mutter horrified apologies about missing the last train home and make purposefully for the door, only to be sighted an hour later deep in conversation at the bar. Publishing parties tend to be both convivial and exclusive, though a rare exception to the conviviality – and possibly the most bizarre and ill-conceived of all such functions – was one given, at about this time, by a brand-new publisher for a book about Auschwitz. The subject matter hardly lent itself to roistering, still less so since the party was attended by several survivors from the camps, all of whom looked sad and grey and sombre. Even the most jocular and rubicund regulars froze as they entered the room; we sipped our drinks in guilty silence, whispering uneasily among ourselves, before skulking off at the earliest possible opportunity. It was at an altogether more conventional party that, during this first stab at the freelance life, I met a dark, black-eyed woman in her forties who, after we'd talked for some time, told me that she was a radio presenter, and that since I had talked to her with such enthusiasm about books and the publishing business, and was regularly employed as a reviewer by *The Times* and the *Sunday Telegraph,* I might like to appear as a guest on her programme. I dreaded the thought of booming out across the airwaves since I had a strong suspicion that my efforts at coherent speech would come over as an inaudible rumble, punctuated by gasps and sudden, spasmodic grunts; but I was in no position to turn down work of any kind, and one thing might lead to another, so I asked her what would be involved. It was simplicity itself, she told me: I should choose two recently published paperbacks and she would do the same; after which we would read each other's choices and discuss all four books over the air. Anxious to do the right thing, I asked her whether I should bring notes with me, or even write out what I was going to say: that was quite unnecessary, she said, and would ruin the spontaneity of the occasion; all I had to do was to read the four books, meet her at Broadcasting House on the appointed day, and let nature take its course. This seemed an ideal arrangement from my point of view, involving the minimum of work and the prospect of a jovial afternoon with this amiable black-eyed lady; we parted the best of friends, and next day I rang with my two suggested titles (both of which I had read before); she gave me hers (neither of which I had read before, or particularly wanted to read), and we arranged to meet in a fortnight's time in the lobby at Broadcasting House.

Obedient as ever, I read her two books, struggling through to the end, made no notes, and turned up at Portland Place on the dot of half-past two. A moment or two later I was joined by my genial party-going companion – only, rather to my alarm, she seemed an altogether brisker personage than I remembered through the haze of alcohol and smoke. She was wearing a smart purple suit, and carried a clipboard in one hand; and after a friendly exchange of greetings she asked me if I'd brought my notes with me so that we could plan what we were going to say before we went on the air. When I replied that I hadn't made any notes because she'd told me not to, a tremor of irritation and alarm flickered across her brow. 'We'd better go and have some coffee,' she said, her voice suddenly less cordial than I remembered, 'and see what we can do to salvage something from the wreckage.' Heading up in the lift *en route* for the canteen I wrung my hands in agonised contrition, but she remained adamant and unforgiving, merely repeating, 'I can't imagine how you thought you could get through a programme of this kind without making detailed notes in advance. Surely that stands to reason?' It did, but my pointing out that she had specifically told me not to bother with notes seemed to make little impression. Over coffee I was so unnerved that, in a throwback to my schooldays, when my hands were forever atremble, I had to keep hold of my mug with both hands; but despite a momentary spasm of indignation, during which I contemplated walking out and letting her get on with it alone, I somehow found myself sitting opposite her in the studio, laying out the books on the desk that divided us and nodding uncomprehendingly while a bearded man in earphones told me how to speak into the microphone and tested my boom for sound. By now my friend from the office party was too angry to catch my eye, and seemed to have disowned me altogether; but at a thumbs-up signal from the man with the beard from the other side of a glass partition she clipped a smile to her face and launched into her introductory patter. After a word or two of welcome I heard her say 'my guest this afternoon is the writer and critic Jeremy Lewis' – neither description was true, but they sounded suitably impressive – at which she made an angry flicking motion towards me with her fingers and, after a moment's hesitation, I boomed out a breezy 'Good afternoon.' That hurdle surmounted, I felt I could relax while she launched into a detailed description of the first of the two books she had chosen. I felt – quite wrongly, as it turned out – that I should lend support to the occasion and add a touch of the spontaneity she prized, so instead of waiting my turn I chipped in every now and then with cries of Wonderful' or 'Quite right too,' which came across – or so I am told – like distant rumblings of thunder, more suggestive of office furniture being moved about in the background than the kind of suave debate or waggish banter normally encountered over the air. Anxious to make amends and to prove myself worthy of the occasion, I fixed my eyes on my mentor with spaniel-like devotion; but far from rewarding me with an encouraging pat or smile, she glared at me as unmercifully as ever, so that the brief surge of confidence excited by my helpful cries of 'Wonderful' quite suddenly ebbed away. I managed to mutter a few pitiful words of praise for the book she had chosen; and then, to my horror, I heard her say, 'And now, Jeremy, the first of the two titles you've chosen is Paul Theroux's *Saint Jack*. Could you tell us why you've chosen that particular book?' No doubt I could have done so had I had some notes to hand, for it was a novel I much admired at the time; as it was, I launched out with some bravado, swiftly tied myself in Laocoon-like grammatical knots, lost the thread of what I was trying to say, let out a terrible cry of 'Oh Christ I can't go on' and buried my head in my hands. At this the man with the beard came rushing round from behind his glass panel, making kindly soothing noises and explaining – for I had no idea of such things – that the programme was being recorded and wasn't going out live, and that we could easily start again as soon as I had recovered my composure. The only problem was that all this had quite unnerved my interlocutor, veteran broadcaster though she was, so that she too began to ramble and forget what she was trying to say. Somehow we stumbled through the twenty minutes or so allotted to us, and after it was over I made a shamefaced farewell and sidled unhappily away. I kept my fingers in my ears when the programme was broadcast next day; Petra told me that, apart from the background rumble of 'Wonderfuls', I featured hardly at all, but had been edited out almost to extinction.

All my life I had suffered – still suffer – from insomnia, sweating heavily into my pillow and sighing loudly in the hope of being overheard and jamming my watch against my face in an effort (usually futile) to read its luminous dial; and about this time I decided that, rather than cram any more pills in my mouth, I would try my luck with a hypnotist. A year or two earlier, Petra – a forty-a-day merchant, the first sound from whom at the crack of dawn had been the rasp of match on matchbox, followed by greedy puffing sounds – had taken her problem to a retired policeman in Pirelli slippers, practising near Harley Street, who had weaned her off smoking in a single session, so I decided to follow her example. Riffling through the Yellow Pages, I came across a Major Knares-Pillow, a licensed hypnotist following his trade in Kingston-on-Thames. I rang the major; he had a very loud voice and sounded as though he was issuing commands on a large and windswept parade ground. I made an appointment with his assistant – the major himself was fully engaged – and, a day or two later, made my way to a red-brick Edwardian house with an overgrown garden and a butter-coloured front door. I rang the bell, which echoed hollowly about the hall; and a moment or two later the door was opened, vigorously, by the major in person, who barked out an order to enter and made his way briskly down an empty, white-painted hall with black and white tiles on the floor. Like his fellow-practitioner in Harley Street, the major was wearing a pair of brown-and-white Pirelli slippers – evidently they were *de rigueur* among the hypnotist fraternity – surmounted by shiny grey worsted trousers, an open-necked apple-green shirt and an orange cardigan. He showed me into a waiting-room as bare as the hall, and then returned to his room next door – he had left a patient in mid-trance, it seemed, in order to open the front door – from whence, a moment or two later, I could hear him bawling instructions at some hapless smoker ('You *will not* smoke again. Do you understand me? You *will not* . . .'). Eventually I was collected by the major's assistant – a mild, middle-aged lady in a white coat – and taken to another bare room, furnished only with a large, rather greasy wine-coloured armchair of the kind that tilts back like an aeroplane seat and comes equipped with a foot-rest, and a small, upright chair in which the middle-aged lady promptly seated herself. Before we could begin, she said, I should remove my shoes – an unexpected hazard, exciting terrible visions of her fighting for air and gasping at the window as the stench of unwashed socks drifted across the room like a cloud of mustard gas – and then make myself as comfortable as possible, resting my arms, palms upwards, on the gleaming arms of the giant chair and closing my eyes in order to concentrate on what she had to say. I did so, and a momentary silence reigned, broken only by the major's muffled cries from the floor below. 'You will lift your right arm, quite involuntarily,' the middle-aged lady told me, 'after which you will be hypnotised. I will make you do nothing against your will, and to break the trance all you need do is to open your eyes;' and with that she began – like a gentler version of the major – to repeat, over and over again, 'You will lift your right arm, you will lift your right arm . . .' Nothing happened: my arm remained firmly on the arm-rest, as though it had been nailed in place; I felt torn between the desire to laugh and feelings of inadequacy and embarrassment on her behalf; and I was just about to open my eyes and suggest, in the nicest possible way, that we call it a day since – much to my shame – I was obviously not an amenable type, when, much to my amazement, my arm began to drift upwards until it was standing at a right angle to the arm-rest. From that moment on I was convinced, and for several weeks thereafter I dutifully hypnotised myself before settling down to sleep, until boredom broke the spell. But I thought fondly of the major and his middle-aged assistant, and recommended them enthusiastically to a small army of smokers and insomniacs; all of whom returned from the Edwardian house in Kingston aglow with admiration.

I had to abandon one of our Seaview holidays halfway through in order to help an MP to write a book which (or so he later assured me) succeeded almost single-handed in preserving the unity of the United Kingdom. Mr Callaghan, the then Prime Minister, was toying with various schemes for devolving power to Scottish and Welsh Parliaments in the hope that this would thwart the nationalist threat to the Labour Party; and a week or two before we left to go on holiday a friend of mine at Jonathan Cape rang to ask if I'd be free to help the Labour MP Tam Dalyell with a book in which he planned to savage the government's plans as an ignoble exercise in political expediency, the only effect of which would be to insert yet another raft of well-paid bureaucrats between the people and those who ruled them. The only problem was that the book had to be ready for the Labour Party Conference in September, at which it would be ignited like a stick of dynamite; it was already early July, and the book was in 'embryonic' form; could I possibly drop everything else, and get in touch with Mr Dalyell at once?

Next morning I hurried along to the House of Commons, reported in to the policeman at the gate, and waited in the Members' Lobby with an agreeable glow of self-importance while familiar-looking faces bustled busily to and fro clutching papers to their lapels and looking self-consciously unself-conscious, and policemen in their shirtsleeves lent over railings and rubbed their chins, and parties of constituents – the men in blazers and ginger shoes, the women in white acrylic cardigans and white shoes, massive white handbags banging about their calves – gazed reverently up at the Victorian mosaics on the ceiling while their local MPs, peeking at their watches as the faces scanned the skies like bespectacled radar beacons, hurried them round the Mother of Parliaments. Some twenty minutes later I spotted, advancing towards me through the crowds, a sturdily built, engagingly shambolic figure with a large, pale face, grey-black hair and the heavy, pendulous head of a voluble Hereford bull: he was wearing a grey suit, the trousers of which concertinaed over his shoes, a green-and-white check shirt and a navy-blue tie with a trade union crest placed firmly in its middle – his sole concession to his party, for his accent was as clipped and plummy as befits an Old Etonian. His right hand was outstretched in greeting, and he spoke in a deep, staccato rumble not dissimilar to my own. He suggested we start with a cup of coffee, and as we moved away he talked, passionately and in minute detail, about the iniquities of Scottish devolution – a subject about which I knew nothing, and had no views on whatsoever beyond a very English feeling that for the Scots even to contemplate going their own way somehow smacked of ingratitude – while at the same time thrusting sheet after sheet of paper into my hands.

Once seated behind a canteen table – and later in those green-cushioned corridor perches on which MPs seem to do so much of their business – I tried to make sense of the deluge of words and paper that flowed, remorselessly, towards me. As is so often the case with those who have become obsessed by a subject, Tam assumed as a matter of course that I – and his potential readers – knew quite as much about the subject as he did, shared his sense of urgency and outrage, and merely needed to be pointed in the right direction and swayed by some burning rhetoric. He appeared to spend a good deal of time shuttling between Strasbourg, London and his home in Edinburgh in the company of a thick pad of heavily embossed House of Commons notepaper: every time he took to the air he returned to earth with some hand-written thoughts on the subject of Scottish devolution, most of them a mere twenty or thirty words long but making up in bulk and aphoristic pungency what they lacked in wordage and linking passages; and it was these that he thrust upon me while we sipped cup after cup of black coffee and I wondered how we would ever make sense of it all, let alone produce a publishable book by the middle of next month. Although he was an experienced and combative journalist, Tam seemed to think – like many others before and since – that books and compost heaps have much in common, and that his random thoughts on House of Commons notepaper, together with the odd anti-devolutionary article wrenched from the *Guardian* or the *New Statesman,* would, if pressed together, somehow mulch down into a finished book by a mysterious process of fermentation; I found it hard to share his optimism, and as the disparate sheets of paper mounted up around me I began to feel symptoms of incipient hysteria. Luckily a division bell put paid to the flow; I gathered together the sheets of notepaper – in themselves as thick as a telephone direct-ory – and the anti-devolutionary fulminations torn from various magazines, and promised to return next morning after I'd read them, with some ideas about how they could be turned into a book.

Sitting in the garden at home that evening, I began to plough my way through Tam's compost heap. At half-past ten I finished my reading, and fell back exhausted; at half-past eleven Tam rang, as he was often to do, from his flat in the Horseferry Road (sited, or so I liked to think, above a public lavatory) with a further flurry of suggestions ('Jeremy, you won't forget, will you, that Paul Johnson wrote a very good piece on the subject' or 'Jeremy, what about the Irish dimension? Ought we to give some thought to that?'); at half-past twelve, with our meeting in the morning racing towards me and not a constructive thought in my head, I made a large pot of tea, said goodnight yet again to Petra – already woken by the messages from the Horseferry Road – and stole downstairs to work out what to do.

One of an editor's most useful (and quite genuine) roles is to act as an uninformed general reader, separating the wood from the trees, letting the author know what such a reader needs to be given by way of background information before he can embark on the arguments proper, and imposing some kind of shape and logic on random arguments and strongly-held beliefs; and the only way in which we could make sense of Tam's polemic was to treat it like a superior school essay, starting out with a brief fulmination to whet the reader's appetite, moving into more placid waters with some historical and factual background chapters, spelling out the whys and wherefores of the devolutionary case, before moving into a higher gear with an unanswerable savaging of Mr Callaghan's ill-laid plans. By half-past two I had a skeletal scheme typed out, and I crept up to bed a good deal less worried about our meeting in the morning.

The product of panic as much as inspiration, my scheme was hardly a work of genius: but Tam – who turned out to be the most generous-minded and appreciative of men – hailed it as a masterpiece ('Jeremy, I have to tell you that I think that is quite *brilliant*'). The torrent of words and sheets of House of Commons notepaper continued unabated, but at least – with the synopsis to hand – we had some idea of where to place them, inserting new sections or altering their order as occasion demanded. As the days went by I became increasingly gripped by the subject, sharing to the full Tam's sense of indignation and – tentatively at first, but with increasing confidence – adding my own suggestions and comparisons, all of which Tam would (rather to my alarm, since I felt quite unqualified to advance any views on the subject) mull over in silence for a minute or so before pronouncing in sonorous tones, 'Jeremy, I think that's rather *brilliant*. We must put it in at once.'

At some stage we agreed that I would start our fortnight's holiday on the Isle of Wight, after which I would fly up to Edinburgh for an intensive week's labour, during which the book would somehow be written and delivered to Cape in time for the Party Conference. Seaview was particularly bright and sunny that summer, with the towers of Portsmouth shimmering through the haze and children burying one another in the sand and becalmed dinghy sailors in tan shorts rapping out orders as their sails flopped limply in the non-existent breeze, and I felt more than ever like an elderly schoolboy on the last day of the hols when the time came for me to say farewell to Petra and the girls and our friends from Sparrows Hanger and their eager black labrador – no longer a mobile watering can, but rushing busily up and down the beach with a branch of wood in its mouth – and take the ferry from Ryde and various sweltering trains *en route* for London airport, a small suitcase in one hand and my portable typewriter in the other.

Tam was waiting to greet me at Edinburgh airport, and as we drove towards The Binns – his eighteenth-century ancestral home, a mile or two outside the city along the Firth of Forth – he filled me in with the latest iniquities of the devolutionists, and revealed that Hugh Trevor-Roper had agreed to write an introduction. Crunching across the gravel drive, I noticed a queue of sightseers snaking out from the front door, and a uniformed attendant waiting to sell them their entrance tickets; and after hurriedly introducing me to his wife and children, Tam bustled me upstairs to an empty attic room where, free from all distractions, we could concentrate on defeating the devolutionary cause. Bare except for an unmade-up metal-frame bed, two upright chairs and a small table which could double up as a desk, it was the kind of room in which a mad or disgraced relation might well have been locked up for life: the walls were empty, the floor was uncarpeted, and from the dormer window one could see hills and the sea and, immediately below, the patient line of visitors. An additional hazard, as far as I was concerned, took the improbable form of the peacocks strutting up and down the terrace and every now and then uttering their raucous cries. I had long been allergic to peacocks – the turquoise of their feathers and the sound of their voices induced a terrible tightening

in the chest and shortage of breath, and more than once I had
woken, sweating, from a nightmare in which a roast peacock was
served at dinner – so when, next morning, I drew back the curtains
and was confronted by a peacock nodding and bobbing on the far
side of the window-pane, I fled back to bed until the intruder had
strutted importantly away.

I had thought, in the Isle of Wight, that the worst was behind us;
but no sooner had I taken my place on one of the two upright
chairs, and removed the lid from my portable typewriter, than I
realised that all my labours had been, apparently, in vain. The
metal-frame bed, on which Tam was now perched, was covered
with sheet after sheet of House of Commons notepaper, all of them
fresh from the master's hand; and as he passed them to me, one
by one, with an appropriate exegesis, Tam would occasionally
break off to tear a sheet from the *Scotsman* or the *Daily Telegraph*,
which he then handed to me with the suggestion that 'Jeremy, I
think this ought to go in somewhere, don't you?' Once again I felt
as though I was about to be seized by an epileptic fit – comparable
to that which might have occurred had the peacock vaulted the
window-ledge and advanced, pecking, on my ankles – and as the
words washed over me I gripped the edge of the table and closed
my eyes and waited for the storm to pass.

For half a day I thought no progress would ever be made, and
that I would have to report a failure to my masters at Jonathan
Cape: but then, quite suddenly, the book began to emerge in strips
of continuous prose, as Tam paced up and down declaiming on a
subject he knew so well, while I pecked on my portable typewriter,
straightening out his syntax and punctuating as we went, making
sure he didn't stray too far from our much-elaborated chapter
breakdown, and occasionally – even at this late hour – coming up
with ideas of my own, not all of which were rejected ('Jeremy, I
think that's *brilliant*'). It was one of the most enjoyable if exhausting
editorial jobs I have ever done, and we got it through to Cape in
time. I had grown very fond of my erratic, independent-minded
companion, who still stands out in the House as a rare free spirit in
a sea of dull professionals: I haven't set eyes on him since he drove

me back to the airport, the completed typescript under my arm, but years later, when the Devolution Bill had long ago been forgotten, he wrote to me out of the blue on that familiar House of Commons notepaper to say that he had been thinking about me, and had decided that I had been responsible for the United Kingdom remaining as it was, since if it hadn't been for his book, the Devolution Bill might well have been enacted, and if I hadn't been to hand he might never have written the book . . . Any other editor could have done the job I did, quite probably without being driven to the brink of insanity; but as I have never made any effort since to involve myself in public life, my venture into Scottish politics has a particular place in my affections.

The Act of Union may have balanced, briefly, in the palm of my hand, and Mr Callaghan may have started uneasily in his sleep at the thought of what his maverick MP was writing far away in the attic of The Binns, but at home I remained a sadly unimpressive figure, still performing tribal dances in front of the television and lacking the gravitas, the income, the company car, the foreign holidays and the pension prospects of my fellow-suburbanites. I loved our house, every inch of which we had painted and papered ourselves, teetering off ladders and stepping in pots of paint, and I loved being able to work at home, and I loved my daughters even more as they cast nappies and babyhood behind them and grew louder and funnier and more articulate with every day that passed: but although I remained as diligent as ever, scrupulously clocking up the hours and taking work with me wherever we went, I found my earnings lagging behind even our modest level of expenditure, and far closer to those of a sixteen-year-old copy-typist than our modest mortgage would allow. I still saw no reason why I should be paid more than a pittance for doing work that I greatly enjoyed, but as the days rolled by and the debts ran up, something would surely have to give.

One afternoon in early spring, when I'd been enjoying the freelance life for about a year, the phone rang and I found myself talking to a man who was – as it turned out – a source of more disinterested goodness and generosity, to me and to many others, than anyone I have ever met. I had come across Hugo Brunner once or twice in my early days as a literary agent, when he was a director of Chatto & Windus, and liked what I remembered; and now he was on the phone from Oxford to say that he had just moved from Chatto to look after Oxford University Press's General Division under the affable gaze of 'Bruno' Brown, and to ask whether I might be at all interested in coming down to work with him; I had, he said, been recommended to him by his former colleague David Machin, who had given me the job of editing Tam Dalyell and had been my more effectual predecessor in the late-Victorian literary agency. I was gratified and flattered by Hugo's words, but had no desire to abandon my freshly-decorated suburban home, with aeroplanes roaring overhead and worried-looking commuters hurrying past the door, and despite the alarming state of our funds the thought of going back into even the most congenial office filled me with dread: but Petra felt there would be no harm in accepting Hugo's invitation of lunch, since we could combine my visiting the OUP dining-rooms with seeing our old friends John and Christine Kelly, who had recently moved from Canterbury to Oxford, where John had been made a Fellow of St John's and was devoting his life to the letters of W.B. Yeats.

It was a bright spring day when we arrived in Oxford, and the buildings glowed like honey in the sun; Hugo Brunner and Jon Stallworthy, the Deputy Publisher of the General Division, appeared to take my potential as a publisher's editor a good deal more gravely than I did; the job, it seemed, was mine, and it seemed madness to resist. But as we headed back home I told Petra – much to her disappointment – that I couldn't bear to go back into institutional life, however benign, and next day I wrote to Hugo and, as gracefully and as gratefully as I could, declined his kindly offer; after which I forgot about the whole thing, and life resumed as before.

About a fortnight afterwards, late on a Friday afternoon, the editor of the *Illustrated London News* rang me with what was, he knew, an unreasonable request, but which, if met, would earn his undying gratitude. One of his regular book reviewers had failed to deliver his copy, and he was a thousand words short; would it be possible for me to read four biographies over the weekend and get him copy first thing on Monday morning? Never knowing where the next job, if any, will come from, freelances are always reluctant to turn down work; I had never written for the *Illustrated London News* before, associating it with my school library and sepia-coloured drawings of archaeological digs; but it paid well, and I was eager to get on its roster of reviewers. Of course I would, I said; within half an hour a helmeted figure on a motorbike had handed over a parcel of books, and I was deep in the life of Montrose. By Sunday night I had struggled through all four books, but felt too exhausted to write a word; I got up at five on Monday morning, but could find no way of threading together seventeenth-century Scotland and English nannies in mid-Victorian Russia and two more recent but equally disparate slices of life; by ten I was still as stumped as ever and the deadline was upon me. I rang the editor and grovelled, and he told me that if I could drop the copy in no later than two o'clock that afternoon all would be well, but not a minute later. Somehow between ten and one I managed to extrude my thousand words and, running all the way, made my way to the Gray's Inn Road via Mortlake station and Waterloo. It was raining and I had forgotten my mack; I hadn't slept a wink, and hadn't found time for lunch; as I padded home through the drizzle I thought of Oxford gleaming gold in the sun and, for the first and only time, felt that the freelance's life was that of a dog, and wished above all else that I had taken Hugo's offer. As I pushed open the front door Petra came beaming out to say that Hugo had just rung, begging me to reconsider. It seemed too good to be true, and I picked up the phone at once and told him I'd changed my mind; and six weeks later, after a 'freebie' trip to Israel to write an unpublished travel piece – so desperate did I become to escape the remorseless timetable imposed upon us by our over-enthusiastic hosts, with not a second left free between canning factories and Druze encampments and the Wailing Wall and Holy Places and a junior minister explaining all kinds of things with the aid of a slide projector, that I took to getting up at three every morning and wandering round by myself, free from the ever-hovering car and driver, and came home in more of a daze than ever – I abandoned the freelance life and the homely joys of the suburbs for the grandiloquent role of the Literature Editor in the General Division of Oxford University Press.

CHAPTER SIX

Oxonian Interlude

FAR AND AWAY the worst thing about moving to Oxford was leaving our house in the suburbs, with its sham Tudor gable, its black-and-white tiled hall, its rotting conservatory, its elaborate ceilings, the plaster mouldings of which could be bought by the yard, its tiny back bedrooms overlooking an unkempt garden and the beanpoled allotments beyond. Only nine months earlier I had, in a flurry of manly pride, applied the last drop of gloss paint to the bottom-most step of the vertiginous staircase that soared up from the light and dancing motes of the dolphin-blue hallway into the blackness and cool of the floor above. We knew and loved every inch of the house, hundreds of identical specimens of which stretched blandly away to either side, to Putney to the east and Richmond to the west; we showed prospective buyers round with a blend of pride and defiance, hoping they'd love it and yet say no, dreading the thought of the hall being covered over with wall-to-wall white fur, or louvred glass windows being installed in the kitchen, or heat-preserving polystyrene tiles adorning the dining-room ceiling, with swivelling spotlights cunningly inset, or our wholesome sheets of Laura Ashley – one tiny room of which we had, in our ignorance of handiwork, papered round and round rather than up and down – being elbowed aside by swathes of fur-coated flock in shades of crimson and silver. In the end we found a buyer; and one terrible Saturday morning I took a deep breath, removed the first picture from the wall, and began the demolition of what seemed like a lifetime together. It was blazingly hot on our last day there: we hoovered the empty rooms for the last time with tears in our eyes, ate a takeaway meal in the garden, eking out the minutes, trying to pretend that nothing had changed, and then drove blindly down to Oxford, like expellees from Eden in a scarlet Renault 4. Six years later, when we moved back to a similar but smaller house only four streets away, our Oxford friends treated us with a mixture of bafflement and pity, as though by preferring the tired anonymity of East Sheen to the self-evident splendours of North Oxford we had been offered Paradise and spurned it from pure perversity. As it turned out, I never liked living in Oxford, congenial as the company almost always was, and couldn't wait to trade in Summertown and St Aldate's for the Upper Richmond Road: and as far as Paradise was concerned, I felt I had had an intimation of it at least in our dim suburban home, whereas Oxford, for all its obvious allure, left me curiously unmoved.

I began my Oxford life as a PG, camping out on the Kellys' floor in a redbrick terrace house belonging to St John's at the bottom of the Woodstock Road, returning to London at weekends while Jemima finished her term at school and Hattie shouted in the background and unwanted prospective buyers poked bird-like about the house, apologetically peering into cupboards and expressing polite interest in my father's Cambridge oars pinned up in the hall. On my first evening in exile, after Petra had driven back to London and I was left, for all the Kellys' bonhomie, feeling more like a prep-school boy on his first day away from home than a middle-aged man seizing an undeserved opportunity to rescue his career from the doldrums, John Kelly and I wandered round to a small pub somewhere off Observatory Street. It was the kind of place I liked, with bare boards on the floor, a ceiling kippered by smoke, two tiny front rooms devoid of music or fruit machines, and an entrenched-looking clientele, some of whom could be spotted perched on broken benches in the garden beyond, where rotting mattresses and rusting bed-frames lay scattered between two apple trees. Among the boozers I recognised, much to my relief – for I longed already for London faces – a drinking companion of the chief accountant and the sea-dog, from the days when they had preferred the rheumy delights of the Museum Tavern to the further shores of Southwark and Kentish Town: a red-faced, wild-haired figure with the battered features of a fallen angel, clad in a greasy fawn gaberdine mack, a roll-your-own dangling from his lower lip, as if held in place by a tiny dab of glue, Tim Hilton was already making his name as an art critic, and went on to write a much-acclaimed life of Ruskin. Meeting him here was pleasing enough, and did something to dispel my gloom; and later in the evening I was introduced to another regular whom, though I never knew him well, I instinctively liked and admired as much as anyone I met in Oxford.

Dan Davin was, as I soon discovered, in charge of the Academic Division – better known as the Clarendon Press – at Oxford University Press: as such, he was the academic equivalent of my boss-to-be, Sir John Brown – who looked after the General Division – and, with the Secretary to the Delegates, one of the three most important people in the Press. He was then, I would guess, in his early sixties: he had a large, heavy head, reminiscent, though more benignly so, of Hermann Goering's, an oddly bare, angular and shiny-looking scalp with strands of shiny hair brushed over it, a wide, slightly frog-like mouth, and bulging, bloodshot eyes, melancholic in expression and narrowed against the smoke that drifted up from the cigarettes he smoked, lighting each from the stub of the one before. With his wife, Winnie, and a select circle of cronies, he spent many of his evenings in The Gardener's Arms, gazing through the smoke in gloomy silence as the bitter edged its way down his glass like the mercury in a rapidly-falling thermometer, or passing monosyllabic comments on the follies of fellow-publishers at the Press, or Oxford academics whose works he was looking after. A New Zealand Catholic of Irish extraction, Davin had had a good war, serving under Freyberg in Crete and the Middle East, and after being demobbed he had hovered on the fringes of Fitzrovia before becoming a full-time academic publisher. What he really wanted, perhaps, was to be taken seriously as a novelist: it seemed to be generally agreed, rightly or wrongly, that those novels which had found their way into print were fairly feeble, but they were more than made up for – in my eyes at least – by *Closing Times*, his sad, vivid and affectionate memoir of the literary life.

Ostensibly a series of six portraits of his friends – Maclaren-Ross, Louis MacNeice, Dylan Thomas and Joyce Gary among them – the book's real interest was as covert autobiography of the rueful, self-deprecating kind, with Davin the part-time roisterer and unsuccessful writer watching and recording his friends from the wings, enjoying his pints in the pub over lunch but always keeping an anxious, office-worker's eye on the clock. At his memorial service a few years later in the Balliol dining-hall – I went with Richard Cobb, who moved restlessly on the bench beside me as speech succeeded speech, each more excessive than the last – much was made of his greatness as a publisher and a writer, and how the world of letters would never be quite the same again. In fact he was little-known in the publishing world at large and remained, in essence, an editor of academic works rather than a fully-fledged practitioner like the Chairman or André Deutsch; but he wrote one excellent book, which is surely enough in itself, and much of what made him such a sympathetic figure came from his own unillusioned sense of the great gulf that lay, for him as for the rest of us, between the dreams of youth and actual achievement, between the words on the page and the evanescent Irishry of the bar-room raconteur. Writers who fail to fulfil their potential or cling to the side of the pool are often easier to understand, more akin to us in their sad perplexity, than those who display a monk-like dedication and an unswerving sense of purpose; and however generous their motives, his eulogists in Balliol hall did this truthful, distinguished, rather melancholic man a sad disservice by attributing to him qualities – or rather achievements – he would, I'm sure, have been the last to claim for himself.

A year or so before my arrival the Press had decided that all but a handful of those employed by its General Publishing Division should join their colleagues from the Clarendon Press and the Educational Division in Oxford, moving away from the marmoreal yet slightly raffish splendours of Ely House in Dover Street to the even grander headquarters of the Press in Walton Street, five minutes' walk from where I had been introduced to Dan Davin in

The Gardener's Arms – a honey-coloured quadrangle that combined printing works and publishing offices, the high walls and gabled skylights of an early Victorian factory with the Corinthian columns and pale blue clock of an eighteenth-century college, complete with a circular, immaculate lawn with a pond and a gigantic beech tree in the middle, and a porters' lodge with grave-looking porters inside, sporting the filigreed crest of the university on the lapels of their dark blue uniforms. The pale blue clock and the lawn and the navy-clad porters and the eighteenth-century ambience – if not the clinical, rubber-floored corridors within, offices sprouting to either side like grapes from the stem of a vine – reminded me of a sober, diligent version of Trinity College, Dublin: but despite these and other enticements, a number of old lags had refused to make the move from Dover Street, suspecting Oxford life of being parochial and incestuous, and were busy finding themselves billets with other London publishers; which was why I now found myself, on the morning after my arrival in the Kellys' house, presenting myself in reception and examining, as I waited for Hugo to come down, the copies of various Oxford Dictionaries and Histories and Companions to this and that which had been carefully laid out under glass-topped cabinets like so many mediaeval manuscripts or priceless fragments of urn.

Far from emerging, as expected, from within the building, Hugo came suddenly striding in behind me, a broad smile of welcome lighting up his face, one hand outstretched, a pair of bicycle clips encircling the ankles of his grey flannel suit. No one has a greater gift for making people feel wanted or at home, and as we worked our way – circuitously – from the main quadrangle in the modern, purpose-built extension in which the new arrivals had been housed, and as he escorted me from cell to cell and introduced me to my new colleagues, each of whom seemed as agreeable and as friendly as the last, I felt a sudden, unexpected surge of happiness, as though I had strayed into one of the sunnier passages of Dickens, inhabited by beaming and twinkling Mr Brownlows or other benevolent characters: I no more wanted to be in Oxford than I ever had, beyond that brief moment of despair when I had staggered home in the rain from the *Illustrated London News,* but now that I was there, I could hardly have chosen to spend my time in more pleasant or congenial company. The introductions made, Hugo then showed me to my office and – after suggesting that I might like to pop into his lair in twenty minutes' time – left me to my own devices. I found myself in a small, bright, modern-looking room with a metal frame window, a grey haircord carpet, a comfortable swivel chair made of black-painted metal and matted black tweed, curiously reminiscent of a blackberry bush, a rather humbler-looking chair for visitors without a swivel built in, and an expensive-seeming desk of teak and more black metal, topped by a gigantic anglepoise lamp like a sunflower wilting at the end of summer. From my window I looked out onto a stretch of honey-coloured wall, pierced by white-painted mullioned windows; from Hugo's rather more important office, overlooking Walton Street and the back entrance to the old Radcliffe Hospital, one could watch visitors coming and going, employees chaining their bikes to the rails, Dan Davin and his cronies making their way to The Gardener's Arms, and the navy-clad porters bustling importantly out to shoo off some irreverent motorist who had dared to park on the cobbles outside the main gate.

Absurdly enough, as it now seemed, I had been appointed the Literature Editor of the Press's General Division; and on the shelves about me stood row upon blue-backed row of those books which, together with the Dictionaries, had made the name of OUP famous throughout the world, and which constituted my particular patrimony: World's Classics (still, then, in their tiny, elegant format, inherited from Grant Richards), Oxford Standard Authors, Oxford Illustrated Dickens, and Oxford Books of verse and prose edited by assorted dignitaries, from Yeats and Sir Arthur Quiller Couch to Helen Gardner and Philip Larkin, plus some daunting-looking works of literary criticism and heavily annotated biographies, most of them devoted to Russian writers of whom I had heard dimly, if at all. It was my job to look after, and add to, this particular and all too visible slice of the Oxford list, and as I gazed about my clean, closely-carpeted office, wondering how to open the window and how to work the pocket calculator with which, I was told, I would soon be totting up overheads and profit margins and suitable royalty rates, I felt both overawed and fraudulent. Not only did I know almost nothing about the nuts and bolts of publishing at this level – I began to gasp for air as a kindly colleague tried to explain a computer print-out – but I had read barely a line of Pope or Milton or Dryden since my schooldays (when, to make matters worse, I had, after O-level, deserted English for geography at the pleading of a heavily tweeded games master). Whether the Oxford Wordsworth was a reasonable text, whether it needed the kind of notes and introduction craved for by modern undergraduates, how it compared with the competition, or which of the eminent scholars snoozing or guzzling or discussing their mortgages in the colleges down the road might be the man to mastermind a new and unbeatable edition were, to me at least, matters of grave indifference. I found almost all literary criticism other than that practised by writers themselves quite unintelligible, and suspected its perpetrators of being charlatans and windbags to a man (the only one who made any sense at all was George Steiner, and I soon learned that, in Oxford eyes, he was regarded as the worst of the lot); exactly what I was doing there, or why someone so obviously ill-qualified for this particular job had been chosen to occupy it, was quite beyond me.

My feelings of inadequacy, never far from the surface, were further inflamed when I realised that one of my predecessors was widely regarded within the Press as a cross between a secular saint and a Fellow of All Souls, after whom I was bound to seem shallow, ignorant and boorishly insensitive. Well-known in the trade – and greatly admired by many – for the pale-blue pencil-marks with which she adorned the typescripts on which she was working, she evinced towards her authors the flattering, reverential awe of a vestal virgin who alone was sensitive and receptive enough to understand what they really had in mind. She despised the notion of publishing as a business, in which the ideal had somehow to be tempered to reality, and books should be made to pay for themselves; although she had elected to stay behind in London, she was still heavily involved in the books she had commissioned – including several multi-volume lives of Russian poets – and when I suggested that perhaps it wasn't feasible to allow the author forty-eight pages of photographs and footnotes on the page while at the same time pricing a book of over 400 pages, of which we could not possibly hope to sell more than 1500 copies throughout the world, at not much more than the going rate for a novel, she greeted my suggestion with a disdainful sigh, with much raising of her eyes to heaven, as though the Goths had broken through and civilisation was crumbling around her. Such impracticality was infuriating in itself, but more maddening still was the implication that she alone was on the author's side. To underprice the book would mean publishing it at a loss, without selling a single extra copy, given the rarefied nature of the subject matter, whereas to publish at the profitable, higher price would benefit both the Press and the author, whose royalties were based on the published price: but such coarse and philistine reasoning was far beneath such a sensitive spirit, who would have been perfectly happy for the author to earn half as much from a lifetime's work rather than dabble in the squalid waters of commerce. In this she was quintessentially Oxonian, reflecting attitudes that were, as I soon discovered, all too common on college high tables and among the bicycling, sandal-shod ladies of the Woodstock and Banbury Roads.

As a recent arrival from London publishing, who knew far more about the business than ever I would, Hugo – much to my relief – took my part in these polite if distant encounters; and before long he joined me in what must have seemed a further and unforgivable act of vandalism. By a pleasing irony, the Oxford end of the business – the dictionaries, the schoolbooks, the academic monographs, the books on teaching English as a foreign language – was extraordinarily well-run, businesslike and profitable, supervised for the most part by sharp-suited middle managers with an eloquent command of business jargon and pocket calculators, and a ruthless insistence on adequate profit margins and returns on capital invested; whereas the former London end was altogether more Oxonian in its literary pretensions, its love of corduroy and tweed, and its very obvious disdain for the notion of publishing as a trade, and for vulgar talk about 'gross margins' or 'stock turn' or 'discounted cash flow' or the other monstrosities dreamed up by American business schools. Among the most attractive embodiments of Ely House amateurishness was a much-admired series of reprints of long-forgotten eighteenth- and nineteenth-century novels, bound in cloth with ribboned headbands, terracotta-coloured washtops, top-quality paper and elegant lettered jackets. They were greatly admired by dons and scholars, still more so since – as was often pointed out, in tones of gratitude and wonder – they cost even less than the sum my predecessor had suggested for the life of Aleksander Blok, while making available books that could only otherwise be tracked down in obscure and dusty second-hand bookshops; and yet, in publishing terms, the series was a disaster. The worldwide market for some of these books was probably in the region of 750 copies; in order to achieve the price they wanted, and for which they were so gratefully admired, the editors at Ely House had committed what is, in publishing terms, the mortal sin of printing five, six or even seven times as many copies as were needed, with the result that the warehouse was awash with beautiful, unwanted books which no remainder merchant would touch, and could not be given away. The only, dreadful, answer was to pulp the lot, making way on the racks for what the men in sharp suits would have described as 'faster-moving lines'.

Light relief was at hand, however, in the more congenial form of those useful money-spinners, the Oxford Books of this and that. Until a year or two earlier anthologies – and Oxford anthologies in particular – had been restricted (wisely, perhaps) to serious subjects like Renaissance Verse or Mediaeval Carols rather than Soccer, Seduction or Office Life, and I suspect that the subsequent mania for anthologies owed a great deal to the enthusiasm with which Jon Stallworthy, followed by Hugo and myself, thought up and commissioned new and more populist Oxford anthologies, including Frank Muir on Humorous Prose (a very late delivery), Kingsley Amis on Light Verse, V.S. Pritchett on Short Stories, John Gross on Aphorisms and – following the baffling success of the rather tedious *Oxford Book of Literary Anecdotes* – innumerable anecdotal volumes from the Military to Politics. At one of our fortnightly editorial meetings some bright spark – suddenly aroused from slumber, perhaps, and anxious to make amends – floated the idea of an *Oxford Book of Satirical Verse*. My colleague Richard Brain, later of the *TLS*, sensibly suggested that Geoffrey Grigson would be just the man for the job, and urged me to get in touch with him. Ever amenable, I wrote off to Grigson's literary agent as soon as the editorial lunch was over and the last glass of wine had been drained. She promised to sound him out, and a day or two later she rang back to say that – despite some earlier feud with the Press, the details of which no one seemed to remember – he would like nothing better than to edit such a book. Terms were agreed, and contracts exchanged; and I headed off down Walton Street to the OUP canteen rubbing my hands together, with the satisfied air of a man who has done a good day's work.

Exchanging contracts with his agent was all very well, but the prospect of having to deal with Geoffrey Grigson – let alone raise possible queries or even criticisms – filled me with dread on two scores. In the first place, he was a notorious literary pugilist, renowned for the ferocity and the zeal with which he savaged those he suspected of fraudulence or bad faith. He had been doing battle since the 1930s, and his scalps included those of Edith Sitwell, C. Day Lewis and Ted Hughes. I had no idea what he looked like, but I saw in my mind's eye a desiccated, wintry beanpole of a man with a cold grey eye, a precise, scornful mouth, hawk features, spectacles (perhaps) of the kind preferred by Herr Himmler, thin grey hair streaming in an arctic wind, and a shirt collar several sizes too large for the wizened, lizard-like neck that protruded from it. How, I wondered, would I be able to sustain five minutes' conversation with so lethal a figure – on satirical verse or any other subject – without being exposed at once and cast aside as a lightweight and a nincompoop? Until now I had, thanks to the kindness of my colleagues and some nimble sleight of hand, managed to bluff my way through my part as OUP's Literature Editor: would I at last be exposed to shame and ridicule by

Grigson's insisting on dealing with someone rather more scholarly and better informed? Matters were made still worse by the fact that, as the keen-eyed child of a Cornish rectory, Grigson was, I knew, something of an expert on country matters, editing anthologies on flowers and the seasons, contributing to Shell Guides, and generally showing himself to be well-informed on matters like ragwort and barley and hedging and ditching. A child of London and the rusty, concrete-strewn South Coast, I had read not a word of Richard Jefferies or W.H. Hudson, found William Barnes incomprehensible, and tended to glaze over when even the most sympathetic of English poets began – as English poets so often did, at least until the moderns – to wax rhapsodical about moss and pansies and delphiniums. My knowledge of birds was restricted to the robin, the ostrich and the chicken, of flowers to the rose and the dandelion, of trees to the Christmas and the palm; I was wary of cows, and terrified of horses. Adrift in the country, I invariably snagged my trousers on any available stretch of barbed wire, or toppled sideways when trying to clamber a fence, landing heavily in the mud on the other side with an angry grunt. I made ecstatic noises about the Arcadian landscapes of Claude Lorrain or the view from a train window, but secretly preferred the unalarming, well-trod paths of Richmond Park, with litter-bins to hand and aeroplanes droning comfortably overhead, to the mud and wildlife and cross-looking rustic folk of Gloucestershire or Norfolk. Like many townees, I had always felt uneasy with – and rather inferior towards – genuine country-dwellers, with their voices like Dan Archer and their shrewd blue eyes and confident dealings with pigs and bulls and weather-beaten faces and easy ways with sticks (tapped knowingly against the rump of a cow or the side of a boot) and Land-Rovers crammed with animal feed and spanners and – worst of all – their twelve-bores, liable to go off at alarmingly short notice, causing me to leap from my skin and hurry for shelter as a shower of rooks thudded to the ground about us. As a child in the 1950s I had always felt, when visiting my grandparents' Gloucestershire farm, irremediably urban and incompetent, and I was quite sure that – like my ferocious and derisive grandfather – Grigson would spot in me at once a suburbanite of the most contemptible variety.

All the same, publishers are supposed, at times, to meet their authors, or at least make friendly noises in their direction, so I wrote the old curmudgeon what I hoped was a no-nonsense, man-to-man affair, saying how pleased I was (how pleased we all were) that he was editing this book for us, how good I was sure it would be (on the strength of a letter alone he might, for a moment, think I was in a position to judge), how much I looked forward to meeting him (here an element of direct untruth intruded) and – in a sudden spasm of *bonhomie* – how delighted I'd be if he came and had lunch next time he was in Oxford. Once the letter was safely in the post, I felt that sense of relief that comes from doing what is right. It seemed most unlikely that the ogre would want to waste a lunch-hour with a menial like myself, but at least I'd shown myself willing; having done which I could lean back in my chair and bend my mind to other, less alarming matters.

I heard nothing for a week or two – I later learned that Grigson was an infrequent and peremptory letter-writer – until, one sunny afternoon, the phone on my desk rang – jolting me, as it invariably does, from some agreeable daydream, or post-prandial slumber, or doodling on my blotter – and a hearty, jolly-sounding lady introduced herself in ringing tones as Jane Grigson, the wife of the ogre and much admired as a cookery writer and (in our household at least) as the inventor of curried parsnip soup. 'Geoffrey was *thrilled* to get your letter,' she informed me in a voice far removed from that of an ogre's wife, 'and he'd *love* to come and have lunch with you. We'll be in Oxford next Wednesday: is there *any* chance he could come and see you then?' So jolly and friendly did she sound – and so great was my fear of the ogre, despite her dulcet tones – that I immediately asked her if she'd like to come as well, partly because I liked the sound of her and partly because I hoped she might shield me from her husband's acid tongue and freezing stare; to which she replied that she'd like nothing better, and that they'd both turn up in reception at a quarter to one on the day we'd agreed.

Even as she spoke I was overcome by a further spasm of dread, temporarily obliterating my other anxieties. Halfway between the main buildings of the Press and the Worcester end of Walton Street, OUP used to have a set of dining-rooms in a redbrick late-Victorian building with Dutch gables and the look of a converted workhouse. Despite its unpromising exterior, the three dining-rooms reserved for important guests were extremely grand, with chandeliers twinkling overhead, college prints on the walls, glass-fronted bookcases stuffed with Oxford books to remind the forget-ful of why they were there, and sideboards crammed with every imaginable variety of drink and covered with open boxes of cigars from which indigent academics and literary men regularly lined their pockets; while crisply-aproned, matronly waitresses in green-and-white uniforms flashed to and fro with silver salvers balanced on their arms and opened bottle after bottle of dust-encrusted wine. The only drawback to this admirable arrangement was that the food itself was identical to that served to the staff in the canteen below – institutional stodge of the battered Spam and chips variety, followed by jam roly-poly and custard – except that by the time the chips had been transferred to the silver salvers and carried upstairs they had cooled even further and lost what little crispness they had ever possessed, while the Bird's had acquired that thick, elastic skin that is so impervious to the probing spoon and so familiar to generation after generation of prep-school boys. For my part, I was more than happy with meals of this kind – I have always relished institutional food, and despised those who recoil with a shudder at the mere mention of prunes or tapioca or liver like shoe-leather or offal of any kind – but the notion of this queen of gastronomes being offered for lunch all that she held most foul was too much to be borne, undoing all the good I had hoped to achieve by asking the ogre to lunch in the first place and alienating my hoped-for ally at a stroke. Surely I should have risked all, in the hope that OUP would foot the bill, and booked a table at the Elizabeth or the newly-opened Quat' Saisons. But by now it was too late: they were speeding towards me from their Wiltshire fastness. I could only wait for the worst.

Shortly before one o'clock the lady in reception rang up to say that Mr and Mrs Grigson had arrived; pausing only to dry my right hand on the seat of my trousers – a soggy handshake followed by soggy chips was surely going too far? – and clipping to my face what I hoped was a frank and manly smile, I hurried downstairs to greet them. Bearing in mind Grigson's rustic enthusiasms I had abandoned jeans and an open-necked shirt for green corduroy trousers, a Viyella shirt (far too hot for the time of year, but a sacrifice well worth the making), a blue-and-white spotted silk tie of the kind worn by puce-faced men swaying on the steps of White's, and a fiery tweed jacket such as I associated with Surtees's choleric Lord Scamperdale and his sidekick Jack Spraggon. I hadn't found the time to bone up on Cobbett or John Clare, nor had I rung my Gloucestershire cousins to check on the state of the harvest, but I had spent the morning turning the pages of Helen Gardner's *New Oxford Book of English Verse* in the hope that this sudden immersion might stop me making too many obvious howlers and somehow soften the look of bovine vacuity which, as far as I could tell from photographs or occasional glimpses in the mirror, invariably illuminated my features in public.

As I rounded the corner into reception I caught my first sight of my dreaded guests; and by the time I reached the spot where they stood turning the pages of the current catalogue I felt an altogether happier man. Both Jane and Geoffrey looked reassuringly ruddy and stout and cheerful and friendly and unpretentious: I felt at once – as I always did thereafter – that I was in the company of old and highly congenial friends to whom one could burble not only about writing and publishing and literary gossip and even, if pushed, foot-and-mouth disease, but about children and cats and holidays and all those less worrisome items which excite a frisson of tedium or disdain in the more austere or self-regarding literary man. Far from being desiccated and severe, with an outsize shirt collar, a cold seagull's eye, a contempt for small talk, and a donnish, inquisitorial tone of voice, Geoffrey looked like a jovial, well-fed farmer of a kind that – had I met him thirty years before – might have given me an altogether less fearful view of rustic life. A well-built, comfortable-looking man with small blue eyes set in a blunt, reddish, windblown face topped with a thatch of white hair, he was dressed in an open-necked shirt, a beige cotton safari suit with button-down pockets and a belt at the back, and – most engagingly of all – socks and sandals. Jane was quite as jolly-looking and friendly as her voice had led me to expect – a round, kindly, convivial-looking woman with an open-air look to her cheeks and a pair of outsize horn-rimmed specs of an unalarming kind. Together they looked like a less mawkish version of the Cheeryble brothers, as well as a walking testimonial to the pleasures of the table, and of Jane's cooking in particular. A moment or so later we were joined by Hugo Brunner, who had kindly volunteered to share the burden of the ogre's scorn; and, talking vigorously, we set off in a foursome down Walton Street in the direction of the dining-room.

As we settled down to lunch and spread our napkins on our laps – the chandeliers winking overhead despite the blazing sun outside, the cigars within easy reach, the pre-prandial gin-and-tonics coursing through our veins, the serving ladies bustling to and fro with plates and silver tureens – I felt that all was working wonderfully well. Only the problem of the food remained; yet even here, it seemed, all was miraculous! The packet minestrone was despatched with cries of glee, and much smacking of the lips; far from toying listlessly with the greasy fish in batter and the sodden chips and the frozen peas (cunningly garnished with a pat of butter and a sprig of parsley) or leaving the greater part untasted or tactfully concealed beneath a provident lettuce leaf, both parties volunteered for more, straining eagerly forward in their seats as fresh lumps of batter were spotted peeping over the rim of the silver salver; as I watched Jane adding the custard to a gigantic mound of steamed date pudding, while Geoffrey waited his turn, barely able (or so it seemed to my frenzied imagination) to master his excitement and impatience, my ignoble anxieties faded into oblivion.

And all this while not only had Geoffrey refrained from referring to William Barnes or Thomas Hardy – let alone silage or mangel-wurzels – but, beyond accepting in a self-deprecatory way our polite noises of enthusiasm, he had made barely a mention of the *Oxford Book of Satirical Verse.* I had braced myself for a battery of questions and keen debate – keen on his side, dumbfounded and inert on mine – about the virtues of Pope and Byron and Betjeman and Plomer and D. J. Enright, about how much Swift there should be in relation to Rochester, or Praed to Calverley, during the course of which he would swiftly and scornfully realise how utterly inadequate I was to be his editor. Yet here was the great critic, the scourge of the pretentious and the sham, a man dreaded and feared by literary men for almost half a century, not only tucking into school food with evident relish, but discussing school holidays and badly behaved dogs and even, no doubt, dry rot and how to deal with elderly relations with far greater zest and interest than he had shown when, at the packet soup stage, I had, to set the wheels in motion, tentatively raised the names and subjects of some other companion Oxford Books which we had recently commissioned. Only at the very end, when we had downed our coffees and dabbed our lips and left the table, and were walking back down Walton Street to the offices, Hugo and Jane in front, Geoffrey and I trailing some twenty yards behind, did he display any relish in a Grigsonian achievement. As we strolled slowly along I said to him that I thought Jane's curried parsnip soup was one of the very great inventions of the twentieth century, far outstripping television, the jet engine or the pocket calculator. Geoffrey stopped in his tracks, his face lit up with pleasure; and then 'Jane, Jane!' he shouted down the road, his white hair blowing in the breeze and his right arm waving above his head: 'Jane! They make your soup!'

I had left OUP by the time *Satirical Verse* was published, and although at Chatto & Windus I commissioned and published Geoffrey's last book, *Recollections* – a rather episodic book of memoirs, containing some sharp and often very funny accounts of his dealings with, among others, Cyril Connolly, Wyndham Lewis and Louis MacNeice – I never saw a great deal of the Grigsons once we had left Oxford and moved back to London. From time to time we visited them for lunch in their rambling white farmhouse on the bare downs beyond Swindon, at which Jane produced vast, delicious meals, with not a battered cod or soggy chip in sight, let alone a roly-poly pudding, and minded not in the least when our daughters, in the way that daughters will, looked askance at some of the less familiar items on their plates: both Jane and Geoffrey seemed genuinely fond of, and indulgent to, children, and I remember being touched by his saying that he thought the younger generation much maligned, and that he found the friends and contemporaries of his daughter Sophie – who had just gone up to Manchester University – more attractive and more idealistic than his own. I remember, too, a birthday party for Geoffrey at which it rained all day, and the cars got bogged down in the fields, and the guests – hundreds of them, it seemed, and all of them cheerful – scurried for shelter from barn to outhouse, a paper plate held up like an umbrella against the rain, and a glass of wine and a plateful of Jane's goodies, somewhat waterlogged, in the other, or bumping into them in St Antony's at the Oxford Food Symposium, of which Jane was a luminary – with Geoffrey sniffing appreciatively about, still clad in the same fawn safari suit and socks and sandals. And then Geoffrey died, and Jane herself fell ill. I wrote to ask her to the publication party for my first book, and she wrote back to say that, alas, she couldn't make it: 'I've been having trouble lately, and am in the middle of radiation treatment at the moment which rather keeps me to the house.' But, she went on, 'thinking of the funny times Geoffrey and I had with you – esp. the gourmet meal at the OUP – always makes me laugh'. I wish I had known them better and seen more of them, for they were the kind of people one could love on the shortest acquaintance. As it is, Hugo and I have the memory of the battered fish and soggy chips; and the *Oxford Book of Satirical Verse* – which, after all, provided our *raison d'être* – remains triumphantly in print.

My particular – and, alas, unsuccessful – contribution to this flourishing branch of the trade was a series of miniature anthologies intended for the classier end of the gift market and designed to slip into whichever long-redundant Edwardian pocket the marketing men had in mind: it included James Lees-Milne on Country Houses, Alan Ross on The Turf, Raymond Carr on Hunting, Jasper Griffin on Snobs, and a good many others before the series was sadly discontinued. Feeling, for some obscure reason, that he was a natural miniaturist, I liked the idea of John Sparrow, the Warden of All Souls, editing one of these small anthologies – presumably on some suitably donnish subject – but felt diffident about approaching so eminent an Oxford figure. Richard Brain, who was a good friend of Sparrow's, told me that I had no reason to be afraid and that the Warden was much less alarming than I might imagine, so I dropped him a line care of the Warden's Lodgings and waited to see what would happen next. A day or two later the phone rang and I found myself talking to the Warden, who suggested that I might like to come and see him next day round about tea-time. He sounded affable enough, I liked the idea of having tea with the Warden of All Souls, and any excuse to get out of the office was very welcome; we agreed a time, and I strode off home feeling rather pleased with myself, there to bone up on the *Lady Chatterley* trial and re-read the Warden's Introduction to the Penguin Collected Housman.

I thought it only polite to look smarter than usual when visiting the Warden of All Souls, so next morning I once again abandoned my jeans and corduroy jacket for my only suit, a wasp-waisted, tubular-trousered affair which had been made for me in Dublin in the early 1960s out of scratchy, seaweed-coloured tweed so thick that the trousers, corrugated slightly at the back of the knees, could quite easily stand up by themselves, like the bottom half of a suit of armour. This suit, to which I was – and still am – greatly attached, had been designed to withstand the unheated damp of Irish digs, and could only reasonably be worn in the depth of winter; it was now a muggy mid-October, and by the time I reached the OUP headquarters I was sweating heavily, my specs sliding down my nose in the way they do in mid-summer, my shirt plastered to my chest with unseemly patches of sweat, and my hair – washed specially for the occasion – glued to my scalp in greasy swathes. This would never do, so as soon as I reached my office, puffing heavily along the corridor, I peeled off my jacket, loosened my tie, turned off the central heating, opened my window as wide as I could (since my office was in a modern block, this involved standing on my desk and doing stretching exercises) and spent the rest of the morning moving as little and as slowly as I could, while the sweat patches gradually dried out and the fiery Donegal tweed scratched my legs like an all-embracing bramble-bush.

That afternoon I let myself out of the office with that guilty, furtive feeling of truancy that the office-worker invariably experiences when escaping even on legitimate business, and set off in the direction of the High Street, moving at an even, unhurried pace so as not to excite another outburst of sweating and steamed-up specs. Some ten minutes later I found myself standing outside the Warden's Lodgings – a honey-coloured eighteenth-century building, square like an outsize doll's house and tacked onto one end of the Gothic arches and pinnacles of All Souls itself. It was, by now, a misty afternoon, and the paving stones seemed to exude the greasy dankness of the Thames Valley at its most lugubrious; peering over the black-spiked railings in front of the house – on one of which an empty Coke tin had been neatly impaled by some disrespectful passer-by – I noticed in the area a litter of Kentucky Fried Chicken boxes and polystyrene cups, rude intruders into a world once peopled by Betjeman and Bowra and the likes of Harold Nicolson. Thrusting such unhappy thoughts aside, I strode up to the panelled black front door, and pealed loudly on the bell.

Like most of those who think of themselves as diffident, sensitive souls, a far cry from those coarse-grained intruders who elbow their way into where they are unwanted, tramping on all finer feelings *en route,* I hate having to ring or knock a second time in case I seem unduly impatient or insistent; but after a minute or so with no answer I pealed again, adding a tentative rap with the knocker as well, and then stood sharply back, as though distancing myself from the crime, to await the cry of rage from within. Still nothing happened; and I was just about to leave, feeling rather relieved, when the door flew open and I found myself face to face with the Warden of All Souls.

I had a fairly good idea from my reading of literary lives of what the Warden looked like – a stocky, muscular frame, a largeish head, and old-fashioned, strong-featured English looks of the kind that involve an iron jaw, jagged eyebrows, and black, shiny hair smoothed back from a widow's peak of a type that, for some inexplicable reason, no longer seems to be available: a craggier version of Denis Compton, perhaps, or a 1930s film star who had disguised himself as a member of the Bar and displayed an unexpected knowledge of the Latin poets of the Silver Age. I recognised the Warden at once, and he was wearing, as anticipated, a blackish, rather subfusc suit with a white shirt and the occasional flash of red braces; but his dapper widow's peak had fallen forward in a cowlick, rather like Henry Green's in Cecil Beaton's well-known photograph, and his large, dark brown eyes seemed to be rolling in his head. It was obvious that he had completely forgotten about my coming, and had no idea who I was, and when I stammered out an explanation he smacked his hand to his forehead and emitted a torrent of apologies. I told him not to worry in the least, and that I could easily come back another day; and I was just moving off when, suddenly conspiratorial, and rather pleased with himself, he seized me by the arm, pulled me into the Warden's Lodgings, and slammed the door shut behind me.

'I'm *so* glad to see you, and I'd be *extremely* grateful if you could help me out by staying for tea,' he said, bending towards me and speaking in a low and confidential drone. He found himself, he explained, in a fearful pickle. He was, he should explain, something of an authority on Housman, and several months earlier the leading Japanese Housman expert had written to him to say that he would be leading a team of other Japanese Housman experts to Oxford in the autumn, and that they would very much like to visit the Warden to discuss Housman's rhyming patterns. The Warden had – not unreasonably – banished the whole thing to the back of his mind, but the Japanese Housman experts had suddenly descended upon him and were busily discussing Housman's poems in his sitting-room even as we spoke. All this was bad enough, but to make matters worse he couldn't understand a single word they said, and was rapidly running out of conversation. Could I possibly help him out? Perhaps, as a younger man, I might be able to make out something of what they were trying to say and act as some kind of interpreter or semaphore-operator, or at least I could help to pour out the tea and keep them smiling and happy? Of course I would, I said, feeling flattered by his friendliness and touched by his predicament; he expressed his undying gratitude, and with that we moved out of the murky darkness of the entrance hall into the sitting-room beyond.

'This is my friend Mr Jeremy Lewis,' the Warden boomed as we entered, speaking very slowly and clearly, as if addressing a party of imbeciles or a delegation of the deaf and dumb. 'He too is something of an authority on Housman, and is eager to join our discussions,' he continued in mendacious vein, raising his eyes in a heavenwards direction as he caught my gaze. The Japanese Housman experts were peppered about the room, perched upright on the edges of the Warden's capacious armchairs and clutching dainty cups of tea, a slice of seed-cake balanced on the saucer. They looked serious and very small, the men in fawn or pale blue lightweight suits, the women in demure, old-fashioned numbers of the kind that might have been worn by Doris Day. I flashed an all-purpose smile in their direction, helped myself to a cup of tea and a slice of seed-cake, found a chair, and prepared to join in the conversation.

'Is Housman a popular poet in Japan today?' the Warden enquired, keeping his sentences simple and speaking in the loud and hyphenated manner I remembered from *Rainbow* and *Tiny Tots*: 'And is he taught in u-ni-ver-sit-ies?' To these and all our other questions – before long I had thought up some of my own, despite my ignorance of the subject – the Japanese Housman experts replied with a series of impenetrable, gargling barks, like so many sea-lions ordering fish, while the Warden and I craned keenly forward in our seats, our faces lit up with the kind of fatuous good-will one associates with up-to-date clergymen trying to consort with the young, or well-intentioned gatherings of international civil servants. Despite the Warden's curious mode of speech, the experts appeared to understand what we were saying, grinning or shaking their heads as the occasion demanded, but their replies seemed to bear no relationship whatsoever to English as we knew it; they seemed happy enough with the way things were going, cheerfully accepting further cups of tea and a second slice of seed-cake, and helpfully supporting one another's arguments, but I found myself wondering, in my insular way, whether it was really possible to be an expert on a poet, in any more than a factual or biographical sense, if you cannot speak his language in a way that is intelligible to his compatriots. As for the Warden, he soon abandoned the fight, exhausted by his labours, but lay back in his chair, shaking with silent and sometimes spluttering laughter whenever I caught his eye, and throwing me off my stride as I racked my brains for what little I could remember of Housman's poems, or the Warden's Introduction which I had so scrupulously re-read the evening before.

By now it was dark in the Warden's garden, and it was time for the Japanese Housman experts to return to their hotel on the Banbury Road. The Warden and I shook their hands with companionable warmth as they trailed through the darkened hall and out into the foggy High Street; and then, as the front door closed behind them, the Warden let out a great sigh, sweeping the back of his hand across his forehead in a histrionic gesture before thanking me once again and suggesting that we both deserved a drink. Back in his sitting-room, he produced a shoe-box crammed with black-and-white photographs of modern undergraduates (male) with jeans and bangles and long hair. We went through these one by one, while he compared them unfavourably with their predecessors of fifty years before. We had another whisky, and then it was time to go; and I tramped home to North Oxford to brief my wife on the foibles of academic life, grateful at last for the warmth of my bristly Dublin suit as I brooded on the complexities of Housman scholarship, and the demonic look of complicity in the Warden's face as he fought to control his mirth.

Much to my regret, I never met the Warden again; later I learned of how, the Warden no longer, he had had to abandon his long-held Lodgings for a flat in the Iffley Road, where – unkindest cut of all – he had to put out his own dustbins. This seemed a sad, unhappy falling-off, and I hope there was no truth in it; but whenever I see a picture of the Warden in his heyday I think – with amusement and affection – of how I bailed him out in his hour of need, when Housman could help him no more.

Although I continued to feel momentary spasms of irritation when faced by a residual outburst of vestal virginry, I greatly enjoyed the company of my colleagues at OUP, and never more so than at our weekly editorial lunch next to the Grigsonian dining-rooms, after which, flushed with wine and camembert, we would stagger back down Walton Street for a well-deserved rest. From Hugo downwards they were friendly, intelligent, enthusiastic and refreshingly free of the side and the endless politicking that makes ordinary office life so hazardous an occupation; and far from discouraging one another for fear of being outshone or losing status to a rival, they seemed to delight in one another's triumphs, however modest, eagerly suggesting ideas and generously pooling their resources. And yet – for such is the perversity and ingratitude of man – I found myself, if not unhappy and bored, a good deal more restless and dissatisfied than I had any reason to be. Part of this was simply missing London; and part had to do with the nature of the Press itself. It was the first large organisation I had ever worked for; it was also a part of the University, a highly successful and shrewdly-run business which was at the same time imbued with the pomp – and some of the pomposity – that went with Delegates gravely meeting in the Clarendon Building to discuss the latest publishing proposals, and learned journals, and academic monographs, and the mere fact of being the world's oldest and most famous university press. I felt, for the first time, that I had encountered the Establishment, a body whose existence I had hitherto doubted, and that I was working – very much under false pretences – for a literary branch of the civil service. The Press was both more bureaucratic and more democratic than anywhere else I had ever worked: rather priggishly, perhaps, I disapproved of the way in which responsibility was spread – or dodged – by consulting all those involved via an elaborate system of memos before even the simplest decision was made, yet the positive side of this was that all of us were kept informed and were free to express our views; and despite the proliferation of formal titles and an occasional chilling *hauteur*, there was far less wearing of rank than in even the smallest London publishing house. And yet, admirable and efficient and likeable as it all was, the old Adam in me pined for the swiftness and the flamboyance and the dictatorial dash I remembered from St James's Place and Great Russell Street: somehow publishing as I liked it seemed a preserve of enlightened despots, more akin to Frederick the Great than the Fabian Society. I found the decency and the good behaviour and the cool common sense and the benign but perceptible aura of superiority claustrophobic, in much the same way as I found Oxford itself claustrophobic; and, as often as I could, I took the early train to London, and did my work instead in the half-deserted, marmoreal offices in Dover Street, where a few dissolute remnants of the *ancien régime* still held court in remote attic rooms of the former bishops' palace.

Chief among these attic-dwellers was Peter Janson-Smith, a convivial, bibulous figure who had been Ian Fleming's literary agent, and was still deeply involved in the intricacies of the Fleming estate. Peter and his fellow-Jacobites came down to Oxford once a week, looking rather red and rumpled among the fresh, eager faces of their Walton Street colleagues, who regarded them with the stiff, suspicious unease that an anxious mother might display towards a debauched and jovial uncle liable to lead her offspring astray: I took to him at once, finding in him a welcome breath of London air, and made a point of hurrying up the interminable flights of stairs to his office as soon as I arrived in Ely House. Very soon we discovered, much to my relief, a justification for my endless trips to London in the form of Kingsley Amis's forthcoming anthology of light verse, which had been commissioned by Jon Stallworthy and nominally formed part of my patrimony: it had been looked after until my arrival by Peter, with a good deal of help from fellow-attic-dwellers, who busied themselves checking Kingsley's references and sorting through the large piles of photocopied pages that formed the completed typescript. None of this left a great deal for Peter and me to do, but since Kingsley was an important author, and the book would make us a great deal of money, it was essential to put our best feet forward and hold a series of high-level meetings to discuss the kind of things that publishers discuss and give an overall impression of purposeful activity. These were held in Peter's office, which was dominated by a gigantic, gleaming fridge, and when I arrived at half-past ten, hot from the Oxford train, I would find the anthologist and his London editor sitting one on either side of Peter's desk, gold half-moon spectacles perched on the ends of their noses to add a serious, scholarly touch to the proceedings, desultorily sifting through the latest batch of photo-copies and wondering what should be left out of the finished version. Since neither Peter nor I had read a great deal of Calverley or Praed, and were in no position to suggest who might or might not have written a scabrous verse 'variously attrib. Milton and Rochester' in the printed version, our contributions to the meeting were essentially jocular and social. On the dot of eleven Kingsley would look at his watch, peer thoughtfully over his spectacles, and say in a surprised voice, as though it had struck him for the first time, 'That's an interesting-looking fridge you have there, Peter'; at which Peter, looking equally surprised, would produce a cork-screw from his desk drawer, open the fridge – which, much to everyone's surprise, turned out to be choc-a-bloc with bedewed bottles of white wine – whip out the cork with a satisfying plop, produce and pour out four glasses (the fourth was for his colleague in the room next-door, who had been waiting to join the conference at this stage), and fall back behind his desk with the satisfied look of a man who has done a good day's work; and so the meeting would progress, with much popping of corks and smacking of lips and an increasingly listless shifting of sheets of paper, until it was time to go to the Italian place over the road for lunch, at which business could be carried a further stage amid the companionable clinking of glasses.

Drink is an occupational hazard of the publisher's life, and it loomed especially large during our dealings with the *New Oxford Book of Light Verse.* Early on in my career at the Press I rang Kingsley Amis – whom I had never met – to say that I would be in London, and to ask if I could possibly come and see him at six o'clock that evening. 'Of course you can,' he said: 'Just in time for drinkies.' When the day came I realised that I wouldn't be able to stay in London that long, so I suggested that I might come at four instead. 'But you'll be too early for drinkies,' a crestfallen voice replied. No doubt, I reassured him, there would be plenty of other opportunities, and we agreed that I would turn up at Flask Walk shortly after four. He met me at the door – wearing a thick tweed jacket and, or so I like to think, a pair of bedroom slippers on his feet – and led me towards a kitchen-cum-conservatory. 'I suppose you'd like a cup of tea?' he asked, in a more belligerent and resentful tone than is normally reserved for so mild an enquiry, and when I said I would he dropped a tea bag into a mug, added some boiling water and handed it to me with an air of gloomy resignation. As I sipped my brew I tried to explain who I was and why I was sitting in his kitchen drinking a cup of tea; but I was uncomfortably aware that he wasn't listening to a word I said, but was watching my every sip, monitoring the level of the tea as it slowly edged its way down the mug. As I drained the last mouthful a look of relief spread across his features; and then – ever the attentive host – he said, even more gruffly than before, holding out one hand in the direction of my mug, 'I suppose you'd like another one of those?' It was a hot day, and I felt thirsty and unnerved, and I said I would, very much indeed: at which another tea bag was produced, more boiling water was added, and the same disconcerting routine was undertaken once again. By now it was twenty past four; and no sooner had I tipped the last drop of tea down my throat than 'Good, it's drinkies time,' said Kingsley, leaning eagerly forward in his chair, the look of peevishness quite gone: a bottle was produced, and everything was right again.

A year or so later, after the book had been published, Kingsley was invited to be one of the guests of honour at a literary lunch of the kind that is attended by ladies with mauve hair and hats like herbaceous borders and ivory handbags apparently crammed with rocks, and presided over by aldermen with chains about their necks and puce-faced men in scarlet tailcoats, much given to banging gavels and shouting 'Pray silence for his Worshipfulness the Mayor!' This particular lunch took place in Stratford-on-Avon; Peter Janson-Smith and Kingsley were driven down from London in a hired car with a bottle of whisky between them on the back seat, while I made my way across country with a sober contingent of Oxford colleagues. We gathered in a motorway hotel on the outskirts of Stratford, the ladies in hats milling busily about and the publishers' publicity girls laying out piles of books on trestle tables in the hall; we ate the regulation lunch of cold chicken and boiled potatoes followed by fruit salad out of a tin, washed down with watery Riesling, Kingsley and his two fellow-authors sitting at the top table with the mayor and the editor of the local paper and the most important ladies in hats, while the rest of us made our way to our places at the circular tables that lay about its feet. Gavels were banged, the puce-faced man in the scarlet tailcoat looked to be on the point of a seizure, the mayor welcomed today's distinguished speakers at inordinate length, laughing a good deal at his own witticisms and losing his way in his notes, and was followed by the editor of the local paper and the most important lady present, while the rest of us writhed in our seats; very much as an afterthought by now, the three authors finally rose to their feet, hurrying through their speeches in half the time it had taken the mayor to finish his preamble and move his hands from his lapels to the swell of his comfortable-looking stomach.

The speeches over, the three speakers were led out of the dining-room and into the hall, where they were seated behind a long trestle table, on which lay piles of their books to be signed for the ladies in hats, who were bustling excitedly about, gathering up armfuls of books and, as if by instinct, forming into patient queues. It was at this critical moment, the whole point of the proceedings, that two of the authors – maddened, perhaps, by Riesling and tinned potatoes and mayoral rhetoric – decided to go on strike:

Kingsley and Reginald Maudling – a large, reassuring figure look-ing like a bank manager in a double-breasted suit – announced that not a copy would be signed until they had something to drink, and that the something should be whisky, sharpish, rather than watery Riesling. By now it was well after three o'clock, thanks to the mayoral speech; the bar was closed, and the management was adamant. In the end I managed to wangle them two large paper mugs of whisky, and disaster was averted; Kingsley and Peter Janson-Smith were swept back to London in the back of their hired car with appropriate refreshment to hand.

Oxford Books were all very well, but my favourite among all the books I took on, at OUP or anywhere else, the one for which I retained a particular, almost parental, love, was an altogether more modest affair, at least in the quantitive terms of physical bulk and number of copies sold.

In 1953 Dom Aelred Watkin, the Headmaster of Downside, sent an account of his grandmother's curious and melancholy life, writ-ten by her daughter, to Evelyn Waugh. Waugh wrote back to say that although he thought it unpublishable in its present form, it was a 'tale of haunting beauty and pathos', and he urged Fr Watkin to revise and improve his mother's version. Three years later they were in touch again on the subject of Maria Pasqua. Waugh felt that some of the story's magic had now been lost, though admitting that 'perhaps it is the novelist in me that wishes to defeat the historian . . . Perhaps I have played with the idea of Maria Pasqua so long in my mind that I have added some inventions of my own.' To Nancy Mitford he wrote that 'it is a most moving story of Beauty in captivity, very sad and full of authentic, bizarre detail. Not a plot for you or me, but it could be made a great work of art by someone. Who?'

Dom Aelred's sister, Magdalen Goffin, inherited Helena Watkin's papers, including Waugh's helpful suggestions for the book's improvement, after their mother's death in 1972; and it was her version of *Maria Pasqua,* brief but highly potent, that landed on my desk one day in 1978. Some of my more austere colleagues greeted my raptures with a disapproving sniff, but I was so bowled over by the beauty of the writing and the sadness of the story that I persuaded I Iugo to allow me to take it on, despite the absence of footnotes and references duly verified, and despite touches more reminiscent of a novel or even an unhappy fairy tale than a scholarly monograph.

Maria Pasqua was born in the Abruzzi in 1856, the daughter of impoverished peasants. Because she was very beautiful, with great liquid eyes, she was soon supplementing the family income with work as a child model in Rome. When she was six she and her father made their way to Paris – and Maria left behind forever a country that would increasingly assume, in her eyes, all the attributes of Paradise Lost. In Paris she was painted by Academicians of the kind that were soon to be elbowed aside by the Impressionists, but did brisk business in the meantime selling their wares to the rich and famous. Among these was the Comtesse de Noailles, who – pipped at the post by a Rothschild also in pursuit of some saccharine study of the beautiful Italian girl – went one further by buying the model herself from her father for the price of a vineyard.

'Madame' was, despite her name, an Englishwoman; as a Baring, she was also very rich. Childless and separated from her husband, she spent her days moving restlessly between Paris, the South of France and various English seaside resorts. Though formidable, she was also engagingly eccentric, with strong views about the health-giving properties of cows' breath – a cow would be tethered by each ground-floor window so as to infuse the room – and rose-tinted glass. She refused to travel if the wind was in the east or stay in a house with an oak tree nearby, wore a fur hat in bed and ate all her meals behind a specially constructed screen.

From a life of Bohemian poverty, Maria was translated into a very different world. She learned French and English, grew more beautiful than ever, and was eventually packed off to school in England – where she encountered the 'black-coated figure' who was to shape, and to blight, the rest of her long life.

Philip Shepheard was a widower, eighteen years older than Maria Pasqua, and as soon as he set eyes on her he determined to marry her. He was a just and conscientious landowner and country squire, but as a husband he was dour, economical with candles, and prone to hurrying his wife and children off to bed at nine o'clock each night. Locked away in a remote Norfolk farmhouse, Maria Pasqua spent the rest of her life pining for a world she had lost and waiting, resentfully, for *le vieux* to die so that she could revisit Italy once again; but by the time he complied, aged ninety-four, she was an old woman herself, and it was too late.

'Can't you take a deep breath & invoke Virginia Woolf & Max Beerbohm and start again with the aim of creating a literary masterpiece?' Evelyn Waugh asked Fr Watkin. It's hard to imagine that Magdalen Goffin's version of Maria Pasqua's sad, compelling life would not have met with his approval; and he might well have been amazed to learn that so touching and terrible an account of the *lacrimae rerum* went swiftly out of stock, and has not been reprinted since.

Among our authors was a man who, after an unusually active and adventurous life, had decided, in middle age, that he should have been a woman all along, and had taken himself off to North Africa for the necessary operations. A year or two later she had written a book on the subject: among the evidence she produced for her having been born into the wrong sex was his hatred, at his public school, of organised games and towel-flicking in the showers, which made me wonder whether most of the people I knew – with myself in the lead – shouldn't be booking aboard the next flight for Morocco; while the idyllic evocation of life as a middle-aged woman with which she rounded off her book seemed to consist of jam-making, gossiping on street corners with other ladies clutching handbags, and being chucked beneath the chin by gallant taxi-drivers.

By the time I met her, she was a cheerful, fit-looking figure with a bush of grey hair, broad shoulders, a light tenor voice, cone-shaped bosoms, bangles on her wrists and the faintest five o'clock shadow dusted over with talcum powder; she was clad, more often than not, in what was referred to in old-fashioned circles as a flower-patterned summer 'frock'. She had always been a wonderfully vivid and evocative writer, with a genius for finding exactly the right epithets with which to conjure up the look and the sound and the smell and the flavour of the places she had been to, and the book she had delivered to us could not have been better done. Haggling with her over the few points under discussion was a slightly unnerving business, in that one never knew quite with whom one was dealing: for most of the time she would employ traditional feminine wiles – batting the eyelids and gazing demurely at the floor, or waving her arms in the air and setting her bangles a-jingle – but then, quite suddenly, she would spread her knees, put her hands on her thighs and become a no-nonsense man again, throwing me quite off balance and instantly gaining her point. She invariably signed off her letters with love; I liked her a great deal, but in those days I was far stuffier about such matters than I have since become, and deciding how I should sign off in reply caused me agonies of wakefulness and indecision. I didn't want to seem rude or ungrateful, but I couldn't get round to reciprocity, so I tended to sign off every letter with some facetious or laboured joke which made any mention of love redundant. Equally problematic was the question of kissing, now that the English were becoming a nation of amateur public kissers, with the preliminaries to parties or social gatherings blighted by a good deal of swooping and ducking, and innumerable false starts. My author was, I had noticed, rather keen on this kind of thing, cocking her head sideways in anticipation of a peck on the cheek: freer, more generous-minded spirits plunged in with the abandon of a kepi-wearing Legionnaire, but – stiff and ungallant to the end – I could never quite make it.

One evening at a party I found myself talking to an old friend of my author's, who happened to be in Oxford at the time. He was a ruddy-faced, hawk-featured man, with the fiery eyebrows and ebullient high spirits of a hard-living eighteenth-century squire. Taking care to remember my 'she's and 'her's, I told him that I was working with his friend on her new book, and how greatly I was enjoying it all. 'Are you really?' he exclaimed. 'And how is the old boy? I do think he looks a bit of an ass walking round in high-heeled shoes and carrying a handbag, but do give him my best, and tell him I'd love to see him one day.' Rather rashly, perhaps, I told him that my author – who lived a long way from Oxford – was coming into my office at three next afternoon, and that if he wanted to see her he could always pop his head round the door. "That's a *very* good idea,' the eighteenth-century squire replied: 'I'll be there on the dot of three – but *please* don't tell the old boy I'm coming, since I'd like it to be a surprise.'

Next afternoon, at a quarter past two, my author arrived in my office. When it came to professional matters she was always extremely quick, efficient and decisive: by a quarter to three we had done whatever needed doing, and she was gathering up her belongings and preparing to make her way back to her car and the long journey home. It seemed too dreadful to think that she was about to miss the welcome surprise her friend had in store; so, at the very moment when she was holding out her hand for a farewell shake, I asked her if she couldn't possibly stay on another ten minutes or so, since an old pal was longing to see her and was even now hurrying towards us from a distant part of the building. At this she turned ashen, and a look of panic shot across her face. 'Christ,' she said, in tones more reminiscent of a persecuted schoolboy than a successful lady writer, 'is *he* here?'; and with that she grabbed hold of her coat and her handbag and her briefcase, flung open my office door, and hurtled down the corridor with giant, manly strides. Five minutes later my door was flung open, and a grinning red face peered eagerly round its edge; but by then the bird had flown, and was driving flat out in a westerly direction.

At some point in my career with the Press I persuaded Hugo to send me to Dublin for a couple of days, since we had one or two authors there whom nobody seemed to know, and I might be able to make use of my Irish connections to drum up some business. My real reason for wanting to go was that I hadn't been back since leaving Trinity over twenty years before, and if I could slake my nostalgia at someone else's expense – and justify my trip at the same time – so much the better.

From this brief, unhappy trip I learned two things: that when it comes to heavy drinking the English are mere amateurs, who should never attempt to take on the Irish; and that it is far wiser never to revisit the places in which one was once intensely happy, but to preserve one's distance and keep the memory intact. Dublin looked, as it always had, both foreign and familiar as I trundled in from the airport on a green-and-white double-decker bus, and my legs seemed on automatic pilot as I strode from the bus station up Westmoreland Street to Trinity to take coffee with the Provost – I had called on him as my tutor once a term so that he could sign a form which entitled me to a student discount on flights between Dublin and London – before moving on to the Shelbourne to drink Guinness with a potential contributor to my series of miniature anthologies; but it was when I went on from there to Merrion Square, to see a poet who was editing a forthcoming Oxford Book, that I began to lose control. The editor was a mild-looking civil servant in glasses, and we ate a civilised lunch of salmon and salad in a room overlooking the square; but the drinks were stronger than I suspected, and when the time came for me to hurry on to my next appointment with a Professor of English at UCD, the mild-looking civil servant pooh-poohed the very idea and, moving swiftly towards the telephone, rang the professor and suggested he join us for a drink. The afternoon wore on, and the lunchtime wine was succeeded by Jameson's; darkness fell on the square outside and the gaslight flared on the great silver lampstands with the arms of the city embossed on the base; other figures materialised out of the darkness, and still the bottle made its rounds. Not a word of business was said or done, and my plans for ensnaring the professor from UCD lay befuddled and unventilated at the back of my barely working brain. After a while someone suggested, in a thick and halting voice, that we might give Seamus a ring, and see what he was up to. Somehow we found ourselves in an old haunt of mine, the International Bar, draining pint after pint of stout and whiskey chasers with bearded men in matted tweeds and Aran sweaters; somehow I managed, just, to remain on my feet, despite knocking several glasses off a curlicued, marble-topped table onto the black-and-white stone floor and standing, ashen-faced and sweating, in the Edwardian downstairs lavatory, my forehead propped against the tiles, the cistern gurgling overhead and a broad, wooden-seated bowl waiting to receive the contents of an unremembered Chinese takeaway; somehow, after the pub had closed and my fellow-carousers had made their way home in their various directions, I stumbled back to my hotel in Kildare Street, where I flung myself fully-clothed on my bed before oblivion intervened.

Next morning I had nothing to do until lunch with my old friend Brendan Kennelly, by now the Professor of English at Trinity and as cherubic and cube-shaped as ever. My head was pounding like a drum; it was raining; I wandered the squares of Trinity like a lined and battered revenant. I knew every inch of the place and every cobble underfoot, and every step and every corner was peopled by the ghosts of those I had loved – by ffenella and Shore and Ian Whitcomb and Charles Sprawson and Suzanne Lowry with her almond-coloured eyes – and yet even the ghosts no longer belonged but seemed redundant and out of place in a city full of strangers; and later that afternoon I trailed back to London paralysed by gloom and determined never to revisit the scenes of my youth. Some years afterward, I found myself back in Dublin, this time disguised as a freelance journalist, and was overcome once again by the same feelings of melancholic displacement, drifting unhappily and superfluously about streets and squares that once meant more to me than anywhere else on earth and looked exactly as I remembered them, and yet were utterly changed in all the qualities that mattered; but by then I had both exorcised and embodied that particular, precious slice of my life in the pages of the *London Magazine* and, later, in *Playing for Time*, so that even when I took up my position on the pavement on the far side of Fitzwilliam Street from which, day after day nearly thirty years before, I had gazed up at ffenella's window in the hope of catching her eye, I felt only boredom and impatience, filling in the hours in an alien city till I caught my flight home.

* * *

Nor was I any happier living in Oxford. I had never lived in a place so full of people I liked, so crammed with kindred spirits; whereas in East Sheen we greeted the few neighbours we knew with, at best, a peremptory 'Good morning,' we hailed their Oxonian equivalents as friends; and yet – by some perverse paradox – I found Oxford's cumulative effect intolerably claustrophobic, narrow and self-regarding in a manner that was, perhaps, inevitable in a rather rarefied community which, however likeable and liberal-minded its constituent parts, seemed as one in regarding its particular ways of thinking and behaving as unquestionably superior to those that prevailed in the barbarian world beyond. No doubt there was some truth in this, but I found myself longing for the anonymity, the vulgarity and the variety of London, for neighbours who had never heard of Brasenose or the Master of Balliol or Chatto & Windus, any more than I had heard of their commodity brokers or double-glazing businesses – both of which, like a college or a publishing house, were self-contained, hierarchical worlds of drama and gossip and intrigue, all-absorbing to those within and meaningless to those without, and (no doubt) demanding kinds of intelligence and knowledge that were different from, but not necessarily inferior to, those that prevailed in the half-fearful, half-arrogant world of North Oxford, the inhabitants of which liked to pretend that, had they so chosen, they could have run any business one cared to mention with far more success than the current incumbents, while secretly suspecting that the world outside might have proved chillier and less respectful of academic excellence than they liked to imagine. And when I overheard some amiable, reclusive don (whose brasher colleagues were hard at work extracting money from Japanese industrialists) speak with disdainful hauteur of the world of trade or industry, my hackles rose on behalf of an army of commuters and tired businessmen. As an editor with OUP I was considered *persona grata*, and was warmly welcomed in by tweed-jacketed men and apple-cheeked, woollen-stockinged women whose tastes and interests and attitudes of mind I found far more sympathetic than those of the average commodity broker or double-glazing salesman, had I known any to judge them by: but Oxford brought out the philistine and the populist in me, neither of which lay far below the surface, and I found myself eagerly championing the case of reps and middle managers, and pining for a glimpse of a chalk-striped suit or a cheeky chappie's pork-pie hat, with a feather in its band.

Nor was I won round by kindly invitations to lunch or dine in various colleges. I longed, in London, to be asked to the Garrick or the Savile or the Travellers' or even the Reform, with its clientele of grave-looking civil servants, Arthur Marshall oddly incongruous among them, and I liked nothing better than to stand at the bar of one of these places hemmed in by red-faced lawyers and literary men tossing back the gin and tonics before moving off in the direction of the dining-room in small, convivial bands; and, in my innocence, I imagined that Oxford high tables would have something of the same stylish bonhomie. Alas, apart from one congenial evening in Wadham, life on high table seemed a sadly thin-blooded affair at which, as often as not, one found oneself sitting with a diffident Egyptologist and a timid nuclear physicist and a polite but reserved professor of mathematics, none of whom (not unreasonably, perhaps) seemed remotely interested in who one was or where one had come from, hurriedly moving the conversation on to the unexciting common ground of college politics or fire regulations. (Light relief was occasionally provided in the irreverent, bow-tied form of that much-missed publisher Colin Haycraft of Duckworth's, who bounced from college to college like a squash ball in specs, signing up fellow-classicists under the nose of his rivals from OUP, whose lumbering approaches were no match for this wily intruder from the Old Piano Factory in Camden Town.)

Every now and then one of my closest friends from Trinity, Dublin, a loud and jovial English don, far from thin-blooded, who had recently become a fellow of one of the richest colleges, endowed with a legendary cellar, would ask me along as his guest to particularly sought-after suppers. Each time this happened I would hope for the best as I hurried down the Banbury Road in my tubular-trousered dinner jacket, overcome by a suitable glow of self-importance, half-persuaded that this time, at last, myth and reality would somehow coincide; and each time I would stagger home after the nuts and port, feeling a monster of ingratitude, half-guilty and half-baffled by the boredom I had felt. One evening, after several such expeditions, our friend and his wife came to supper. They were late, as he had been held up on college business; and after a couple of drinks he suddenly banged his fist on the table and shouted '*Christ*, they can be *so* boring!' Somehow I felt better after that, and less of an odd man out.

Even more claustrophobic than the dons themselves were the well-scrubbed, high-minded ranks of North Oxford wives in sandals and flower-patterned dresses, twittering on the sidelines, jostling one another for jobs as proof-readers or editorial assistants on learned magazines, and keeping a steely eye out for their husbands' rivals within a faculty or college. Nor did it seem possible, as it was in London, to separate or counterpoint one's social, professional and domestic lives, each providing a perspective on the other and suggestions of light and shade: partly because Oxford is a small town, but more importantly because of the homogeneity and the sameness of North Oxford life, and the prevailing academic ethos, one came across the same people, the same gossip, the same attitudes to life, at work, in the University, in the shops in Summertown, while waiting outside our daughters' schools, at dinner in the evening. (This sense of a self-regarding, middle-class community anxious to distance itself from the cruder world outside received farcical confirmation when our youngest daughter reported for duty at a play school in one of those large Gothic houses just north of the Parks. The new arrivals were seated in a ring, and before the first lesson began the headmistress went round the room, asking each child what his or her father did for a living. 'And what does your father do, Rebecca?' 'He's a Fellow of St John's' – followed by a lecturer in Latin and a surgeon and an editor at Blackwell's and a Reader in Political Theory and so on. For some reason Hattie had come to believe that I sold lavatory brushes for a living, and when her turn came round she told the class that this was indeed my calling. 'No, Hattie, what does he *really* do?' the headmistress asked, seized by a sudden sense of panic. 'He sells lavatory brushes,' Hattie persisted, and the searchlight was hurriedly moved on to the next child, the son of a biochemist.)

Once clear of the ring road or safely on the train to London, my spirits soared and I felt myself again; back in Oxford – sodden, low-lying, the streets awhirr with bicycles ridden by men in socks and sandals and biscuit-coloured linen jackets whose faces seemed oddly unlined and unmarked by life, and by pedalling, upright women wearing reasonable smiles of sweet superiority – I longed only to escape. In this I proved myself as selfish and as self-absorbed as ever; for Petra, Oxford was an interlude of peace, a haven of picnics and sunlit children's parties and outings to the Cotswolds and touring opera companies, before office life and the scramble to work claimed her once again. Ten years after we returned to the suburbs, the same sense of suffocation overcomes me whenever the ring road hoves into sight; and I remain as glad as ever that we spurned the delights of Paradise for the humdrum pleasures of the world below.

CHAPTER SEVEN

William IV Street

ONE EVENING in the spring of 1979, just as we were getting ready for bed – Petra clutching a book and a hot-water bottle, two cats weaving between her ankles like clouds of theatrical smoke – Hugo rang to ask, in tones of tamped-down excitement, if he could possibly pop round for a minute. Hugo was always a welcome visitor, and within minutes he came bounding through the front door, his eyes bursting from their sockets with the strain of containing news that he longed to impart, and a crooked, conspiratorial smile twitching about his lips.

Since leaving Oxford, Hugo had divided his publishing career between Oxford University Press and Chatto & Windus. He had started out working for OUP in the Far East, and had then moved to Chatto as a shareholding director. A year or so later Chatto merged with Jonathan Cape and then with the Bodley Head, in the hope that sharing costs would better enable these three literary lists to keep coarse-grained predators at bay: each firm retained its own office and publishing independence, but a service company – which Hugo had helped to set up – looked after such mundane if vital matters as warehousing, sales and distribution. In 1976, Hugo had moved back to OUP, this time to their Oxford headquarters, but for some months he'd felt uneasy about developments in the Press, which he was beginning to find less congenial than he'd hoped; and now, as if by telepathy, the powers-that-be that ran Chatto, Bodley Head and Cape had written to him with the revolutionary news that Norah Smallwood, the alarming and legendary old lady who had, in effect, run Chatto since the end of the war, was finally planning to retire, and invited him to replace his old boss as the firm's managing director. All this was exciting enough, but I thought with a pang that OUP without Hugo would be a duller and lonelier place, and that although I would never expect to be offered a job as a managing director – or, indeed, as a director of any kind – it seemed too bitter that Hugo, who much preferred living in Oxford, should be lured back to London, whereas I, racked by homesickness for Bloomsbury and Covent Garden and the suburban wastes of south-west London, seemed condemned to permanent exile. But more, it seemed, was to come: for after waving away our congratulations with a self-deprecating smile and a sideways raising of the hand, as though halting a line of traffic, Hugo leaned forward from the edge of his chair and proceeded with further revelations. He knew how keen I was to get back to London, and to London publishing; although he had no intention of uprooting his family yet again, and would have to reconcile himself to the life of a commuter, he was very tempted by the Chatto offer – but only if I would agree to come with him, since we had worked so happily together at OUP. If the idea appealed to me, he would make my coming with him and being made a director of Chatto a precondition of his accepting the job. As it turned out, Hugo – so generous in friendship, so inept in self-interest – would have done far better to insist on other, more Draconian, conditions of acceptance: in the meantime I told him that of course I'd be happy to come with him, and that he could count me in when negotiating our arrival at Chatto and our departure from OUP. But, I asked – sensing, perhaps, the great gulf between rhetoric and deeds, promises and their fulfilment – was Mrs Smallwood, after forty years at the helm, *really* about to retire? At this Hugo looked more conspiratorial than ever and, delving into his jacket pocket, fished out a sheet of dark-blue writing paper; and – after thwacking it approvingly with the back of his hand – he passed it over to me to read. The address, embossed in scarlet on royal-blue paper, was Vincent Square, halfway between the Army & Navy Stores and the Tate; the writing, both tremulous and bold, covered the paper in a series of impatient loops and swerves, as if about to hurtle off the edge. Like all good handwriting, it was dashing and almost illegible: before long it was to become all too familiar, rapping out orders or issuing rebukes on the backs of envelopes or torn-up pages of typescript, but for the moment it took time to decipher, short and to the point as its message was. 'Dear Hugo,' it read (in effect): 'I'm thrilled you're coming back to Chatto and I'm dying to retire, love Norah.'

This seemed unambiguous enough, so much so that I poured us a celebratory whisky, while Hugo carefully folded up the scrap of paper and stored it away in his wallet; after which he settled back with a sigh, as though he had rid himself of a burden. Within minutes our futures had radically changed, and life looked a good deal brighter than it had half an hour earlier, when I'd been filling Petra's hot-water bottle and preparing for an early night; and after Hugo left we walked down to the Cherwell and back in our dressing-gowns and bedroom slippers, discussing the implications of it all.

For as long as I'd been in publishing I had heard unnerving accounts of the ferocious Mrs Smallwood; and although I loved the idea of working once again for a small and distinguished literary publisher, I knew perfectly well that life at Chatto would be alarmingly *ad hominem* and wearing on the nerves after the benign bureaucracy of OUP, where one's mildest move was preceded by a flurry of memos and consultative documents, diffusing responsibility and making it hard (or at least unkind) to point the finger at the guilty man. As I knew from my days at Collins and at Andre Deutsch, many of the best publishers were dictators of varying degrees of benevolence, the fiercest of whom were regarded by their colleagues and the trade with a mixture of terror and affection, enlivening a gossip-ridden, introverted business with tales of slamming doors, sobbing secretaries, flying paperweights, echoing cries of rage and loyal retainers reduced to a trembling pulp. Compared to tycoons in more lucrative and cut-throat trades, publishing autocrats may well seem mild and well-mannered, since humour and a certain innate civility have a way of breaking through: but this is cold comfort at the time to their employees, who tend to be vaguer, more diffident and less driven than their more carnivorous contemporaries in merchant banks or advertising agencies.

Mrs Smallwood had long occupied an important niche in this colourful and – in publishing terms – highly effective pantheon. Her father, I learned, had been an improvident artist with a large brood of children. Like many distinguished publishers Norah had not been to university, but had joined Chatto as a secretary some time in the late 1930s. She was then, or so I like to think, a pretty, bashful girl, with a slim and elegant figure, high colouring, penetrating bright blue eyes and a cloud of curly, reddish hair, ambitious in a bashful way but uneasily aware of her lack of education and of how little she knew, and very much in awe of Chatto's reputation and of the company in which she found herself.

Chatto had been founded in 1855 by a dubious figure called John Camden Hotten, who made his fortune by publishing pirated editions of American writers like Mark Twain and Walt Whitman. His successors, Messrs Chatto and Windus, were a good deal more respectable, publishing Trollope, Wilkie Collins and R.L. Stevenson, paying their authors royalties, and establishing the firm's reputation as a literary list. When Norah joined, the firm's chairman was Harold Raymond, a much-admired pillar of the book trade, best remembered as the man who invented book tokens; but the bright young spark was her near-contemporary, Ian Parsons, a scholar of Winchester and Trinity, Cambridge, who was responsible for establishing the firm's well-known list of lit. crit. through Cambridge acquaintances like Leavis, William Empson, Basil Willey and E.M.W. Tillyard. In 1945 Chatto bought The Hogarth Press, and Leonard Woolf became a colleague, puffing his pipe in the corridors and distributing to grateful members of staff apples from his orchard in Rodmell: twenty years earlier Chatto had caused a stir by publishing Lytton Strachey, and Leonard Woolf's arrival reinforced the Bloomsburyish flavour of the firm that still prevailed in the early 1980s. Chatto already had a distinguished stable of authors, including Aldous Huxley, William Faulkner, Norman Douglas, T. F. Powys, Richard Hughes, V. S. Pritchett and Compton Mackenzie, not to mention Little Black Sambo and *The Young Visiters*; Leonard Woolf brought with him an equally resonant team of writers, Virginia Woolf, Freud, Isherwood,

William Plomer, Henry Green, Laurie Lee, Edwin Muir, William Sansom and Laurens van der Post among them. All this must have been heady stuff, and implanted in the youthful Norah implacable notions of what publishing was all about, and how publishers should go about their business. Like all good publishers-to-be, she was ready to try her hand at everything when not typing the partners' letters – including helping Ian Parsons with *Night and Day*, the short-lived equivalent of the *New Yorker*, which was edited by Graham Greene and published by Chatto, and included among its contributors Evelyn Waugh, John Betjeman, Cyril Connolly, Elizabeth Bowen, Osbert Lancaster and Peter Fleming, with cartoons by Nicolas Bentley and that unjustly forgotten comic genius, Paul Crum.

The outbreak of war presented Norah with her great opportunity, which she seized with customary vigour. Many of the male staff, including the ebullient Ian Parsons, went off to fight, leaving Harold Raymond and Norah in charge at William IV Street. Nights might be spent fire-watching on the roof with Stevie Smith, but during the day the once-diffident secretary set out to turn herself into an all-round publisher and an indispensable member of the firm. She began to deal with authors and their agents, haggling over terms, drawing up contracts, fixing schedules and publication dates; she got to know fellow-practitioners like Rupert Hart-Davis and Jonathan Cape and Jock Murray and Allen Lane of Penguin Books; she learned about the different branches of the business, but particularly involved herself in design and production, commissioning jackets from artists like John Minton, Edward Bawden, Charles Mozley and Leonard Rosoman, drawing up estimates, negotiating with printers, paper-merchants and block-makers, making sure that delivery dates were met and prices adhered to. To make up for her lack of education she read everything she could lay her hands on: she proved herself a shrewd and decisive judge of a typescript, and authors and colleagues came to respect and value her views; but – and here a sense of inadequacy remained with her to the end – she would never attempt to edit a book or to write a blurb or even a difficult editorial letter. Such work was best left to those who knew about such things – to Ian Parsons, or C. Day Lewis (who joined the firm in 1960 as a reader and poetry editor), or Day Lewis's successor, D. J. Enright, himself a Chatto author. Gradually publishing in general, and Chatto in particular, became her absorbing interest and then her entire way of life, and still more so when her husband was killed in the RAF after only a few months of marriage. She grew fiercer and harder and more domineering and, on the surface at least, immeasurably more self-assured; by the end of the war she was, in effect, running the firm, and when Ian Parsons, the heir-apparent, was demobbed from the RAF he soon discovered that he would be forming part of a duumvirate under the chairmanship of Harold Raymond; that the firm itself, once benign and easy-going, seemed rather more strident and embattled than he remembered; and that the timid, fresh-faced secretary who had helped him with *Night and Day* had become a formidable and domineering publisher.

I had known about Chatto for as long as I could remember, since one of my parents' closest friends was Harold Raymond's stepson. During my last year at university I had folded myself into my sister's pram-sized baby Fiat and driven across the Weald to visit Harold Raymond, a cardiganed, suede-shod, silver-haired figure on the lines of Wilfred Hyde-White: although he had retired from Chatto a year or two earlier, he was happy, over a lunch of lamb chops, to give me some avuncular advice about getting into publishing, but I was too vague and too unsure of what I wanted to do to follow it up. Nor had I had much to do with the firm since I'd been in the trade. Like many of my contemporaries, I was glad to know that Chatto existed, and I respected the quality of its list; but I thought it, for all its virtues, to be dull, dusty, parsimonious and dingily old-fashioned. As far as I could gather, it appeared to be staffed almost entirely by men with private incomes who were prepared to work for nothing or, better still, put money into the business, and the sweet-natured, inevitable contingent of nervous maiden aunts in cardigans and sandals and porridge-coloured skirts who had devoted their lives to the firm and earned half as much as a typist in the City.

As England's most ineffectual literary agent I had sold one or two academic books for inclusion in their lit. crit. list, invariably (and rightly) for extremely modest sums of money: much to my relief, none of these negotiations had involved Mrs Smallwood – perhaps I had excelled myself and asked for less than they were prepared to offer, or even for nothing at all? – and I had found myself dealing instead with D. J. Enright, who seemed entirely unalarming and, from the sound of his voice on the phone, very much the kind of man one might like to know. Emboldened by my success, and desperate to abandon a way of life for which I was so obviously unfit, I decided in a sudden spasm of self-aggrandise-ment that I would write to Mrs Smallwood just in case a job came up at Chatto. A day or two later her secretary rang to say that, alas, there was nothing on offer, but that Mrs Smallwood would be prepared to see me at such-and-such a time. I dreaded my meeting with this legendary figure who, I felt sure, would send me away with my tail between my legs, but perhaps I could sweeten the pill by calling on Dennis Enright as well? I gave him a ring and we agreed that I would see him first, and that he would then shunt me down the corridor for my appointment with his Leader.

On the appointed afternoon I turned up, for the first time, at the old Chatto offices in William IV Street. After pushing my way through a pair of blue swing doors, I found myself in a bare and gloomy corridor. A broad staircase of incongruous grandeur swept upwards into darkness, baroque barley-sugar banister-rails blend-ing oddly with the dark-blue lino on the treads; to the right, behind a sliding-glass panel, a figure with the features of a heavy-smoking Roman emperor sat at the controls of an elderly upright switch-board, a cigarette smouldering in one hand while with the other he plunged a plug into a hole in the switchboard (so connecting the caller and the called), or, with a bold, imperious gesture, yanked another from its resting place (more often than not, as I was later to learn, cutting off both parties in mid-sentence). Tentatively sliding the panel aside, I asked the emperor where and how I could find Professor Enright; he gave a nimble display on the plugs, announced my arrival, and suggested that I took the lift to the second floor, where the Professor would await me.

I would have been better advised to set off up the baronial staircase, since the lift was of that unrestful pre-war variety that involved holding open with one's elbows two tightly-sprung wooden doors while struggling to pull aside a black metal grille, like part of an old-fashioned camera, which lunged hungrily at one's head and shoulders and nipped the ankles of the unwary. After a good deal of opening and closing of doors, and wrestling with the metal grille, we began to move, very slowly and with a good deal of juddering, in the direction of the second floor. Once there the lift stopped with a sudden jerk, throwing me off balance; after which I had once more to do battle with the grille, holding it firmly in place with my foot while struggling to push open another pair of equally well-sprung wooden doors. (In later years I disdained the services of this boisterous lift. Mrs Smallwood, on the other hand – frail, arthritic, carrying a walking stick – made regular use of it; but it may well be that she had, early on in her long career, quelled it with a glance.)

I stumbled, dishevelled, onto a darkened landing, the walls of which – like those of a prep school or a lunatic asylum – were painted in dark-blue gloss up to waist level, and pale blue above; on the floor was the same blue lino that I had noticed in the corridor below and on the stairs. Peering through the gloom, I saw before me a ruefully smiling figure with a wide, expressive mouth, a bush of grey hair that shot away from his head like a coil of smoke in a high wind, and pale, rather rubbery features that combined – in the most engaging way – the lugubrious and the comical, the sardonic and the benign. He was clad, almost certainly, in a fawn or green shirt with a green or fawn tie; fawn trousers; shoes with tractor soles, and a bottle-green (or, perhaps, a fawn cotton) jacket. I like to think he had a pipe in his mouth; be that as it may, he shook my hand in a resigned and doleful way, and – like a kindly jailer – beckoned me to follow him past an array of pigeon holes and down a maze-like corridor, painted in the same institutional shades. We passed a door with the words 'Norah Smallwood' painted on a small wooden plaque; and as we did so Dennis raised his eyes to heaven with a woeful look and pressed his finger to his lips, so that we stole past the dragon's lair on the tips of our toes.

After another imposing-looking door with 'Ian Parsons' emblazoned on its plaque – 'IMP', as he was known, was still the joint managing director – we turned left, right and left again before coming to Dennis's lair: a small, sunny room with a greenhouse door, khaki-coloured bookshelves on two walls, post-war Utility furniture, and the same blue lino on the floor. On Dennis's plain wooden desk was a black upright typewriter, several typescripts, a set of proofs, an ashtray (heavily laden), a reading-lamp and an ancient Bakelite telephone with a brown twisted cord running away from it. Taking a look out of the window – the frame and sill of which had been painted a virulent pink – I realised that the Chatto offices were built round a well, on the far side of which other members of the firm could be spotted making coffee or tugging at filing cabinets or filing their nails or trading office gossip in conspiratorial, outraged tones, or gazing blankly back across the well in a day-dream. Above us, to the right, the illuminated globe on top of the London Coliseum spun slowly round and round, while through the open window came the sudden screech of a soprano practising her scales, like a knife upon a plate. This, I learned, had been C. Day Lewis's office before Dennis's arrival: much later I was to spend some years in it myself – Dennis had moved to a room on the floor above – editing typescripts, writing blurbs, studying the small print in contracts, correcting proofs, coming back far too late from over-convivial lunches, and listening, with a kind of frozen horror, to Mrs Smallwood's voice advancing down the corridor, and the tap of her stick on the lino.

Dennis was, as expected, altogether less alarming: I liked him at once, and many years later he was to become, with Hugo, my closest friend in the firm. In the meantime, as he told me about life at Chatto, and what he did there – his voice a throw-away mutter, interspersed with laughter and the sudden pulling of faces – he busied himself cleaning and filling and tamping his pipe. After half an hour of chatting peacefully we were interrupted by a ferocious blast on the telephone. Dennis gave the rude intruder an admonishing sideways glance from under momentarily darkened brows and then, with a sigh and a shrug, picked up the receiver. An imperious female voice rang round the room. At the first syllable, Dennis sat upright in his chair as though he had been plugged into the mains; and as the voice spoke on and on, he held the receiver out at arm's length – every now and then bringing it back to his mouth when his views were sought ('Yes, Norah') – and, jabbing the forefinger of his free hand in the direction of the voice, accompanied its every word with a running commentary in mime. The voice eventually revealed that its owner was ready to receive Mr Lewis, and would Dennis kindly show him the way? Dennis rose wearily from behind his desk, and we retraced our steps back along the corridors of institutional blue. On the threshold of Mrs Smallwood's office we paused, and he placed a kindly hand on my shoulder, as though I were a young officer about to go over the top, before knocking and ushering me in. My last glimpse of him was standing rigidly to attention in the doorway, like a parody of a military man; and then, 'Thank you, Dennis' came the cool, commanding voice from within, and he disappeared back into the darkness.

I remember very little of that first encounter with Mrs Smallwood; far more understandably, I was of no interest whatsoever to her, and made no impression at all – a suspicion sadly confirmed when Hugo reported her bewildered irritation on being told that my coming along was a condition of his taking the job. Nor did she seem any more enthusiastic when, shortly after accepting the job, Hugo arranged for the two of us to call in at William IV Street so that he could show me round and introduce me to his former and future colleagues, all of whom greeted him like a prince come into his own, or the vanguard of an army of liberation.

The Chatto offices, I now discovered – for I had seen very little on my previous expedition, some five or six years before – occupied three floors of a tall, Venetian-looking mid-Victorian building; those that were not occupied by Chatto were sub-let to a publisher of scientific journals and to A. M. Heath, the literary agents. The ground floor consisted of an austere and uncomfortable waiting-room, painted battleship-grey, on the walls of which hung sepia photographs of Mark Twain and Andrew Chatto, a framed letter from Robert Louis Stevenson, and the contract between T. S. Eliot and The Hogarth Press for the first publication of *The Waste Land*; a bare white lobby, cluttered with bicycles and the familiar litter of brown-paper parcels and large buff envelopes waiting to be collected by visored messengers on motorbikes; the small glass cubicle that housed the Roman emperor and his collection of plugs; the post-room, where post and parcels were sorted and sent out; the file copy library, a silent, windowless cell with the old-fashioned whiff of a Boot's lending library; and an airless, wood-panelled stock-room which had been implausibly converted into a board-room. Once on the second and third floors, where the Chatto publishing took place, one found oneself in an austere and elegant cross between a conservatory and a penal institution. Most of the offices, other than those that faced across William IV Street, looked out across the well: light streamed in from it through tall, ceiling-high windows, and was then bounced and reflected through the building by the gleaming gloss paint of the corridors and a glittering galère of internal skylights and win-dows; on bright, windy days, when the clouds were scudding overhead and the sunlight sparkled on the windowpanes and the Coliseum's revolving silver ball, one might almost have been at sea. At the far corner of the well was a cast-iron staircase, useful for stealing back after late lunches, and a pair of old-fashioned lavatories with cisterns high on the wall, flushed by jerking a perished rubber ball on the end of a length of chain. Outside the men's lavatory was a wide, shallow wash-basin such as one might have found in a barber's shop, topped by a mottled mirror and a white-painted wooden box containing an ancient ivory-backed hairbrush and an equally ancient tortoise-shell comb. I became convinced that neither had been used since the 1950s: had the straggly grey hairs still caught in the brush be-longed to Leonard Woolf, I wondered, or had Harold Raymond left them there before hurrying out to lunch at the Garrick or a meeting of the Publishers' Association?

The first to welcome us on our arrival was the Roman emperor, who – as he always did when greeting familiar visitors – slid open the glass panel, thrust out his arm, and shook us both warmly by the hand. George was by now in his late sixties. A cigarette dangled permanently from his lower lip, and his face and his hair – which was longish, and swept back from his noble Roman brow – seemed to have been stained a muddy brownish-yellow by years of nicotine. Even as he greeted us, he broke off to deal with an incoming telephone call, which gave me an opportunity to examine the technique of a master. He donned a pair of enormous earphones which, when not in use, hung about his neck like a fox-fur round that of a maiden aunt, inserted a shiny brass plug on the end of a flex into the appropriate hole in the pinboard – at times the flexes seethed about him like a basketful of serpents – and addressed some soothing words into a black mouthpiece shaped like a lily. George's voice and telephone manner were, I soon learned, greatly admired in the trade; he combined dignity with deference, and enjoyed a flattering ability to recognise the voices, the occupations, the work-in-progress and even the family histories of those who called in from outside. Fellow-publishers would tell Norah how much they envied her George, much as Wodehousian country-house owners coveted a neighbour's cook or butler. Unlike the tetchier kind of butler, George had no side or snobbery: he was, however, a master of *realpolitik,* summarily unplugging lesser callers in mid-conversation if Mrs Smallwood needed to ring out and no lines were free, and hurrying her favourite authors to the head of the queue. He spent a certain amount of time listening in to important and high-level conversations about matters of interest to us all: at times like these it might well prove impossible to get a line, while George himself could be spotted slumped over his pile of flexes, a frown of concentration puckering his brow and a bare half-inch of cigarette glued to his bottom lip, keeping intruders at bay with a wave of his hand or a cautionary finger raised to his lips. George would then pass the confidential items on to Les the office packer, after which they would – if Les thought it right and proper – enter the office bloodstream well in advance of any official pronouncement.

George seldom left his cubicle, but when sighted away from his natural habitat he turned out to be a good deal shorter than his large, imperial head might have led one to suppose. Before becoming a full-time switchboard operator he had played violin in the band of a Cunarder on the Atlantic run, and in the past he had been persuaded to bring his instrument along to office parties, accompanying Ian Parsons on the banjo. His wife, also a keen smoker, was keener still on housework, and on hoovering in particular, and at home George spent more time than he might have wished lifting his legs in the air while she hoovered underneath, or retreating from one room to the next, ashtray in hand, while the Hoover roared and wheezed behind him. He came in occasionally after he had retired, wheezing heavily and looking as putty-coloured as ever, casting regretful looks at the tiny glass-partitioned cubicle in which he had spent so much of his life. He had dreamed of spending the happy, lazy days of his retirement edging up English canals in a long-boat, violin and cigarettes to hand; but – as is so often the case – death unkindly intervened.

After shaking hands with George we moved further back into a windowless region of cardboard and string and jiffy bags, of post office scales and franking machines and wooden-handled knives and pots of glue: the domain of Les the Packer. Leslie Booth was a rangy, humorous-looking individual clad in a brown cotton over-garment of the kind worn by old-fashioned ironmongers or country grocers, and his long, narrow face, bushy eyebrows and mutton-chop whiskers gave him the look of a mid-Victorian poacher, straight from the pages of Surtees. He spent his days standing behind a long plywood counter, sorting the incoming post, packing parcels, franking letters, lugging huge bags of mail to the post office over the road, passing on useful items of gossip and beating vast sheets of cardboard into shape with a sideways rap of his hand. Much to Mrs Smallwood's indignation, Les was Dennis Enright's closest friend in the firm: she would refer to 'Mr Booth' as 'your friend' when speaking of Les to Dennis, adding a savagely ironical twist to the words as she did so. I could quite see why Dennis enjoyed Les's company for he was shrewd, wise and often extremely funny, and I soon took to joining them for lunch in the Marquis of Granby every Tuesday – a tradition which still continues, though Les no longer makes it after retiring to the far end of the Metropolitan Line. Only in his alleged defiance of Mrs Smallwood was Les, perhaps, a little unreliable: over drinks in the Marquis he would tell us how he had, in effect, driven Mrs Smallwood from the packing-room ('You stick to editing those books, and leave the parcels to me'), but somehow it never quite rang true.

Moving up from these subterranean depths to the air and light of the publishing offices, we hurried from room to room as Hugo introduced me to my new colleagues, rising from behind their desks – one finger marking the place in a pile of proofs, or a hand hurriedly clamped over the mouthpiece of a telephone if interrupted in mid-call – to shake me by the hand and mutter a polite enquiry or a jocular word of warning before subsiding with a sigh of relief as the door closed behind us and the caravan moved on to the room next-door. All this was agreeable enough, if utterly confusing, but both of us were uneasily aware of postponing the moment of truth; and as the hands still waiting to be shaken grew fewer, our smiles grew more nervous and more forced, and the pleasantries offered up and the defiant little quips so much whistling in the wind. All of a sudden the sunny, windswept offices with their potted plants and gleaming tongue-and-groove and middle-aged ladies drinking mugs of milky coffee seemed bleak and grey and forbidding; the air grew colder and the twittering ladies fell silent, like birds in a garden when a snake hoves to. I wished we had embarked on none of this, that I was happily back at OUP, writing long and helpful memos in triplicate, working out elaborate costings with the aid of my pocket calculator, and looking forward to a long and convivial editorial lunch under the chandeliers in the Walton Street dining-rooms.

Mrs Smallwood's door was open, as ever. Hugo knocked; a

forceful, slightly metallic voice commanded us to come in; like Dennis before him, Hugo raised his eyes to heaven, straightened his tie, and we advanced to meet our fate. We found ourselves in a light, L-shaped room, the tall conservatory-like windows of which looked out across William IV Street. One entire wall was covered with bookshelves; the others were made of white-painted tongue-and-groove, and the overall effect was that of a South Coast yacht club which had been taken over by an outpost of Bloomsbury. The parquet floor – worn and uneven, its tiles rattling loosely together – was partly covered by a faded Turkish carpet. Mrs Smallwood's desk – an Edwardian kneeholer, with a red leather top and brass handles to the drawers – occupied the shorter arm of the 'L'. Behind her was a shallow, curved alcove filled with books; to her right was one of the room's two windows, with Ruskinian curlicues visible through the panes, greasy-looking pigeons fluttering and cooing on the window ledge, and plant pots suspended from hooks in the ceiling; in front of the desk were two white-painted wickerwork chairs, comfortably cushioned and waiting to receive us. The desk itself was crammed with typescripts, proofs, contracts, letters, photographs, little boxes containing paperclips, and all the familiar detritus of a busy publisher's office; and propped against the Bakelite telephone and the odd little boxes were cards on which someone had written, in a looping, thick-nibbed hand, various instructions of a medical and cautionary kind ('Don't forget to *take your pills*' and 'Remember to keep your feet up *as much as you can*'). Unwisely ignoring this last request, the subject of these injunctions was hobbling briskly towards us, one hand clutching a knobbed black cane and the other raised in greeting, while the sun streamed in through the windows behind her and the motes danced in the dusty air.

Mrs Smallwood was a thin, elegant woman of medium height, with a cloud of snow-white hair, apple-red cheeks and dazzling ice-blue eyes. She could well have been beautiful as a girl, and was still extremely distinguished; the combination of large eyes, high cheekbones and hollow cheeks gave her the frail, slightly skull-like look I associated with pictures of Jean Rhys. Her age, as I soon discovered, was a source of endless and ungallant speculation, with wilder spirits claiming that she was well into her eighties or even her early nineties: in fact she was only in her early seventies, but chronic and crippling arthritis made her look years older, though her mind was as sharp as that of someone a third of her age. Cortisone had thinned her blood, and made it hard for cuts to heal; she was too impatient to lead the life of a semi-invalid, and her legs – already as thin as broomsticks – were often swathed in bandages as a result of her banging or cutting them while hurrying about her house or the office; during the years that I worked for her I became accustomed to awestruck announcements that Mrs Smallwood had banged her leg again, and was not in the best of moods. For some time now she had walked with the aid of an ebony walking-stick, scurrying along the corridors like a graceful, long-legged crab: for she remained, despite her ailments, a stylish and even a dashing figure, much given to forceful shades of scarlet and to broad-brimmed black felt hats, one of which I noticed hanging behind the door.

We met in the middle of the room. Hugo bent forward and kissed her on the cheek; I felt this might be a shade presumptuous, so – eager to prove myself unalarmed – I grasped her warmly by the hand and prepared to pump it up and down. At this she let out a screech of anguish and thrust the afflicted hand between her other arm and her body, as though plunging it into a vat of ice, while her pale blue eyes suddenly brimmed with tears and the papery skin on her face – the whiteness of which contrasted vividly with the almost feverish bloom of her cheeks – turned paler than ever. Only then did I realise how the arthritis had twisted and wasted her hands, which looked like pathetic, misshapen claws: the agony I had unwittingly inflicted seemed to endure for ever, and by the time she had recovered her poise – waving her stick in my face with an unnerving, unanswerable mixture of levity and menace – I had been reduced to a grovelling pulp of apology and self-abasement, and the ebullience with which I had left Oxford earlier in the day had entirely drained away.

All this not only got us off to an uneasy start, but proved sadly symptomatic of life in the weeks ahead. As day succeeded day it became increasingly obvious that Norah – as I was now allowed to call her – had no intention whatsoever of retiring, that she had quite forgotten the contents of the letter on royal-blue writing-paper which Hugo had so carefully folded away in his wallet, and that far from seeing him as an heir-apparent or an unwelcome usurper, she was delighted to have his help in the day-to-day running of the firm, but was otherwise intent on keeping him at the same level he had occupied before leaving Chatto for the calmer waters of OUP. Ancient habits, long engrained, soon reasserted themselves: with every day that passed Norah seemed sprightlier and more authoritative, eagerly looking forward to the future and giving not a moment's thought to her pension scheme or the delights of an old people's home, while poor Hugo looked greyer and more worried and more weary, like someone who realises all too painfully that he has ended up where he started out, and is resigned to playing a reluctant (though invariably courteous) supporting role to a demanding prima donna. It was equally obvious that, for all their brave words and decisive rhetoric, the powers-that-be in the publishing group were – as reserved, amiable Englishmen of the gentlemanly kind – quite incapable of dealing with an elderly and domineering woman who was fully prepared to exploit her age, her femininity, her frailty and her strength of personality to get what she wanted and remain where she was. They alone were in a position to tell her to go but were, understandably if a shade ignobly, far too unnerved or exhausted to tackle the problem in person and more than happy to leave matters to Hugo, egging him on from behind the scenes but seldom engaging in battle themselves. Hugo was the kindest, the most unpolitical and the least cynical of men, always eager to believe the best of those about him and too convinced for his own good that reason and good will would prevail in the end; no one could have been worse suited, by temperament or previous experience, to act as a hatchet-man. As I knew from OUP, he was an excellent and underrated publisher – enthusiastic, literate, much liked by his authors, encouraging and helpful to those who worked for him, insistent on high standards, unfashionably sensible about such matters as advances and print-runs – yet instead of getting on with publishing books and reviving the fortunes of the firm, he wasted his days in agonised and fruitless discussions about how to get rid of his chairman. On the train back to Oxford he would regale me in tones of resigned good humour with the latest developments, such as they were; and although I was as terrified of Norah as anyone else, and would never have dared to stand up to her, let alone show her the door, I came to regard the antics of my seniors with angry despair. I learned, for example, of a lunch at the Garrick to which Hugo had been invited by a former Chatto eminence, a bluff, likeable man, now retired, who had been widely and rightly admired as a publisher and had spent forty years of his working life being bawled at and harried by his volatile, irrepressible lady colleague; no doubt he remained extremely fond of her, but for years he had found her behaviour intolerable, and he too felt that, for the sake of the firm, she should be made to hand over. As the meal progressed and the glasses of claret were drained, the elder statesman – a keen luncher and imbiber, a stiff white napkin tucked into his shirt collar, obliterating the salmon and cucumber of his Garrick Club tie – became ever more emboldened. 'Don't take any nonsense from that woman, Hugo,' he thundered, banging the table with his fist and helping himself to a fortifying swig, his kindly features suffused with righteous indignation: 'You've got to be firm with her and tell her to go.' All this was gratifying enough, as daring and subversive rhetoric always is: but at the coffee stage the eminent publisher, suddenly paler and graver and altogether less inflamed, looked nervously about the room and, leaning across the laden table, muttered, 'Does Norah know we're having lunch together?' Of course she does, Hugo told him; at which his host wiped his brow with his table napkin and whispered – fearing, perhaps, that his former colleague might be hidden under the table or concealed behind a screen or even, for so pervasive were her powers, cunningly disguised as a waiter or as one of the grey-suited, purple-featured fellow-lunchers contentedly chomping about them – 'Tell her, if she asks, that we've been discussing group overheads and how they can be brought down . . .'

I relished stories like this, passing them on at once to Les the Packer, but they filled me with gloom: and I wished, for his sake above all, that instead of trusting that misleading scrap of royal-blue paper, Hugo had made it a precondition of his taking the job that Norah should be off the premises before he returned. But for all my frustration and irritation, I didn't envy those involved: the powers-that-be were decent men, if not heroic, and although my instinctive feeling was that a clean cut would be swifter, tidier and kinder than a gradual whittling away – which was how it turned out in the end – the nobler part of their reluctance to strike no doubt reflected an unwillingness to hurt a long-serving colleague who had done fine things for her firm and of whom they were, in civilian life at least, extremely fond; and the awesome realisation that in removing Norah's job they were also removing her life and her *raison d'être*. Norah knew this better than anyone, and was more than ready to exploit the timidity and the gentlemanly reticence of her opponents. Doing battle with her at any level was an exhausting and alarming business, and within days of our arrival I began to see how formidable and how frightening she was.

Like most publishers of her generation, Norah had no time for meetings, forms or paperwork, preferring to deal directly on the telephone, scribble messages and memos on whatever scraps of paper happened to be at hand, and work out her advances and her costings on the back of an envelope – the results of which were exactly the same as those deduced via elaborate forms, pocket calculators and lengthy consultations with production managers, salesmen, accountants and the rest, but were arrived at within minutes rather than hours. She had grown up in a world in which publishing firms were managed and run by the publishers them-selves, the best of whom were instinctive businessmen, combining the roles of entrepreneur, literary critic, impresario, salesman and accountant; accountants, like salesmen, were there to serve rather than to rule, and their tedious jargon had to be re-explained at every three-monthly board meeting ('Remind me again of what turnover means' and 'Where in this document do I find the profit?' – the truthful answer to which was 'Nowhere' – were Norah's unfailing cries on these occasions). All this made for an autocratic, direct and very personal way of running the firm, and one in which the rest of us, however grandiloquent our titles and our names on the notepaper, were expected to play subservient and supporting roles: and whereas up-to-date publishing houses would appoint at least some of their directors on the basis of their function in the firm, Chatto's directors were – as they always had been – essentially editorial with, preferably, money invested as well. Once a week four of the five directors – Dennis couldn't face it – would gather in Norah's office for a mid-morning editorial meeting at which, in theory, we could ventilate our ideas about possible books and authors and report on what we had read. Norah perched behind her desk like a bird of prey while the rest of us clustered before her, like rodents waiting to be devoured. When it came to discussing our views, she refused to play by the rules, to observe those discretions and areas of reticence so precious to those of us who are condemned to remain in the ranks forever. Everything was personalised and heightened: like a possessive, passionate parent, she bridled at any outside criticisms of those within the fold and fought to defend her flock, but felt at liberty to cuff us about the head as briskly as she liked. Such plain speaking came as a shock after the tactful circumlocutions of the OUP, and the sneers with which she would greet what seemed an entirely reasonable suggestion would have unnerved far sturdier spirits than mine. Nor was fighting back necessarily the answer: I soon discovered that Norah was far quicker-witted than the rest of us, and one of those maddening individuals who can always trump one's argument, however watertight it seemed in advance.

One of Norah's most effective techniques was to invoke the great names of the past, accompanied by a mournful shaking of the head and appropriate tut-tutting noises. Seeing herself as the guardian of a sacred flame, '*Whatever* would Leonard think of that?' or 'Cecil must be *turning in his grave*,' she would intone: no doubt both men would have groaned to hear her words, finding them all too familiar, and instinctively sided with those beneath the lash, but the net effect was to leave one feeling more inadequate than ever, a vulgar intruder on some solemn private rite. Equally unnerving was her refusal ever to admit her own ignorance. Like all of us, she had her blind spots, but 'Oh dear, *surely* you knew that? Where *have* you been all these years?' she would wonder, a wintry smile flitting across her features, whenever – like some loyal, rather half-witted spaniel producing a long-lost slipper and longing for a pat – one came up with an item of red-hot gossip or a piece of publishing information of which one felt particularly proud. And although Chatto meant more to her than anything else in life, she wanted it to be *her* firm and for the books that we took on to be *her* books, and resented and disparaged those that the rest of us took on – if we dared – as though they were impoverished, rather common cousins who were only allowed in on sufferance. Like all worthwhile publishers, she took on books which we all knew would lose money and sell a derisory dribble of copies, but were worth doing because they were good in themselves and, with luck, would lead on to greater things, and even make some money in the long term; but she was lethally swift to prophesy doom for comparable titles which the rest of us suggested. 'And how many copies would Hatchard's take of *that*?' she would ask with a wicked gleam. 'At this rate we'll all end up on the Embankment' was her invariable and unusual rider, evocative of Edwardian rakes fallen on hard times: the thought of Chatto directors and staff spending their nights in cardboard boxes off the Strand or raising bottles of meths to their lips was too terrible to contemplate, and the book in question would be smartly sent on its way. Most alarming of all was her habit, when angry or in violent disagreement with what someone else was saying, of shuffling objects about the surface of her desk in furious, staccato bursts. The rest of us would find ourselves hypnotised by those terrible, twisted hands shunting a stapler or an ashtray to and fro; the speaker – by now utterly unnerved – would falter and dwindle and finally dry up altogether; Norah's hands would slow down and grow still as the opposition fled; the tension and the anger and the sense of an imminent storm would lift and Norah – a kindly, triumphant smile playing about her lips – would keep us happy with an entertaining or scurrilous anecdote or, as if to make amends, pass round a tin of boiled sweets which she kept in a drawer for occasions such as these. No doubt more resolute characters would have refused to put up with all this, and sent her packing in the direction of Leonard and Ian and Harold and Cecil and all those other ghosts by whom we were haunted: but we were all the mildest and feeblest of men, anxious to be friends and to behave in a reasonable, kindly, civilised way, hating rows above all else; and we were as putty in her hands.

None of this would have mattered were it not that the firm was dying on its feet. Norah was – to her credit – a parsimonious, cheeseparing publisher of the old school, keeping a stern eye on the overheads, paying her authors advances that could safely be re-couped from sales of the books themselves, only allowing a few, better-selling titles the luxury of a full-colour jacket, keeping a close and cautious eye on print-runs, review copies, publicity ex-penditure and the like, and relying on loyal and long-suffering staff to put in long hours for very little pay and still less to look forward to by way of a pension; and she knew by instinct what the pub-lishers of the 1980s so happily forgot – that while large fortunes can be made from professional or academic publishing, where markets, however modest, are predictable, price is no problem, advances and royalties are vestigial or non-existent and the bookseller's discount a reassuringly modest affair, literary publishing has always been a risky, marginal trade, more dependent on the whims of luck and fashion than on the predictions of market researchers, and dependent on a finely judged balancing act between the demands of literature and commerce. And yet for all her frugality the firm made a loss every year, and was only kept alive by the lucky chance that Cape, the largest and the liveliest firm in the group, was profitable and could afford to carry its partners. Norah had, over the years, brought in and looked after authors who had, ideally, proved both profitable and well-regarded, like Iris Murdoch and, more recently, Dirk Bogarde; she fought like a lioness on behalf of her writers, most of whom were devoted to her, and she was respected as well as feared within the trade; and yet by the 1970s she had become something of an anachronism. Partly because of her reluctance to allow her colleagues to take on books of their own, and partly because literary agents were unwilling to sell their big books to Chatto, finding Norah too parsimonious and exhausting to deal with, she was not publishing enough books to pay those overheads – rent, salaries, lighting, heating and so on – which form so large a part of a publisher's outlay and of the published price of a book, each one of which must help to pay its way. The firm was quietly haemorrhaging, and as long as Norah remained *in situ* it seemed likely to continue that way.

Norah may have been out-of-date, but her dislike of profligate publishing seems, in retrospect, eminent good sense from a publisher's if not an author's point of view. Her generation despised and resented those whom they condemned as 'chequebook publishers', always on the prowl to snap up authors whom more scrupulous publishers had taken on and encouraged from unpromising beginnings. Writing out large cheques was the easiest thing in the world, made easier still if you had a loud voice and a forceful personality; what made literary publishing an art was the ability to spot and to cultivate one's own authors while at the same time getting the figures right, and to finance the new, the difficult and the untried with the well-established and the successful – and, ideally, a remunerative, steady-selling backlist of books about gardening, fishing or bridge, librarianship, birds or model aeroplanes. In the brash new world of the 1980s such careful husbandry seemed a dim, unglamorous affair; and hitherto sensible publishers – flattered by the notion that publishing, briefly favoured by the City, was a blend of big business and show business, and eager to spend money that may well have belonged to some remote corporate owner – became ever more extravagant, with disastrous end results. Nowhere was this more apparent than in the matter of publishers' advances, reports of which misled the public into assuming that writing had become a well-paid job. Whereas old-fashioned publishers would base the advance to an author on the royalties to be earned from a modest proportion of the initial print-run – usually between 40 and 50 per cent – and puritanically refuse to take into account possible earnings from subsidiary rights, their up-to-date equivalents – often competing with one another in auctions masterminded by literary agents – would, if desperate to capture a particular author, or prevent him from drifting away, throw into the pot all the royalties from the publisher's own editions, all the hoped-for income from serial and paperback rights and, if needs be, a few thousands or tens of thousands of extra pounds as well. The huge advances which hit the headlines were relatively few and far between but raised authorial expectations in general, so that even fairly modest titles tended to carry advances that would never be earned back, and were saddled with a burden of debt that could never be recovered. Jesuitical accountants were nimble in explaining to their masters that none of this mattered, that unearned advances, like unsold stock, could be written off in the accounts and so consigned to oblivion; common sense told one that this was nonsense, that money poured down the drain was lost for ever, and that unearned advances – whether of £1000 or £500,000 – must, cumulatively and in the long run, prove a disaster. Publishers eager to make their firms seem vibrant and competitive would justify an initial lashing out ('It's well worth our overpaying this once since it'll put us on the map'), but soon discovered that sinning was addictive.

Nor was that the end of the story. Showing no signs of gratitude, books for which publishers had overpaid sold as many or as few as they would have done under the old regime; but instead of cutting their losses, panic-stricken publishers poured good money after bad by overprinting in the hope that they could somehow buy or bludgeon their way out of trouble; and, when that failed to do the trick, wasted a further fortune on publicity. And all this time publishers' overheads were rising as the property boom got under way, and publishers began to pay themselves, as well as a few of their authors, wages a notch or two above the national average, and to set money aside for pension schemes as well; while the new bookselling chains, with their bright high-street shops and extended opening hours, were not only demanding bigger discounts from publishers to pay for all these improvements, but filled their stores with up-to-the-minute titles bought on sale or return, many of which ended back in the publishers' warehouses but had the immediate effect of encouraging publishers to overprint or, still worse, reprint a title which seemed – albeit momentarily – to have gone out of stock, so converting what might have been a modest profit into a thumping loss. Despite running up bigger and bigger losses, general publishers continued to be bought up by conglomerates, after which many were merged or closed down; while their more level-headed colleagues in less dashing branches of the business – in academic or educational or professional or legal publishing – continued to make profits undreamed of at the more glamorous end of the trade. In Chatto's case at least, all this lay in the future tense; in the meantime, although the virtues of parsimonious publishing would become apparent long after Norah's retirement, the firm over which she presided seemed ever more anachronistic, a relic of a vanishing world in which printers' readers could be relied upon to pick up authorial or editorial blunders, and the two-colour lettering jacket – at its best the most elegant outfit of all – was an everyday occurrence.

Never the bravest of men, I was, before long, as terrified and demoralised as the rest of William IV Street; and I came to dread that cold, sarcastic voice, and that twisted, emaciated body hobbling angrily down the corridors, far faster than expected, on its shiny ebony stick. And yet, like all shrewd autocrats, Norah always knew when she had gone too far, when even the most cringing worm was about to turn, so that in the last resort she never failed to sweeten the vinegar with a necessary dash of honey. Every now and then, after an especially nerve-racking week or two – when the arthritis had been at its worst, proofs had failed to come in on time, the reps had proved unusually obtuse or unreceptive, a jacket had the wrong price on it and the office had rung to blood-curdling cries of rage, the slamming of doors and the gulp of a sobbing secretary scurrying for safety – Norah would, like a latter-day Queen Bess, make a procession through the office to visit and console her loyal subjects, limping gamely from room to room, exuding smiles and an irresistible charm, showing an apparently genuine interest in children, dogs, family snaps and holiday plans, and winning round in an instant the angry, the resentful and the disaffected. And on more than one occasion as I sat in my office, seething with impotent fury and despising myself for not being brave enough to defy this dreadful old lady when I knew her to be wrong or unjust, the door would swing open and – preceded by her stick – the object of my fury would let herself in and set herself down in the cane garden-chair on the opposite side of my desk. 'And how is dear Petra, and those nice little girls of yours?' she would ask (she was fond of Petra, and vice versa, but the nice little girls had – not unreasonably, since children and offices never mix – received a cold eye on their only visit to William IV Street); or, worse still, she would deposit her tragic, twisted hand in the middle of my desk, like some frozen root vegetable recently unearthed, and, while I gazed in horror at this emblem of age and mortality, she would talk about death and dissolution and how, as a lonely, childless old woman, she would be all too soon forgotten. Only the flintiest-hearted could have resisted such pluckings of the heart-strings, and only the most ingenuous could have failed to recognise what she was up to. I fell for it every time, and always with my eyes wide open: how could I, my better half insisted, have harboured such ignoble, petty thoughts about this fine, unhappy woman? She was my friend, after all (minions ache for the friendship of tyrants, and tyrants for ever dangle – and then withdraw – the possibility of friendship); her temper and her sneering and her domineering ways were only the arthritis speaking; from now on everything would be different, on a new and more equal footing. We parted in a glow of mutual affection and esteem, Norah placing her hand in blessing on my shoulder, the tears welling up in my eyes; but no sooner had I been softened up, and my anger and resentment transmuted to gratitude, understanding and even a curious kind of love, than with one mighty blow I was reeling on the ropes once more, and the whole unhappy cycle started all over again. Nor were my colleagues and I alone in this, for the very giants whose names

Norah evoked with much misty reverence had suffered too under her dominion. Leonard Woolf and Harold Raymond were probably too senior and too elevated, but the amiable Ian Parsons had quailed as she hurtled into his office unannounced, eyes blazing and forefinger wagging at some offending item of paper in her other hand; more than once after his retirement he was rash enough to stick his head round the door of Norah's office during the tail end of an editorial meeting, on his way back from a lunch at the Garrick, only to be bustled out of the room with much flicking of the wrists and shooing movements more appropriate to a dog about to foul one's front garden than to a much-respected senior publisher, incessantly quoted to us as a model we could never hope to emulate. C. Day Lewis, according to office lore, had almost been prevented from giving a series of lectures at Harvard on the grounds that he couldn't possibly be out of the office for so long; Dennis Enright's name – preceded by 'Professor' when the pulling of rank was in order – would be invoked to impress or to quell a hesitant or recalcitrant author but, once invoked, its owner was despatched as summarily as the rest of us, albeit with an extra ounce of affection and respect.

Leonard Woolf – or so I was told – would raise his sad, bloodhound eyes to heaven at the sound of slamming doors or shrieking voices, and offer dry, avuncular comfort to the sobbing or distraught; and this was a role that Dennis found himself playing more often than he might have wished. Unlike his fellow-directors, Dennis came from a working-class background (his father had been a postman in Leamington Spa); and although he had worked his way through scholarships to Cambridge, and had spent most of his life as an academic, teaching in Egypt, Germany, Thailand, Japan and Singapore, he remained a natural democrat, choosing his friends – as he chose his books – because he liked and respected them, rather than because they came from a particular class, or had been educated to a particular level, or were fellow-writers or academics. His friendship with Les caused, as I have said, a certain raising of eyebrows in a firm in which the Bloomsbury tradition of leftish principles combined with old-fashioned snobbery still prevailed. Literary publishing is, almost by definition, a snobbish and sometimes a sycophantic trade, since publishers hunger after, and depend upon, the famous and the well-connected, and intellectual snobbery and social snobbery are compatible more often than one might think. I sometimes felt that the walls of William IV Street were, like those of a seaside hotel, briny with secretarial tears: Dennis's role in the firm was a good deal more than that of an unusually well-read district nurse or human fire-extinguisher, but – to the relief of those afflicted – he was often at hand to comfort and assuage and, more importantly, to make them see their travails in some kind of perspective.

This ability to see things in perspective was one of Dennis's great qualities – and limitations – as a publisher's editor. In even the most literary firms the great majority of the books published will, inevitably, be evanescent and, by the highest standards, second- or third-rate; but the good publisher must – and not entirely cynically – persuade himself and others, if for a season only, that a particular novel or biography or travel book is 'the most amazing thing I've read for years' or 'fantastic' or a 'masterpiece', and that the forthcoming seasonal list is (yet again) 'the best I've ever known'. This suspension of disbelief – or, rather, this momentarily quite genuine readiness to make, and believe, exaggerated claims – is essential to the workings of the literary business and to the well-being of those who depend upon it, and is happily indulged in by reviewers, literary editors, booksellers, agents and, it goes without saying, those authors who benefit from it in terms of sales and self-esteem; and without it the world would, no doubt, be a duller place. Caught in the cross-fire of claim and counter-claim, it's sometimes hard to take the long view, or to remember – when confronted by reviewers' ecstatic claims – that from the great age of the Victorian novel, only a handful of names survive.

Dennis was far too sceptical, far too aware of the long-term, and far too committed to the highest standards, to have made a publisher, as opposed to a cautious and meticulous editor: left to his own devices he would have published, perhaps, two or three books a year, which might well have made sense *sub specie aeteruitatis* – if erring, perhaps, on the side of excess – but would never have paid the bills. (Much of this century's most interesting and adventurous publishing was, in fact, undertaken by 'amateur' or part-time publishers – writers like John Lehmann or the Woolfs or Alan Ross – who, untroubled by enormous overheads, published only those few books they really believed in.) Nor did Dennis have the proprietorial urge so essential to the successful publisher: he seemed loath to mix friendship and business in the sense of inveigling fellow-authors onto the list; and whereas the true entrepreneur feels – for an hour or two at least – a sense of outrage if a sought-after author chooses another firm instead of his own, Dennis seemed perfectly happy so long as *someone* was going to publish that writer's book (assuming he thought it any good), and indifferent if he thought little of it anyway, whatever its commercial potential.

In an ideal world, all self-respecting literary publishers would have a Dennis to hand, with his knowledge, his high standards, his scepticism, his eye for the excellent and the meretricious, his mumbled mockery of the exaggerated claims and fleeting enthusiasms that are an equally necessary part of the publishing process. And although he regarded the whole self-important business with a cool and comical eye, he treated his work with a seriousness that his businesslike colleagues sometimes found frustrating. He had no airs or affectations about himself and his work as a writer or publisher, and combined modesty, self-deprecation and a mocking, affectionate attitude towards those with whom he had to deal, with a strong if world-weary sense of what was right and good; but he asked, and expected, high standards from those authors with whom he worked, and still grumbles about a well-known writer whose new book consisted of pages torn from various magazines and stuffed into an envelope. Norah may have been puzzled and even rather bruised by Dennis's preference for pints of bitter washed down with whisky and water in the Marquis of Granby to more glittering literary occasions, but she greatly valued his judgement, his wisdom and his knowledge. Her affection and her regard were amply repaid: Dennis may, in turn, have disapproved of her ferocity and her waspishness, and mocked her weakness for titled grandees, but he admired her courage, her wit, her clarity of mind, her humour, her taste and her ability to cut through waffle and obfuscation. One of Dennis's major undertakings was supervising and editing the Terence Kilmartin revision of Scott Moncrieff's translation of Proust, and fighting off Norah's efforts to get it into the shops before it was ready ('But, Dennis, we need the turn-over . . .' – the publisher's permanent cry); less time-consuming, but equally tricky in the execution, was explaining the steamier passages in modern novels to Mrs Smallwood. Asked, on one occasion, to explain over the internal telephone an intimate sexual practice found baffling by his leader, he began, with much clearing of the throat, to edge his way towards elucidation via the Latin words for, in the first place, 'tongue' – the trickier part came first, in fact – only to have that cool, incisive voice slice across his mumbled explanation with 'I see, Dennis. One of those filthy words,' followed by the crash of the receiver being replaced on its stand.

One of Norah's more congenial editorial tasks – preferable, I imagine, to puzzling over four-letter words or sexual techniques – was replying to race-relations experts and self-appointed guardians of public morality who wrote in on a regular basis to complain about the fact that we published Helen Bannerman's 'Little Black Sambo' books, and demand their instant withdrawal. For years Chatto had kept in print the six titles in the series, issuing them in a tiny boxed set which sold extremely well and made an ideal present for children (and adults) who enjoyed reading about Sambo and his nimble-witted friends. None of those who wrote in appeared to have read a word of the books themselves. All com-plained that Sambo reinforced the stereotype – their stereotype, not ours – of the African as being somehow slower-witted than the European; Norah wrote back, patiently but firmly, pointing out that Sambo, Quibba and the rest were Indians and not Africans, that they seemed to be particularly sharp-witted (this being the point of the story), and that if anyone was entitled to complain it was the RSPCA, given the terrible fates meted out to tigers, pythons and the rest. Sad to say, Norah's defence of this particular part of the

Chatto tradition proved, in the long run, in vain. After her retirement the Chatto children's list was sold to the Bodley Head, whose
editors shared the views of the irate librarians and education
officers whom Norah had so gallantly kept at bay; and although
Max Reinhardt, after he left the Bodley Head, managed to keep
Sambo himself in print, his fellows were cast into outer darkness
for ever.

Compared with our colleagues at Jonathan Cape – whose chairman, Tom Maschler, was far and away the most stylish and exciting
general publisher of his time – we felt ourselves to be dowdy if
eminently respectable country cousins; and yet, on breezy spring
mornings, when Norah was away or in mellow mood, it was still
possible to recapture some of the excitement she must have felt in
her early days with the firm, when the books were warehoused on
the premises, and the bowler-hatted London traveller called every
morning to report sales of the new Compton Mackenzie or Ann
Bridge to the senior partners, and the youthful, fair-haired Ian
Parsons set out for the weekend in his open sports car with the
typescript of Malcolm Lowry's *Under the Volcano*, only to have it
stolen by some literate thief from the bucket-seat beside him.

Equally evocative of a vanishing world were the six-monthly sales
conferences, which were held in the windowless, wood-panelled
board-room immediately behind Les's packing-room. By now most
publishers were adopting a brisk and functional approach to sales
conferences, introducing an entire spring or autumn list to the reps
in a couple of hours and restricting the editors to half a minute at
most per book, on the very reasonable grounds that the blurb and
the jacket told the salesmen all they needed to know about the
contents, and it was far more fruitful to provide them with a few
easy reminders of how a particular book differed from the competition, or what was being planned by way of promotion, than to
swamp them with soporific details of the plot. Norah, however,
remained a devotee of the old ways. An entire day would be given
over to the presentation of some thirty books; editors tied themselves up in knots trying to unravel the plots of novels in which dons

and literary types thought a good deal before running off with one another's wives ('Oh, God, I forget to tell you that some years before Carol had had an affair with Colin's half-brother Ralph'), or were carried away by life in pre-Homeric Greece or Coleridge's debt to German philosophers, while the reps fidgeted and dozed and loosened their ties, and the airless box of a board-room grew hotter and hotter, and the speaker's voice was, from time to time, obliterated by the sound of Les chopping up pieces of cardboard in the room next door, or banging nails in a packing-case. At eleven there would be a short break while one of the directors hurried out to beg Les not to make quite so much noise, and a very old lady in a flowered pinafore, her hair in a turban, pushed in a trolley laden with milky coffee the colour of Horlicks; but what we were really looking forward to was the buffet lunch in the largest upstairs office, when the wine flowed in copious quantities, topped up for those in the know by draughts of whisky from Dennis's hip flask. After lunch the reps' faces were a good deal redder, and their sleeping more brazen. The East Anglian rep, who held stronger views than most of his colleagues, and was never afraid to let them be known, invariably hogged the only comfortable chair, a broken-backed *chaise longue*, leaving his fellows perched bolt up-right on grey plastic chairs of the kind that can be endlessly piled one on top of another; after the lunchtime imbibing he would wake every now and then with a convulsive start and wild staring of the eyes, and harry the speaker before relapsing back into slumber, while the editorial voices droned peaceably on in the background and Norah – who soon began to show signs of impatience, but refrained from intervention – stirred uneasily in her seat or shuffled her papers about the long board-room table behind which the directors were seated.

One of the perks – or putative perks – of publishers' sales conferences is a chance to exchange pleasantries with those authors who have been invited to address the reps. Up-to-date publishers limited this to coffee and a ten-minute address, but under the old order they were invited to lunch, and encouraged to ramble on for anything up to half an hour. As often as not a red-faced author would address the conference clutching a brimming glass of wine, slurring his words and trailing away into absent-minded silence. One distinguished major-general, who had written an authoritative study of Dunkirk, was so overcome by alcoholic fumes that he failed to make contact with a map of the Pas de Calais which had been pinned to a blackboard behind him, lunging wildly about him with the stick he held in one hand; eventually he toppled off the podium altogether, and had to be helped to the door while the reps – roused from their slumber by the crash of a falling body, with a trestle table in its wake – applauded loudly from the floor.

Almost as exciting was a conference at which the main speaker was a Central European writer of spy novels. His book dealt with a le Carré-like world of double agents and men in mackintoshes: it was written in a language that was only occasionally discernible as English, and I found it completely incomprehensible, but since I am invariably baffled by stories of this kind I put down part of my failure to my own ineptitude. The author himself made up for any inadequacies on the part of his book. He was a sallow, black-haired man in heavy black-rimmed glasses, the lenses of which had been tinted grey, and he lived in a large white house in North London with a gold-plated bathroom and wall-to-wall royal-blue carpeting on the ceiling as well as the floor. On the one occasion I visited him there he served me an elaborate American cocktail, all cherries and pulverised ice and frosted sugar round the rim; just as I was raising this to my lips, a beautiful blonde woman in a diaphanous nightie floated past the door but, to my disappointment, never reappeared. He was one of those suave, worldly Europeans who make the average Englishman feel gauche and innocent and lacking in *savoir faire*; I enjoyed my mysterious and oddly inconsequential meetings with him, but – given my views on his novel – I was astonished to learn that although his book had not been scheduled for publication, he was due to address the forthcoming sales conference as the main speaker of the day. He had, it seemed, laid siege to Norah, deluging her with gigantic bouquets of flowers and kissing her hand whenever they met; she had melted in an instant – how very different he was from the stiff, embarrassed Englishmen by whom she was usually surrounded – and, without finding out how good his book was or when it was going to be published, invited him to address the conference. On the appointed day he arrived in a blue overcoat with a velvet collar and a pearl-grey suit beneath; in one beringed hand he clutched the familiar outsize bouquet, while the other waved a large cigar. He was accompanied by a voluptuous blonde in a black pencil skirt and a leopardskin coat, who must have been half a head taller than he was, and as she wove her way to the back of the room – taking a seat between two of the reps, who straightened their ties and ran their fingers through their hair as they saw her advancing upon them – I recognised her as the girl in the diaphanous nightie. Norah introduced her guest speaker in rhapsodic vein, shedding little light on his novel – it would have been unkind to give the end away – but becoming eloquent on the subject of his charms, while the recipient gazed up at her, his eyelids fluttering behind his smoke-grey specs and a roguish smile lighting up his features; and as he rose to speak, stubbing out his cigar as he did so, Norah buried her nose in the bunch of flowers and gazed fiercely out at the reps, as if defying them not to admire. Sad to say, though full of good will they were able neither to admire nor to condemn, for the author's accent was so thick as to be unintelligible, and after half an hour or so they rose from their seats more bewildered than ever. Nor did the book see the light of day, at least under the Chatto imprint; after the conference Norah decided that perhaps she had better read it, shared my sense of utter bafflement and – regretfully, no doubt – urged its author to try his luck elsewhere.

At some stage during the sales conference Norah would invite the reps round to her house in Vincent Square for a drink. I like to imagine them perched on the edge of their chairs in her first-floor sitting-room of Pompeian pink, the ceiling-high windows of which looked out across Vincent Square, where boys from Westminster School were practising cricket in the evening light. No doubt the reps themselves looked as scrubbed and pink-and-white and ill-at-ease as schoolboys, jumping nervously from their chairs to help her open a bottle of tonic or grapple with a packet of crisps. On occasions like this Norah would be at her most gracious and condescending, affable and even joshing but making quite sure that the barriers that separated mistress and servants were firmly kept in place. Although she would call the reps 'Frank' or 'Fred' or what-ever – 'Mr Booth' alone was exempted: maybe she instinctively recognised in him a subversive element – there was never any question of their calling her 'Norah'; nor would they, even at their boldest and most relaxed, have dared to take such a liberty. Only once do I remember this code being breached, and the shock waves throbbed through the building for years to come, entering into folklore until (as is the way with office folklore) the parties concern-ed and those who remembered them were dead or long retired. My friend Ron Cortie – a regular at the Marquis of Granby on Tuesdays – had worked as the London rep for forty years and, at the moment when disaster struck, was on the point of retiring. A jovial, convivial character, Ron regarded Norah with a familiar mixture of terror and affection. He liked nothing better than to tell stories of her misdeeds over a pint in the pub, banging the table with his fist and spilling the beer as he described imaginary bursts of defiance; and, like the rest of us, he both resented her power and dreamed of being her friend, of being admitted at last on terms of equality and intimacy. Shortly before Christmas one year Norah – a lady of the manor dispensing largesse among her tenantry, or the Queen dropping in for a cup of tea at an old people's home – agreed to join a contingent of Chatto staff for a seasonal drink in the pub after work. By the time she arrived, a loyal lieutenant dutifully trailing two paces behind her, her briefcase in his hand, the party was well under way; Ron was about to order a round and was moving from table to table with a five-pound note in his hand, an expectant smile lighting up his features. At the sight of his mistress he hurriedly broke off and, appointing himself mine host, rushed to greet her with cries of 'How nice to see you, ma'am' and 'Now then, Mrs Smallwood, let me find you a chair' (this last accompanied with a winkling motion in the ribs of the production assistant, designed to oust him from the chair of Ron's choice). All this was well enough, and Norah was looking gratified and benevolent, with her subjects spread about her and her patient lieutenant still standing two paces behind in his black undertaker's mackintosh; but all of a sudden Ron – bowled over by the intimacy of the occasion, and slightly inflamed by drink – made his fatal mistake. 'And what can I get you to drink, Norah?' he asked, bowing in her direction and – or so I like to think – simultaneously winking and rubbing his hands together, like an old fashioned *maître d'*. All at once the little party fell silent, the laughter and the gossip draining away; even the bartender, as if aware of an act of hubris, strained eagerly forward, his hand frozen on his beer-pull, as Norah's eyes turned to ice, and those terrible hands began to shuffle the salt and pepper pots to and fro on the table before her, banging them angrily against one another and against the discus-shaped ashtray with its cargo of ash and crumpled crisp packets. And then, 'Mrs Smallwood to you, Ron,' she pronounced in a voice like caustic soda; and the unhappy Ron, his dreams of friendship shattered for ever, crept humbly away, while the rest of the party, after a deathly silence broken by coughing and stirring in seats, resumed the festive spirit in a sobered and thoughtful frame of mind.

Such tales were enough to freeze the blood; and yet, as the months went by, I found myself becoming surprisingly fond of this alarming and uncompromising figure. I admired her energy, her ruthlessness, her dedication, her wit and her sense of style, and – as is often the case with office tyrants – I soon became fond of her in civilian life: still more so since – and here she differed from comparable figures for whom I have worked – she was perfectly happy, once away from the office, to talk to spouses and those shadowy, domestic figures who inhabit the other life of the office worker, never making them feel, as they are often made to feel in the over-bright, incestuous world of publishing, dowdy or tedious or *de trop*. As for the spouses themselves, they resented the toll that she took on their beloveds – the sleepless nights, the churning guts, the sweating and hollow eyes at the thought of things undone or rows in the offing – but tended, when faced by Norah at her most emollient, to melt in exactly the same way as I melted whenever she asked me (her voice tremulous with concern) 'And how are Petra and those dear little girls of yours?'

One drawback of the tyrant's life is that courtiers – dreading a row above all else, and fearful of losing favour or even their jobs – tend to be stiff and deferential in the presence of the Almighty, joshing and jokes giving way to a look of grave concern; as often as not this makes the tyrant lash out more wildly than ever, with the result that he or she is regarded in a still more dreadful light, and treated still less like a fellow human being. Once away from the office, however, Norah became like anybody else. Presumably some of her neighbours – those few who were interested in publishing and its ways – knew of her formidable reputation, but since they weren't in the same line of business they had no immediate experience of it; no doubt they regarded her as something of a character, as the Vincent Square equivalent of one of those intrepid Englishwomen who lived among tribesmen and told them what to do, or threw their weight around at meetings of the W.I. None of this would have worried Norah in the least, though it would have smacked of *lèse majesté* back in William IV Street: she had a nimble sense of humour, and – except when it came to office politics, or being improperly addressed by the firm's non-commissioned officers – was happy to laugh at herself, and to be teased and laughed at by others. No one was better at this than Jerry Epstein, her next-door neighbour in Vincent Square.

Jerry was, when I got to know him, a round, mole-like figure in his fifties, very much along the lines of a jovial garden gnome. He was a shortish man with a huge head, enormous prune-coloured eyes, a black beard flecked with grey and elephantine ears that seemed to stretch the length of his head and were, as befitted a garden gnome, slightly pointed on top, like an ogee arch. He suffered from asthma – fatally, as it turned out – and found London, which he loved, insufferably damp and cold: he spent a good deal of time huddled in front of his kitchen stove with his feet in the oven, and, whatever the weather, he would be clad in a short brown coat with an imitation fur collar and a red woollen scarf, the ends of which swept the floor, however many times it was wrapped round his neck. Although he had lived in this country for more than twenty years, his accent was undiluted Brooklyn: his delivery was of the rapid, buttonholing kind, alternating between a conspiratorial whisper and shouts of merriment or greeting, and accompanied by much rolling of the eyes to heaven and theatrical mutterings behind the hand. The most generous and affectionate of men, he liked nothing better than to entertain his friends to a lunch of salt beef and bagels and beetroot soup, specially ordered from Blooms, and every Christmas he would putter out to the suburbs in a rust-encrusted car crammed with fruit cakes and candles and jars of this and that, all wrapped in lurid mauve and orange foil. (Expeditions of this kind took him at least one and a half hours each way; he must have been the slowest driver at large beyond the South Coast, hogging the middle of the road and followed by a snake of angry motorists.) He had spent most of his life in films and the theatre, and had become a particularly close friend of Charlie Chaplin, working with him on *Limelight* and *A King in New York*, and producing *A Countess from Hong Kong*; and the Chaplin family used Jerry's house as a base and port of call whenever they were in London. Both Jerry's house and Norah's were at the ends of terraces along one side of the square, and from Norah's kitchen or landing it was an easy matter to keep an eye on the comings and goings over the road; and whenever the Chaplins hoved to Norah would find an excuse to hobble across the narrow road between, and make herself known to the new arrivals.

Sad to say, Jerry's hospitality was not always reciprocated. Norah had become a very close friend of Dirk Bogarde, whose memoirs she had published, and whenever he was in England he would visit her as often as possible. From time to time Jerry intimated that he would love to come over and meet Bogarde, in much the same way as Norah had got to know the Chaplins. These intimations, culminating in an outright request, were in vain. 'If I may say so, Jerry, I don't think Dirk would be terribly interested in meeting someone like *you*,' Norah once informed him, after which he crept back to warm his feet in the kitchen stove and restore his battered self-esteem. Later that week Jerry went to a reception at the

National Film Theatre, and at the far end of the room he spotted Dirk Bogarde, with Norah and another Chatto director hovering respectfully beside him. No sooner had he sighted the little party than he strode purposefully towards them, his prune-coloured eyes ablaze, his hand outstretched, his red schoolboy scarf unravelling behind him. According to his version of events, Norah turned white with indignation as she glimpsed him loping towards them, like a blasphemer in a holy place, and she spun on her heel as if to repel a boarder; but then assumed a look of tearful bafflement when Bogarde – who had known Jerry during his time in the film business – sprang eagerly past her with a cry of 'Jerry, how *wonderful* to see you!', slapped him warmly on the back and, taking him by the arm, prepared to introduce him to his companions of the evening.

Despite such setbacks, Norah and Jerry were extremely fond of one another. She liked to portray him as a buffoon and a vulgarian, albeit with a heart of gold; he liked nothing better than to regale us with her latest outrages, but treated her with an affectionate raillery, his Brooklyn accent sounding more subversive than ever in the pink and gold of her sitting-room as he chid her with cries of 'Aw, come off it, Noraaaah!', dragging out the last syllable of her name to comic effect, raising his eyes to heaven and – like a jocular Jewish stereotype – tapping the side of his nose if he happened to catch one's eye. Once again, as with the Central European charmer with his large cigar and bunches of flowers, such an approach was far more effective than our resentful English reticence and conventional good manners, and bore fruit when Jerry assumed the role – as he sometimes did – of an amateurish literary agent. Not long before Norah's eventual retirement, Jerry sent us a novel by John Hopkins about the adventures of a young Princetonian in the swamps of Central America. I found it funny, exciting and colourful; Norah was uncharacteristically irresolute, so she decreed that she and I and Jerry should meet in the Pompeian sitting-room to discuss the matter. Literary agents are, on the whole, sober, watchful people, parsimonious with emotion, anxious to give nothing away, adept at saying nothing and letting the publisher dig himself into a pit. Jerry's approach was very different; for after singing the praises of his author at inordinate length, he suddenly flung himself on his knees and advanced across the room towards Norah with his hands uplifted in prayer before him, very much in the manner of Al Jolson singing 'Mammy'. 'Oh, do get up, Jerry, and don't be so *silly*," Norah commanded, her voice a blend of irritation and amusement; but Jerry – quite unabashed – continued to advance towards her on his knees, uttering low moans of 'Norah, please,' until at last she relented. 'Oh, very well then, Jerry,' she said – at which he sprang nimbly to his feet and walked back to his chair, dusting the knees of his trousers and giving me a conspiratorial wink on his way.

Some ten years later Jerry died in the Westminster Hospital after a devastating attack of asthma. His old sparring partner had preceded him by seven years; and as we gathered in his house for the memorial service I looked across the narrow road that divided the two houses and noticed that the Pompeian pink had been painted over in a pale dishcloth grey, and that the glowing gold pineapples of the paper on the stairs had given way to an anaemic Regency stripe.

Back at Chatto, in the meantime, signs of change were becoming apparent despite Norah's refusal to budge; and the first of these was the departure of George, for whom the call of the Hoover had become irresistible. His replacement at the switchboard was a puzzle to us all: no one knew (or admitted) who had appointed him, where he came from, or why he should have been considered the right man for the job. Louis was an elderly leather enthusiast, who revved up to the front door on a black and silver second-hand motorbike and came clumping through the hall in a black leather jacket and trousers, both embellished with important-looking zips and studs, black knee-length boots (again with zips), black leather gloves and a black globular helmet so large that one feared his neck might snap or his head be borne to the ground by its weight, like a wilting, waterless flower. He looked like a cross between an old-fashioned deep-sea diver and an under-sized SS man, and we drew back in dread as he stamped towards George's cubicle and, after removing his helmet with a stateliness reminiscent of Archbishop Fisher at the Queen's Coronation, settled himself behind the controls. Unvisored, he turned out to be a clerk-like figure in his early sixties, with unwashed hair dyed a boot-polish black, haggard, ashen features, and humourless, messianic eyes gazing out from behind black-rimmed spectacles, the bridge of which had been taped together, scout-master-fashion, with a strip of elastoplast. Deprived of his helmet he had the soft, exposed look of an insect wriggling on its back: we never saw him out of his leather gear and his steel-tipped boots. He kept himself to himself during his brief interlude at Chatto, speaking to no one and regarding the goings-on around him with undisguised disdain.

Louis may have been a demon behind the controls of his gigantic motorbike, but as a switchboard-operator he was an unusual and disconcerting practitioner. Though silent and sullen in person, he liked nothing better than to listen in to and even join in conversations with authors and agents, suddenly and unexpectedly chipping in to air his views on literary matters and offer his advice on publishing practice. Most of us were too surprised and overawed to complain, and Norah herself was not immune to his interpolations; those bold enough to beg Louis to keep his views to himself, or to grumble after he had – in a spasm of boredom or disapproval – pulled out the plug in mid-conversation, were told in sulky tones to do it themselves then, with a good deal of flouncing and waving of disconnected plugs.

All this was very unnerving, and even Mrs Smallwood – fearing, perhaps, that the ubiquitous Louis was somehow listening in, and would exact a terrible revenge – was reduced to discussing his unconventional technique in a low whisper at our weekly editorial meetings; but before long she had rallied, and Louis's days were numbered. What brought about his downfall was an insufficiently respectful approach to Mrs Smallwood's authors. George had realised, almost instinctively, that without authors a publisher is nothing, and adopted a suitably deferential line in dealing with even the most pestilential callers. Louis, on the other hand, was – as his leather gear suggested – something of a rebel, with strong views on literary matters: a keen reader of science fiction, specialising in apocalyptic works about inter-galactic warfare and the imminent destruction of mankind, he referred to even our most eminent authors with a patronising sneer, as if they were the fossilised remains of a frivolous civilisation that should long ago have been consumed by fire and molten lava. Norah was a stickler for correct modes of address, the grander the better, and for Louis to announce that he had 'Colonel' van der Post on the line rather than 'Sir Laurens' was bad enough, earning him a thunderous rebuke once the sage had rung off; but for him to speak lightly of Dirk Bogarde was going too far, inviting immediate expulsion and disgrace. George had known very well how important Bogarde was to the firm, and to Norah as a close and affectionate friend, and would unplug even the most eminent caller to clear the line should his voice be heard ringing in from the South of France. Louis, on the other hand, made no effort to clear the decks: not only did he keep Bogarde waiting, but when at last he got through to Norah he informed her that 'I've got that actor chappie who writes books on the line. Do you want a word with him?' Ten minutes later Louis, his career as a switchboard-operator in shreds, was zipping up his leather jacket and donning his helmet, and clumped out of the office without a single farewell. None of us was sad to see him go, but we all felt that we had moved from a world of uncomfortable certainties into one of equally uncomfortable flux.

Life was beginning to change, but, as I learned later, Louis was only the latest in a series of surprising appointments. One of my predecessors had, some years earlier, given a job in the packing department to a Glaswegian wino whom he had spotted shouting and waving a bottle near Charing Cross Tube station. Maybe he thought he recognised in him a former member of the firm who had taken too literally Norah's cautionary words about ending up on the Embankment, but the wino was rapidly installed, much to Les's indignation, breathing scrumpy fumes over the incoming post, swaying heavily against passing secretaries, and emitting belches and four-letter words as he fought, in vain, to cram a book into a jiffy-bag half its size or, with much lurching and trembling of the hands, to tie up a parcel of proofs with a piece of string the length of a shoelace. After a day or two of unproductive labour he was set to work painting the outside of the boardroom in thick stripes of pink and white and blue: apart from treading in an open pot of paint and leaving footprints the length of the packing-room floor, and swaying perilously on top of a stepladder when working at heights, this kept him out of harm's way for several mornings. As is so often the case in the office, his afternoons were a washout; after revisiting his old haunts on the Embankment he would return inflamed and thickened of speech, and spend the rest of the day asleep under Les's workbench, occasionally releasing an onion-flavoured fart or an angry cry of 'Fock!' Eventually he disappeared altogether, taking with him the contents of the petty-cash box; and Les, to his great relief, was allowed to continue unaided.

Compared with my immediate predecessor, Christopher Mac-Lehose – who went on to become one of the most stylish and literate publishers in London – I was, I knew, a very dull dog indeed, not least in Norah's eyes. Haifa head taller than I was, with the hawklike features of Sherlock Holmes, and a pipe and loud-checked overcoat to match, he cut a dashing and unconventional figure in the office, where his exploits were described and discussed in awestruck whispers long after his departure. He would sometimes, I was told, arrive in the office just as everyone else was leaving, on his back a mountaineer's rucksack containing crampons, pickaxe, goggles, a coil of rope and a woolly hat, as though he planned to spend the evening scaling the south face of William IV Street under hazardous conditions. He would then spend the next few hours ringing New York and getting on with his work uninterrupted before bedding down on his office floor for a well-deserved rest, setting off home again just as his colleagues were clocking in next morning. Norah was, understandably, ex-tremely fond of him, and saw him for a time as her heir apparent; he lived on the ground floor of the house in Vincent Square, and when her arthritis was particularly bad, and he wasn't in mountaineering mood, he would drive her to work, carry her up the baronial staircase and deposit her behind her desk, which he had thoughtfully festooned with the hand-written health warnings I had spotted on my first day in the office.

Hugo was the kindest and most thoughtful of men, but it would never have occurred to him to carry Norah upstairs in his arms, let alone report for duty at six o'clock in the evening disguised as a mountaineer; yet all this time he had been coping with the far more distressing and distasteful job of getting Norah out of the office once and for all, and locking the door firmly behind her. Gradually, by a process of attrition, Norah was nudged to the point at which she could cling on no longer; and one morning Hugo – looking even paler than usual – came into my office, closed the door behind him, and revealed that he was off to Vincent Square to tell her that her days were numbered. I envied him not at all, while sharing his sense of relief; that afternoon he called in again, looking a good twenty years younger, to say that she had accepted the inevitable with good grace, and the deed was finally done.

Norah, as it turned out, still had a surprise or two in store; but Hugo's days were as numbered as her own. Both Hugo and I had done good things at OUP, but neither of us had made much of a mark at Chatto: he had spent his days on office politics, trying to winkle out his boss, and whereas I had flourished as his lieutenant at Oxford, I was quite incapable of providing him with the support he needed at Chatto, since within minutes of my arrival I had been cowed and put in my place, and had been far too frightened and outwitted to raise my head ever since. Hugo had the potential to be a first-rate publisher of the kind best suited to Chatto and The Hogarth Press, but instead of entering into his inheritance at last, he found himself in an even more intolerable position than he had been under Norah, when life was made bearable by the prospect of her eventual departure, however ghastly the stages in between.

Hugo, it was decided, had not done enough to enliven Chatto during his three embattled years with the firm, and an approach was made to Carmen Callil, the formidable Australian founder of Virago Press, to come in as joint managing director with Hugo, while Virago itself – which Carmen had founded on her kitchen table – was to be incorporated into the group. Carmen had started life as a publicity hound, working for, among others, André Deutsch; and at some stage, while working as a freelance publicist, she had done a brief stint at Chatto, in the course of which she had inevitably had dealings with Norah, and no doubt been bruised in the process. She realised perfectly well that, tough and wily as she was, Norah was equally tough and wily, and that, even in old age, she might well come out on top if engaged in hand-to-hand conflict. Since Carmen was supremely realistic and a nimble politician, she agreed to come to Chatto on the understanding that Norah was off the premises before she arrived; and since she also knew that to allow Norah the smallest fingerhold would be fatal – and that liberal-minded haverings and compromises such as the rest of us were instinctively drawn to would prove, in the long term, messier and unkinder than a clean and final break – she hardened her heart against offering her any of the honorific or consultative posts with which more sentimental and craven spirits sought to sweeten the pill of departure. Later on, after the dust had settled, and Carmen was happily ensconced in Norah's old office, it was often assumed that she had got rid of Norah with dreadful brutality, banishing a harmless old lady from Paradise for ever and callously blighting the evening of her days: in fact Carmen behaved in a perfectly honourable and eminently sensible way as far as Norah was concerned, though given her ferocious reputation many outsiders found this hard to believe. Norah, for her part, recognised in Carmen the only participant in the whole sad saga of equal weight to her own; but she too was happy to blame her woes on the new arrival, denouncing her as a crude vulgarian from Australia with no sense of what Chatto was all about. Like Hitler in the ruins of Berlin, she seemed eager to pull down all about her and to make Carmen's accession as uncomfortable as possible, setting her authors against the raw intruder (in vain, for the most part) and secreting away explosive devices which, it was hoped, would detonate loudly after her departure, causing maximum embarrassment to the new regime. One of my colleagues – a kindly, decent, worried-looking man – drew me aside while preparations for the

Götterdämmerung were in full frenzy and addressed me on the subject in a confidential tone. The publishing equivalent of a senior civil servant in his readiness to provide whoever happened to be in power with the same logical, meticulously sensible advice, without partiality or comment, his cool intelligence was blighted only by a failure to take into account the irrational and the emotional as ingredients of human behaviour, or to recognise the great gulf that usually lies between rhetoric and action, promise and performance. For years he had worked late most evenings, seldom leaving before his leader and then ushering her gravely to the lift, holding back the walnut doors and the black and lunging grille as they fought like tigers in his grasp. Now, for the first and only time, he felt she was going too far. 'I have to confess,' he told me, 'that I am *most* surprised by Mrs Smallwood's behaviour' (I could only assume that she had been caught red-handed priming some especially explosive device). Of course Norah was behaving badly, and of course it was unfair to the new regime, I told him: but surely he shouldn't be too surprised, or think too badly of her. Chatto was, after all, Norah's life, and she was fighting to survive, like an animal being torn from its lair. Such strength of feeling might seem incomprehensible to less committed souls like ourselves, who went to work with one eye on the clock, but given the way she felt it was entirely understandable that she should use whatever weapons came to hand, and go on fighting to the end. He seemed unpersuaded by this, and vanished down the glistening prep-school corridor, shaking his head sorrowfully from side to side.

While all this was going on, Hugo was left on the touchline: he had finally persuaded Norah to go, but was now being discarded as irrelevant to the new Chatto. At some stage in the proceedings, eager to find out what Carmen was like, I called in at Virago in the attic of OUP's sepulchral London offices, and took her out for a drink in a pub nearby (not something I would have dared to suggest a year or so later). I liked her well enough, but sensed a formidable presence; and on the train that evening I told Hugo that, as far as I could see, he had traded in one demanding mistress for another. Anxious as always to believe the best of people, Hugo told me not to worry, and that all would be well. Alas, how wrong he was. Under the new dispensation he was to be chairman and joint managing director, but since Carmen – like all those autocratic publishers I secretly admired – insisted on being solely in charge, it soon became clear that rule by a duumvirate wasn't on. She also, I suspect, refused to see Hugo as a human being, but somehow converted him into a symbol of all that she most disliked about upper-class Englishmen and gentleman publishers. As for the powers-that-be, they saw her as embodying the future, and were eager to protect and placate their new investment – and no doubt they very soon learned that Carmen could be every bit as determined and as terrifying as Norah. If Carmen wanted Hugo out, Hugo would have to go, irrespective of his qualities, and the affection and admiration he aroused among all those with whom he had worked.

But this is to jump ahead, for Norah was still eking out her last days in the firm, and Carmen was hovering in the wings, maintaining a scrupulous distance. Leaving party succeeded leaving party, each grander and more bibulous than the last; speeches were made and triumphs recalled, to the accompaniment of unseen choirs and invisible Hammond organs; tears, both real and crocodile, were shed; paintings and bouquets and items of glassware, suitably engraved, were handed over to little cries of admiration and much falling on necks and wringing of hands; everyone agreed that none of us would ever forget and that eras were coming to a close and that nothing would be quite the same again. On the morning after one of these farewell celebrations I came across Norah in the corridor outside her office, struggling to open a lavatory-glass-fronted door opposite the pigeonholes. She was busy clearing out her things – her office was crammed with tea chests and cardboard boxes – and had just rediscovered in a desk drawer the key to this particular broom cupboard, which hadn't been opened for years. After a good deal of tugging and pushing and jiggling of the key I eventually got the door open, and Norah – brushing me aside with her elbow – stepped eagerly inside. A few seconds later she emerged, lightly dusted with grime and clutching a waisted and belted dark green mackintosh. 'So *that's* where it got to,' she said; and went on to explain that she had lost it during the war – perhaps after a fire-watching session on the roof? – and that it must have been incarcerated in the unopened cupboard ever since. I found this time warp as evocative as the mysterious hairbrush outside the men's lavatory with its freight of thin grey hairs; and a moment or two later the past came surging back once more when she asked me if I would try to tug open a long wooden drawer under the pigeonholes which had been painted shut and – like the broom cupboard – hadn't been opened for as long as she could remember. Opening the drawer proved a far sterner challenge than the cupboard door; it was a warm summer day, and as I heaved and struggled my shirt began to plaster itself to my chest and my specs to slide down my nose, while Norah stood impatiently by, tapping her stick on the lino. Eventually the drawer flew open, sending me reeling back against the glass-fronted door; and as it did so we were enveloped in a gritty grey cloud, as though a pea-souper had been preserved intact in the deep, capacious drawer, like the air in an Egyptian tomb. The inside of the drawer was coated in a thick black soot of the kind that I remembered from my childhood in London in the 1940s, blackening one's collar and the grass in Battersea Park, and leaving a ring of grime on a finger thrust up the nose. Under the dust were several rolled-up examples of jacket artwork from the forties and early fifties, including one by Nicolas Bentley, that elegant and emollient figure from my days at André Deutsch. I asked Norah if – since no one else knew of its existence – I could possibly have the Bentley, but she snatched it out of my hand with a reproachful look, stuck it under her arm along with the other scrolls, and scurried back to her office.

Norah's final exit was, inevitably, rather an anti-climax. I remember that, at her penultimate board meeting, the waggish Clive Ryder-Runton – a fine figure who had recently joined us from the mustard business as Company Secretary, addressed Norah as 'Ma'am' (much to her delight) and liked to escort her to her seat at the head of the table with a flurry of bows and reverential sweepings of the hand, at the same time winking at me over the old lady's shoulder – suggested that, to mark the solemnity of the occasion, her fellow-directors should attend her final meeting in morning suits, hired especially for the occasion, but was instantly voted down. No doubt she cherished fantasies – as even the most hard-headed publishers always do – of the firm collapsing into chaos after her departure, of bereft authors signing round-robins begging her to return, of her driving her enemies before her and resuming life at the helm in triumph. Senior publishers, like the rest of us, like to think of themselves as indispensable, and all too easily believe the windy rhetoric of leaving speeches, the consoling, flattering lies about imminent collapse and the impossibility of staggering on without them. Even the wiliest politicians and masters of *realpolitik* persuade themselves that they are somehow exempt from the passing of time; yet the sad truth is that after the initial flurry of departure, the waters close over at distressing speed, and life resumes as though they had never been. Authors remember former publishers with (one hopes) gratitude and affection, but soon adapt to, and may even prefer, the new arrivals; professional friendships – with agents, fellow-publishers, booksellers and the rest – are genuine enough within the context of the trade, but more often than not fail to survive retirement or dismissal; for a while the former leader lingers on as a kind of King over the Water, vainly evoked when the deeds of the new regime seem particularly crude or disrespectful, before fading into oblivion. Sayings and stories from the old order are passed on, but mean less and less to rising generations, and slowly pass out of circulation; those who remember the old days gradually depart the scene themselves and even the most forceful figures are forgotten, lingering on as names in sheafs of yellowing correspondence or as signatories to long-forgotten contracts. Although she never again set foot in the publishing offices after her departure, Norah used, from time to time, to appear in Les's lair on the ground floor, and ask him to pack up a parcel of books or carry out to her car various possessions and mementoes – including, for some reason, a lawnmower – which had been housed in the office. On one such occasion, some six months after her departure, a secretary burst into the office, pop-eyed with excitement and a sense of good deeds done. A bossy and obstreperous old lady, she reported, was hanging round the packing department and bullying Les, who seemed unable to defend himself: should someone go down and see her off the premises? I'm glad to say that no one did; but it served as a sad reminder of the transience of fame.

Not long after Norah's retirement, Dennis Enright too decided that enough was enough. Even the most recent arrivals were sad to see him go; but the break was less absolute, in that he continued for a while to be a Chatto author, and the well-informed knew that he could be reached every Tuesday at lunchtime in the Marquis of Granby, less than a hundred yards from the front door of the offices. Dennis had never been the kind of publisher who boasted in the Garrick about the deals he'd done or astronomical sales figures; his work as an editor survives in the publisher's ultimate *raison d'être*, on the pages of the authors with whom he worked. For my part – having an incurably trivial mind – my memories of Dennis at Chatto are of his advancing down a corridor, his hair on end and his face illuminated with a lop-sided grin, to impart in a sardonic mumble the details of some fresh folly on the part of a colleague or an author; or of his sampling and re-sampling with Les the various bottles of home-made wine brewed by our author Mollie Harris, and making such inroads on the rose-hip, the parsley and the nettle that the bottles had to be topped up with water before they could be enjoyed by the reps at the forthcoming sales conference, at which Mollie was billed to introduce her book on rustic wines; or of his playing truant from a more formal affair in the office in order to join Les for pre-Christmas drinks in the Welsh Harp, and leading a hurried exit from the back door – I like to think it was the back window, but find to my disappointment that it is heavily barred – after Mrs Smallwood and a fellow-director had been spotted inching their way purposefully through the crowd of revellers to retrieve their errant colleague.

The last two years of Norah's life were spent in a kind of limbo. Like many of her former colleagues, I suspect, I only fully enjoyed her company, and became really fond of her, after she had retired, and was no longer in a position to harry or to dominate. By now we were living near Richmond Park; and every now and then we would call on her in Vincent Square to see how she was and to listen to her reminiscing about the old days in William IV Street. She was funny and kind and affectionate; only if the conversation turned to present-day Chatto did the old Norah make a brief and alarming reappearance. Her eyes would freeze, her body stiffen, her mouth tighten into a slit as she referred to what she considered to be the follies or the barbarisms of the new regime, of which I was now part; her hand would tremble on her ebony walking-stick and she would pace angrily up and down the Pompeian sitting-room until – by cunning or good luck – the conversation could be turned into blander, less painful channels. The doings of her neighbours – of Jerry Epstein in particular, and of a clock-maker whose boiler had blown up, destroying his house in the process – provided an alternative to the goings-on in William IV Street, for Norah was an avid and inventive gossip; so too did her cat Chatto, the gift of a thoughtful literary agent, who soon established himself as an important presence in Vincent Square, and the focus of all attention. A large, black, benign-looking fellow, Chatto was extremely long-suffering: he was never allowed out of the house, was carried around in Norah's arms like a purring baby, and was expected, at mealtime, to sit up on a stool at the kitchen table and play a full part in the proceedings. He was fond of his doting mistress, but from time to time he would forget himself and, mistaking her stick-like legs for those of a chair, sharpen his claws on them, with terrible consequences.

Chatto's outbursts might well necessitate a trip to the Westminster Hospital so that Norah's legs could be rebandaged; and before long the Westminster was to become all too familiar to the indomitable old lady and to a steady stream of well-wishers clutching bunches of flowers. Twice in her last year she was admitted for what turned out to be major surgery. The first visit ended up as a rather social occasion, with ripples of excitement running through the public ward as well-known faces were spotted picking their way past the trolleys and the movable screens in Norah's general direction. Dirk Bogarde was an early and a loyal visitor – and, unlike many of the writers, however esteemed in the literary world, he was a genuine celebrity. His visits raised Norah's standing in the ward to fresh heights; and Norah herself, like a queen dispensing largesse, deigned to introduce him to a select few, hand-picked from among the other old ladies in the ward. Humbler callers from the office – among them Ron, the former London traveller, who knew her far too well to bear a grudge – were made welcome, but were uneasily aware that, a publisher to the last, Norah had one eye on the door for more important visitors: no sooner was one spotted than she would stiffen against the pillow, the current conversation would be hurriedly curtailed, and the sales manager or production director would quietly sidle out, briefcase in hand, as, with both arms extended, Norah greeted whichever grandee happened to have made his or her appearance. I remember bringing her the portable telephone so she could ring one of her eminent friends: Petra helped her into a sitting position, and she felt as light and as frail as a paper kite.

Shortly after her return from hospital I went to see her during a lunch hour, and we walked, very slowly, from Vincent Square to a fish-and-chip shop in Wilton Road of which she had become very fond. Formica tabletops and paper cups of Coke and tomato-shaped ketchup dispensers seemed a long way from lunch at the Ivy with Aldous Huxley or Compton Mackenzie; but she assured me that the cod was delicious, which it was. She was as sharp and as funny as ever, and her malicious, throaty chuckle as contagious as it had always been; and, thank God, we managed to steer clear of present-day Chatto, but remained in the anodyne plains of the past. Meeting old bosses – particularly old bosses one especially admired, or of whom one stood in awe – is often a tricky and melancholy business, and still more so after their retirement. The bosses seem to feel that, once deprived of power, they are of little real interest to those who linger on in what they see as the land of the living, and sometimes display an embarrassing gratitude and even deference to former underlings prepared to take the time to seek them out ('You don't want to waste your time with an old has-been like me'); the underlings still see their former bosses in an altogether more heroic light, and feel awkward and let-down and even faintly irritated by this uncalled-for humility, while at the same time relishing the surprise of being able to talk on an equal footing for the first time. With Norah there was none of this. I had always, even at my most resentful and afraid, admired and respected her; and now I liked, and even loved, her as well. We had, it seemed, become friends at last.

Not long after our fish-and-chips lunch Norah was taken into hospital for what proved to be the last time. Once again her friends prepared to rally round, relishing the finer nuances of life in the public ward and swigging tooth-mugs of champagne at the foot of the bed; but it soon became apparent that this would be a less convivial affair. I went to see her once, and she looked more skeletal than ever: but her cheeks were pink like those of a clown or a face in a drawing by a child, and her eyes were as bright and as blue as ever. A day or two later we called again, on our way back from work. A nurse took our flowers from us, and told us that Mrs Smallwood was too ill to see anyone, but if we'd like to leave a note with the flowers she'd make sure she got it. I felt certain as I wrote that she would never read it; and next day we learned, in the office, that she had died in her sleep in the night.

Norah's funeral was a dismal affair in the cemetery at Putney Vale, with a grey sky overhead and a harried clergyman with one eye on his watch, hurrying through his fifth cremation of the day and referring in Christian-name terms to the matchless virtues and peerless character of a woman he had never heard of before. Her memorial service was altogether more appropriate. Norah had, from time to time, hobbled across the road from the office for memorial services at St Martin-in-the-Fields, and Hugo did the same for her when her time came. Authors, agents, fellow-publishers, friends, family and old retainers turned out in force; Laurens van der Post gave an address and Jill Day Lewis read the lessons; and afterwards we gathered for drinks in the airless, windowless board-room. Three years later, Chatto – by now a very different firm, for good and for bad – moved from the building in which Norah had, forty-five years before, been interviewed for a job as a secretary, and in which she had spent her working life, and set up house in Jonathan Cape's former offices in Bedford Square; and not long after that the entire group, which had recently been bought by an American conglomerate, moved into open-plan offices at the far end of the Vauxhall Bridge Road. Whatever would Norah think, the veterans asked themselves, tut-tutting and raising their eyes to heaven: surely she must be turning in her grave?

CHAPTER EIGHT

Heroes of our Time

LITTLE LOVE had ever been lost between Carmen and her predecessor, and no sooner had the new arrival installed herself in Norah's old office – hand-painted furniture and a whiff of the Omega Workshop ceding place to a jack-in-the-box Mrs Thatcher and a huge oriental tapestry pinned to the wall in which pop-eyed cats indecently clad in nautical jackets but no trousers strutted up and down with cigars in their mouths – than she began, like an animal marking out its territory, to obliterate, wherever possible, the physical presence of the *ancien régime*. Salmon-pink and royal-blue windowsills were painted over in pulsing romantic purple; a pair of bogus baronial doors, embellished with gothic arches and metal studs and plastic bottle-end windows, and painted in the same purple, replaced the plain, elderly couple that had once led onto the street; the blue institutional lino in the corridors was covered over with porridge-coloured wall-to-wall carpeting; offices innocent of ornament other than a squash racquet propped against the wall or a faded photo of some long-forgotten partner found themselves plumped out with cushions and curtains and pelmets and pots of flowers. The men's lavatory, once white with dark-blue pipes and cistern, simmered in apposite shades of yellow and brown; triangular lampshades of white-tinted glass, redolent of spider-haunted milking-sheds and prep-school changing-rooms, were elbowed aside by bulbous affairs in brown and orange, that cast a gloomy amber light more reminiscent of boarding houses between the wars than of a publishing house, ancient or modern; white-painted tables found themselves smothered by tasselled tablecloths of chestnut-coloured velvet, lacking only the gypsy's crystal ball; the austere traditional writing-paper, black lettering on white, the names of directors who had died or retired knocked out with a line of 'x's while those of new arrivals were carefully typed in below, was swiftly removed from service and replaced by a cream laid paper with the firm's colophon picked out in purple and the reading matter in black.

All this was very much Carmen's work, for the rest of us were perfectly happy to trundle along as we always had, and saw no reason for carpets or curtains or amber-coloured lampshades in reproduction art deco. As we soon discovered, she had far more energy, enthusiasm and strength of character than the rest of the office combined, and was determined to involve herself not just in the publishing side of the business – acquiring new authors, starting new lists, revitalising sales and publicity and subsidiary rights, wooing literary agents and literary editors, charming and bludgeoning gossip-columnists and feature-writers into devoting whole columns and even pages to the 'new Chatto' and its redoubtable supremo – but in every aspect of office life, even to the extent of taking away the office towels every Friday night, putting them through her washing-machine and bringing them back, fragrant and neatly folded, on Monday morning.

One morning I came into my office – the tiny, sunlit cell overlooking the well – to find it darkened by a pair of chocolate-and-orange curtains; from the cell next door came the tinkle of broken glass, for my colleague Mike Petty – frustrated by bubbly lavatory glass from peering across the well at the new publicity girls who had been brought in to liven up that side of the business – had complained, implausibly, that his office was far too dark for detailed editorial work, and the lavatory glass was, at that very moment, being replaced by a sheet of gleaming plate. Hardly had I settled behind my desk, leafing through my post with listless fingers and wondering where to start, than my door flew open and our new leader stood before me, her black eyes gleaming with missionary zeal. 'Darling,' she said, 'that cushion you're sitting on is a *disgrace*, and something must be done about it.' As far as I knew, the cushion she referred to was an unobtrusive affair wrapped in oatmeal-

coloured tweed, mounted on a frail-looking Utility chair which must
have been stronger than it looked, having supported C. Day Lewis
and Dennis Enright in earlier incarnations. I rose uneasily from my
seat and peered at the cushion below me, like a dog about to sniff its
mess. 'But what's wrong with it?' I asked, feeling less sure of my
ground as a dreadful vision rose before me of our new managing
director prowling the corridors long after I'd left for home and
discovering the dried encrustations that had built up, like a sedi-
ment, on the underside of my chair as, over the years, I had absent-
mindedly picked my nose while leafing through a typescript, wiping
the end products on desk and chair alike. 'But, Jeremy, can't you see
– it's *disgusting*,' she went on, with some justification it seemed:
'Couldn't Petra make a loose cover for it?' I didn't see why Petra,
who was working full-time and had a house to run, should spend her
evenings running up loose covers for Chatto & Windus, and said that
she didn't have the time. 'Well, I suppose *I'll* have to do it, like
everything else in this place,' the leader replied, holding out one
hand for the oatmeal-coloured cushion with its shameful encrustations. A day or two later it was returned to me with a perfectly-fitted
flower-pattern cover, tied underneath with strips of white ribbon. I
took care to treat the new arrival with suitable respect, but six months
later, as I was leaning back on two legs for a meditative pause in
mid-blurb, the Utility chair suddenly crumpled beneath me, and its
splintered remains were hauled away to the dump.

  Nor was this the end of the refurbishing of Chatto. Since time
immemorial the office waste-paper bins had been square-sided,
khaki affairs made of sheet metal; they performed their primary
functions perfectly well, quite apart from which they were waterproof, cigarette stubs could be ground out against their walls, and,
placed upside-down, they could be used as extra seating in an
over-crowded meeting. All at once a decree went out that these
reliable veterans were to be replaced by raffia baskets from a shop
in Covent Garden, which were a good deal more graceful but had
none of the subsidiary advantages of the older models. Each
member of staff was to be responsible for replacing his or her
basket, and the job was to be done at once. Far too cowardly to defy

this unusual order, but unable to take the matter as seriously as I should, I went on filling my familiar metal bin, and made no effort to head back from lunch via the raffia shop in Covent Garden where the new baskets, made of yellowish straw with circular chocolate bands, stood waiting on the pavement. Every now and then an angry-looking head would shoot round the edge of my door, startling me from slumber or from editing the adventures of a Littlehampton lavatory-cleaner, and ask in an accusing way why I hadn't replaced my bin; still I failed to act, until one morning I arrived to find that my old friend had been taken away for scrap and a raffia-work intruder stood in its place.

Our new leader was a short, neatly-built Australian with flashing black eyes, curly black hair, and a vigorous, disruptive turn of phrase, at once humorous and hectoring. She could charm or savage with equal effect, with not a great deal in between, and as she did so she would bend all her energies and all her emotion and all her attention on the recipient, who was left in no doubt about the force of her opinions, whether favourable or not; but on those rare occasions when she wasn't carried away by the passions of the moment, her face became a perfect blank, like that of an actress waiting to assume a role or resting between parts. She flung herself into her various roles with an abandon that carried all before it. She dominated our lives in the office, harrying and bullying and flattering and inveigling, yet encountered out of context I would find myself staring past her at a party, vaguely wondering why her face seemed familiar: coming back from lunch one day I saw two women talking on the pavement in front of me, not far from the Chatto offices, and after greeting the taller of the two, whom we had published at OUP, I half turned to her companion, as if waiting to be introduced, only to realise with a stab of surprise that this was the same person who had carried away my cushion and whose rasping tones I had overheard with dread as she hurried past my door only an hour or two before, hurling instructions over her shoulder at an alarmed-looking colleague padding dutifully in her wake, notebook at the ready.

Like Norah, Carmen was far cleverer and far sharper-witted than the rest of us, outflanking as well as overriding a feeble opposition; and, like Norah, she believed in the *ad hominem* approach – so alien to the nicely-brought-up Englishman – with the result that a discussion of even the dullest and most neutral-seeming subject soon became highly personalised, with suggestions of moral, personal and intellectual inadequacy adding zest and bias to the debate. Unlike Norah – and this came as a relief after those withering charades of omniscience – she was perfectly happy to admit her ignorance and confess to the odd blind spot: 'Darling, you *are* clever,' she would tell one, batting her eyelids (a favourite phrase of hers, issued on arrival to trainee publicity girls) and gazing up through swimming black eyes: 'You tell me – I know fuck-all about it.' Like Norah, she dangled before one the possibility of friendship, of a final breaking through, only to whip it away once more; like an elusive, titillating lover she offered just enough come-hither charm ('Jeremy, you rat-bag') to keep one's affections alive.

Like the rest of us, I suspect, I felt towards her a familiar mixture of *odi et amo*, of admiration and resentment. I admired her energy and her enthusiasm, her informality and her lack of pomposity, her willingness to break the rules and give it a whirl; I relished her indiscretion and her love of gossip, her refusal to respect the established order and her readiness to savage the mighty with quite as much ferocity as she savaged her staff, and never more so than if one of her flock had come under attack; I respected her chilly Darwinian view of life as a struggle for survival and her unsentimental realism about her life and the parts she was playing, so that although the rest of us tried to console ourselves for our feelings of cowardice and inadequacy by telling ourselves, in the way people do, that her bad behaviour and her tunnel vision and the smoke pouring out from under her door were somehow compensating for what we hoped (in unkind moments) was an unhappy and lonely private life, none of this quite rang true – not least because Carmen herself had got there first, and was far bolder than the rest of us when it came to confronting the bleak realities of love and friendship and work and growing old, and showed few signs of not living life to the full outside the office as well as within.

Despite some exorbitant claims made on her behalf, she was not, I felt, a great publisher, either in a literary sense or in the more prosaic sense of running a business and making a profit: her greatest success had been as a reprint publisher, and she was too worried about being up to the minute, and too swayed by reputations already made, to have been an outstanding spotter of talent, and too extravagant to successfully balance the books. As a publicist – of her authors, her list and herself – she was incomparable; but what really marked her out from all the other publishers I have known was the energy and the enthusiasm and the care she devoted to those authors on the list whose work she admired and of whom she was fond. Though never trained as an editor, she would – within days of receiving a typescript – type out page upon page of detailed and often highly perceptive comments for the author, and pamper and fuss about them thereafter, like a bossy, affectionate nanny. Publishing is, in the last resort, a business like any other; but it is also, and equally importantly, a matter of spreading the author's word, of making him or her a name, and in this Carmen was unmatched. As often as not, the beneficiaries of her enthusiasm were long-standing Chatto authors, coaxed blinking into the limelight by a flamboyant impresario: Antonia Byatt, hitherto admired but little-known, found herself, deservedly, a household name, among the book-reading classes at least; the octogenarian V. S. Pritchett was persuaded to produce new collections of essays and stories, and earlier works were reissued in sumptuous full-colour jackets.

The horrors of office life are soon forgotten once one has left the scene, in much the same way as summer holidays spent gazing angrily out while the rain drums against the windowpane and the clouds scud across a Cornish harbour are eclipsed, in retrospect at least, by occasional flashes of watery sun. For my own part, I had less cause to complain than most: no doubt I was the most tiresome of colleagues – stubborn, disaffected, irresponsible, absent whenever needed, indifferent to much of what Carmen was trying to achieve – and no doubt such wrath as came my way was, as often as not, largely self-induced.

One of my authors of whom Carmen disapproved was Dick West, a free spirit who spent as much time as he could roaming his favourite parts of the world – I liked to think of barmen in Montevideo or Saigon or Durban or Zagreb setting their watches by his seasonal migrations, and setting out the glasses in anticipation of his arrival – and whose pursuit of uncomfortable truths was fuelled by an instinctive, anarchic reaction against whatever happened to be the prevailing orthodoxy, whether of the left or the right. Round-headed, bespectacled, irremediably adolescent, respectably clad in a light tweed suit and woollen tie, with a mackintosh on top, Dick could usually be found with a drink in his hand, his shoulders juddering up and down with barely suppressed mirth, his gaze firmly fixed on the floorboards, as he regaled those about him with derisive gossip and unfashionable views, both delivered in a low and confidential mutter, so that his listeners found themselves having to lean forward for the latest information. Since his dismissal in the early sixties as the *Manchester Guardian*'s Yorkshire correspondent, Dick had been his own master, covering the Vietnam War and South America and the Horn of Africa and his favourite European stamping-grounds, Poland and Yugoslavia. I had always found him the most stylish and sympathetic of journalists, witty and commonsensical and original and unafraid, and I could never understand why he appeared to arouse such antipathy among the *bien pensants*. Like many journalists, he was essentially a sprinter, best on a thousand words, but during the last days of the *ancien régime* I had commissioned him to write a book about his travels round England, his gloomy diagnosis of which seems wretchedly accurate in retrospect.

Through Dick I met Michael Wharton, better known to the world at large as 'Peter Simple' of the *Daily Telegraph*. Michael composed his column while making his way by bus from Battersea to Fleet Street; and every lunch hour, at 2.30, his labours concluded, he would move from the *Telegraph* building to a crowded, slot-like pub next door called the King and Keys, where he would take his stand exactly halfway along the bar and consume an identical lunch of one corned beef sandwich washed down with double brandies and dry ginger ale. To either side of him red-faced, grey-haired men from the *Telegraph* could be spotted trying to catch the barman's eye; as Michael points out in the second of his fine autobiographies, these *Telegraph* men tended, by a pleasing paradox, to behave far worse than their equivalents on more scabrous popular papers, lingering on in the King and Keys till well past closing time and running off with one another's wives long after the men from the *Sun* and the *Mirror* had caught the last train home to Edenbridge or Potter's Bar. Like Dick, Michael spoke in a low mutter, aiming his words at the floor, so that once again one had to strain forward to retrieve his observations: quite apart from relishing his writing, with its combination of comicality and melancholy – during the last days of Norah's rule I signed up his opening volume of memoirs – I found him another kindred spirit, who shared my admiration for romantic, literate adventurers like Leigh Fermor and Denis Hills, and for disruptive sages like Mr Chaudhuri.

Both Dick West and Michael Wharton were keen admirers of an unusual writer called Roy Kerridge, whose picaresque adventures round Britain were beginning to appear in the *Spectator*. Kerridge came across in his pieces as a kind of holy fool, picking his way through a world of Rastas and horse-copers and clerkly Hari Krishnas, his worldly goods in a pair of polythene bags and a cosy idyll evoked in beaming family groups and cheering cups of tea. I liked his combination of innocence and experience, of stylistic naivety and worldly sophistication, and found his journalism funny and perceptive and original; so when Dick suggested one day that it might well be worth my dropping him a line – warning me at the same time to expect the unfamiliar – I wrote to Mr Kerridge care of the *Spectator*, and waited to see what would happen.

A day or so later a disapproving voice from reception rang up to say that a Mr Kerridge was downstairs asking to see me. Leaving my unexpected visitor time enough to grapple with the lift, I sauntered round to the landing, ready to greet him on his arrival and prevent him from being stunned by one of the two walnut-panelled doors as he fought with one foot to keep the lunging trellis gate at bay. Minutes passed and no one appeared, nor could I feel any of those tremors from the lift shaft which suggested that the initial bout of wrestling was over, and the passenger was very slowly inching his way to the second floor on the end of a greasy metal rope. I was about to rush down the baroque staircase in search of my missing visitor – perhaps he had wandered off behind the scenes and been locked in error in the file copy library, or had struck up a friendship with Les the Packer and was busy discussing ways of cutting up cardboard – when below me in the darkness I spotted a small figure in glasses, a polythene bag in either hand, advancing very slowly up the staircase, pausing every now and then to lay down his bundles and mop his brow with a grey-looking handkerchief. A second or two later he rounded the top of the stairs and, spotting me with hand extended, came to a sudden stop, like an animal caught in the headlights, gave a little cry of 'Oh' followed by 'Pleased to meet you, I'm sure' – the end of the sentence lilting upwards before coming to a very definite conclusion, as if accompanied by an inaudible smacking of lips – and extended a warmish hand of his own. Ceremonial greetings exchanged, he followed me round the labyrinthine corridors, muttering as he went ('Well, well, my oh my, this is all very nice, I'm sure') until we reached my cell, where I waved him into a wicker chair – urging him as I did so to make his polythene bags at home – and took my place behind my desk like an old-fashioned family doctor.

Roy Kerridge was a small, mole-like figure. His face was round and benign and shaven in patches, and he spoke at times with a stammer: when overtaken by a fit of stammering he would – like my friend Ian Whitcomb – swat the side of his face with comical effect, so bringing the flow of words on stream once more. His hair was short, like that of a Prussian general, and as he spoke he ran his fingers through the stubble, pausing from time to time to examine his findings over the top of his specs. He was wearing a thick check shirt with a knitted tie, a shiny dark-blue suit-top, short in the body and tight about the waist, with all three buttons done up, and a pair of sand-coloured trousers, the cuffs of which had come unravelled at the back and were trailing over the heels of a pair of silver winkle-pickers, only one of which was equipped with a lace. The lenses of his glasses looked as though they had been smudged with oil, and were so bleared and cracked that I wondered how he peered about him, moving his head from side to side as he did so. The two polythene bags, as I quickly discovered, were crammed with grubby-looking folders containing even grubbier pages of manuscript and typescript, all of which were soon laid out on my desk: like many writers of an older generation than ours – Cyril Connolly and Alan Ross among them – he had never learned to type, and often spent the modest fees he earned on the services of a typist. Until recently, he told me, the *Spectator* had been prepared to work from his original, hand-written versions: he had a round, clear, child-like hand, and the margins of his articles and stories were decorated with meticulous drawings of deer and unicorns, each of which peered out at the world through large, doll-like eyes replete with curling lashes.

The typescripts safely stored away on a shelf, I led him back through the maze – his silver winkle-pickers and frayed trouser cuffs exciting a raised eyebrow from a colleague more accustomed to the memoirs of retired diplomats and major-generals – and took him to the pub downstairs, where I ordered him a cheese sandwich and his favourite tipple of pale ale with a dash of Rose's lime juice. Over lunch, he told me something of his background and his circumstances. He was about the same age as I was and, like me, had divided his life between London and Sussex; he had recently moved back to London from Littlehampton, and was now living over the road from the office in St Mungo's – the former Charing Cross Hospital, and a temporary shelter for tramps – before rejoining his mother and other members of his family in their new home in Kensal Rise. 'You see, I am very blessèd,' he said, taking an appreciative swig of his pale ale and lime, 'in that I have a private income.' Though slightly surprised at this news, for he hardly looked like a member of the *rentier* class, I made envious mumbling noises while Roy hurried on to provide the details. 'Yes,' he continued, 'I have an income of £30 a month, which enables me to live as I like.'

Roy's parents, he told me, had met before the war at a Young Communists party rally. Not long after Roy's birth his father had left home, and had become a geography don in the provinces. Roy had never met him, but finding himself one day in his father's university town, he had discovered the pub in which he regularly ate his lunch and had sat opposite him, sipping a pale ale and lime but never saying a word, until his father had finished his meal and the two of them went their separate ways. After the war Roy's mother had married a Nigerian, who liked to lie in bed reading the *Daily Telegraph*, marking in red ink evidence of imperialist misdeeds. Roy had some half-brothers and sisters, one of whom, Zenga, was also a writer, and rightly admired by the men on the staff of the *Spectator*. Roy was convinced that Zenga had a great future as a blues singer, and somehow got it into his head that Ian Whitcomb – who had, years earlier, reached No. 5 in the American hit parade, and now spent most of his time in Los Angeles, returning once or twice a year to see his mother on Putney Heath – might be able to provide some useful tips. Eager to do what I could to help, I invited all three to supper in East Sheen. Hardly had we pulled up our chairs to the table and poured out the first glass of wine than Roy – looking more mole-like than ever, his hands on either side of his plate, clutching the table edge – began to agitate, and continued to do so throughout the meal. 'Sing for them, Zenga, sing for them now,' he commanded, while the rest of us urged him to let her be, at least till she'd finished her meal. Eventually, at about half-past twelve, Zenga was bullied into giving voice, producing a mighty melodious bellow like Bessie Smith at full volume – while I, translated in seconds from would-be bohemian and man of the world to anxious suburban clerk, raced to close the windows (it was a sultry summer night) and made frenzied shushing noises, forefinger raised to my lips, for fear of waking the neighbours.

Like many good writers, Roy was relentlessly self-absorbed: one day he rang to tell me something, and when Petra said I'd been in hospital for the past ten days, he said simply, 'Oh well, I'll try again later,' and rang off. He lived for his writing – and his writing, at its best, was very good indeed, if a shade repetitive when taken in bulk. He too was essentially a sprinter, more at home with the essay than the full-length book: but from the stained and smeared typescripts that he had left on my desk, individual chapters of which were held together with rusty paper-clips or grimy bits of string, we put together a book which combined one magnificent long item – an account of his experiences as a lavatory-cleaner on the South Coast – with picaresque bits and bobs in which he wandered about the country, joining religious cults and consorting with those whom the rest of us pass by on the other side. On the cover of *The Lone Conformist* we used a photograph of Roy peering anxiously out at the camera, one hand clutching a polythene bag, the other raised up as if to ward off a demon, and on the back I printed the opening stanza of his fine Bellocian poem, 'The Bog-Cleaner's Lament'. Few books, I suspect, in the history of Chatto have ever sold quite so badly, but whenever I pluck it from my shelves – where it sits alongside Dick West's *An English Journey* and Michael Wharton's two volumes of autobiography – I find myself rocking with laughter, and sobered once again by the gulf that so often separates literary excellence and literary reputation.

A yard or two north of Trafalgar Square, William IV Street could hardly have been more central, so it was hardly surprising that figures from my past – and not only Charles Sprawson, grinning like a satyr as he leaned against my door post – should have materialised from time to time in my office. Among them was the unusual, goat-like individual in horn-rimmed glasses who, years earlier during the sporting events that formed part of Trinity Week in the summer term, had entered the annual walking race in a thick, moss-coloured three-piece suit, a walking-stick in one hand and a pair of orange brogues on his feet, and rapidly shot ahead of his rivals in vests and singlets and steel-spiked running shoes. Later in his career at Trinity he had acquired a certain *réclame* by rising in chapel to denounce a visiting preacher; and when he appeared, unannounced, in my office one day, I soon discovered that he had retained his youthful interest in theology. He looked much as I remembered from twenty-five years before, though rougher and wilder than of old: he was unshaven, his glasses, when they caught the light, carried a Kerridge-like imprint of thumb-marks over the lenses, and he wore round his neck, on a thick leather thong, a huge wooden cross, at least a foot long, which thumped against his chest as he made his points with the same comicality and vigour I remembered from the days when he and I and Ian Whitcomb used to meet for a breakfast of porridge and kippers after arriving off the Holyhead-Dun Laoghaire boat. He explained that he was now living in St Martin-in-the-Fields, and he had recently applied for a post as the professor of theology at a university somewhere in the American Deep South. He was, he said, fairly confident of being appointed – had rumours of his intervention in chapel filtered through to Kentucky and Arkansas in the intervening years? – but he needed another reference to clinch the matter. We were old friends, and had known one another for years: would I be a pal and ring Canon X – here he gave me the name of a well-known clergyman – who was acting as a go-between, and put in a word for him? This put me on the spot, since although I was very fond of my old friend, and had long admired his intellect in general and his triumph in the walking race in particular, I was in no position to assess his powers as a theologian. I told him as much, adding that I thought it would be wrong for me to express an opinion either way, though I'd be happy to provide some kind of character reference, for what it was worth. At this he looked rather crestfallen but – being a reasonable and decent fellow – said he could see my point of view; after which he rose to his full six feet four and made his way sadly out of my office, the great wooden cross swinging from side to side like a pendulum, in time with his melancholy lope. Later that afternoon I rang the eminent clergyman, who seemed to be awaiting my call; from time to time I spotted my old friend striding about London as if in training for another walking race, but no more was said about the professorship of theology.

* * *

Among whose who had watched the aspiring theologian surge ahead of his rivals in the Trinity walking race was ffenella, who had stood beside me in skin-tight white jeans and a guernsey sweater that emphasised the hypnotic swell of her bosom, her auburn hair lifting gently in the breeze and what seemed at the time to be a smile of infinite wisdom playing about her lips as the walkers strained and gasped before us, seeking, in vain, to narrow the gap between their mud-bespattered limbs and the flickering walking-stick and well-polished orange brogues of the man who led the field. In all the years since I had seen her last I had wondered how different my life might have been if, far from disdaining her naked back in the Greek prison cell we had shared together, succumbing instead to an attack of nervous diarrhoea, I had grasped with both hands the opportunity of a lifetime; and sometimes at night, unable to sleep, I had woken Petra to discuss at some length the feasibility of my presenting myself at ffenella's Chobham mansion, convincingly disguised as a Hoover salesman or encyclopaedia rep, and then, once inside the door, peeling off my gaberdine mac and false moustache to reveal that I had come to claim my own at last.

One evening, towards the end of our time in Oxford, the phone rang, and a husky voice – unheard for over twenty years – said 'Jeremy, it's ffenella here.' She was in Oxford for the night, and was keen to come and see us. Pausing only to change my trousers and straighten my hair in the mirror, I hurried away to collect her from her hotel, bestowing on her cheek a kiss of the kind I had never dared to impart during our time together in Greece. Seen in the bright light of our kitchen, she looked exactly as I remembered, her auburn hair and large green eyes and slightly hawk-like features seemingly untouched by time; and, to make the illusion even more persuasive, she was wearing exactly the same clothes (or, rather, their early 1980s equivalents) as those in which I remembered her striding across the Front Square of Trinity or perched on the steps of the Examination Hall, a gaggle of admirers gathered about her feet. She carried, in one hand, a broad-brimmed black felt hat; a poncho was draped over her shoulders, below which she wore a tight, sand-coloured guernsey, with vividly coloured

African beads in rows round her neck; her legs were encased in skin-tight black corduroy trousers and knee-length black leather boots. Of lines and grey hairs there were none; everything about her – her voice, her manner, her looks – seemed exactly as they were, as though time had been suspended, or suddenly put in reverse.

She was still living in Hong Kong, she told us, but would be coming home later in the year: she was keen to find a job in publishing, so perhaps we could meet for a drink in London when she got back? This seemed a good idea, and when, some six months later, she rang me at Chatto, I eagerly arranged a time and place to meet. Over the next couple of years we met sporadically in pubs and Greek restaurants and press clubs off Fleet Street: I was always pleased to see her again, and thought her as handsome as ever, but we met more as affable strangers without a great deal in common than as intimates (or would-be intimates) who had shared a small slice of our lives. I had no desire to revive the past – and nor, I'm sure, did she – but I longed with a sudden spasm of nostalgia to devote long, drunken lunches to raking over such past as we had together, to finding out what, if anything, she had felt about me all those years before, and whether my feelings for her had been in any way reciprocated; she wanted to talk about the present, about possible publishing jobs and where she could write reviews, and seemed oblivious to the directions in which I struggled to turn the conversation. She would claim, on the phone, to be suffering from a hangover and hint at an excitingly depraved way of life, but raised a disdaining hand when I suggested a second bottle of wine, and, far from setting the afternoon aside for nostalgia and carousal – as I was more than happy to do, braving the palimpsest of yellow stickers and losing her in expenses as a well-known lady novelist – she would start looking at her watch soon after two for fear of missing the quarter to three from Waterloo. I was glad when she wrote to say that my account of our adventures together in *Playing for Time* was accurate enough: but by writing about her, it seemed, I had – rather to my regret – exorcised her from my system. The ffenella I had known – or thought I had known – lived on for me in the pages of my book, and it seemed wiser to leave it that way.

In between providing references for would-be theologians and trying to nudge ffenella into the past, I struggled, without much success, to make my mark as a publishing editor. Although the success of a lucrative, specialised backlist – books on bridge or cacti or model aeroplanes – depends entirely on the expertise and the enthusiasm of a particular editor, Carmen was eager to experiment with areas of publishing in which neither the firm nor its editors had the necessary experience; a boom in cookery books was under way, and when I mentioned my liking for Jane Grigson she suggested I appoint her our cookery adviser and get cracking with a list to rival those of Michael Joseph, Penguin and Macmillan. I don't think Jane was entirely convinced by my powers as a cookery editor – no doubt she cherished memories of the cod in batter and date pudding with which we had regaled her in the OUP dining-rooms – but she kindly suggested one or two names we ought to pursue, the best-known of whom was Frances Bissell; but when the first of these books was actually delivered, and I found myself puzzling over basting tins and metric measurements and slow ovens and the like, I persuaded Carmen that it would be far wiser to pass the whole enterprise over to my old Trinity friend Hilary Laurie, who was a keen and competent cook and better qualified than I was to deal with such matters.

My travails as a cookery editor were not quite done, however. Among the authors I had inherited from the *ancien régime* was a colourful Cotswold lady called Mollie Harris, best known to the world at large as 'Martha' in *The Archers*. Over the years we had published innumerable books by Mollie about Gloucestershire life and lore, including an elegant little handbook on home-made wines – Mollie's samples of which, specially provided for the sales conference, had corrupted Dennis Enright and Les the Packer – and a scatological volume called *Cotswold Privies*, which sold in its tens of thousands and was crammed with noxious details of lavatory life through the ages. This was followed – rather than preceded, as might have been more logical – by a book of traditional Cotswold recipes as passed down from generation to generation, one of which began 'Take a tin of new potatoes'. Clearly this was not a book to be included in our classy new cookery list, so despite my ignorance of temperature conversion tables and imperial versus metric weights and measures, I was left in charge of the proceedings. Mollie's recipes were, on the whole, fairly simple and easy to follow, but my ignorance let us both down after she had forgotten to specify how much flour to include in her farmhouse Christmas cake. It never occurred to me to ask, nor did anything seem to be missing; but every December for years thereafter I received irate phone calls from puzzled middle-aged ladies – gingerly clutching the phone in butter-smeared fingers, the oven roaring in the background – who had got halfway through Mollie's recipe only to discover that it gave no indication of the amount of flour to be used. Every year I promised myself that I would write down or memorise the quantities concerned, so as not to delay the baking too long, but every year I forgot and had to refer my callers to the author, who may or may not have been at home; and after that I decided that perhaps I should give cookery books a miss.

This was probably well-advised, but I had not – as yet – entirely severed my connection with books about food and eating. We were now in the age of the 'foody', when the colour supplements were crammed with sweaty-looking men in chefs' hats and white hospital uniforms holding out for the reader's admiration two octagonal French plates, one containing anaemic-looking prawns laid out in the shape of a fan, the other some half-cooked vegetables in a similar formation, plus a mound of what looked like molten jam: as a coarser-grained omnivore who thought tripe and onions vastly superior to *tripe à la mode de Caen* and treacle pud in a different league to *tarte aux pommes,* I regarded such goings-on with a bluff and manly derision; but the history of food had always seemed a subject worth exploring, and early on in my time at Chatto I had commissioned Christopher Driver to write *The British at Table,* a learned and enjoyable slice of social history from the Woolton Pie to the present day. A scholarly-looking figure in specs, with a grey Assyrian beard – his upper lip was carefully shaved – Christopher was the editor of *The Good Food Guide,* and every now and then he would invite me along to sample a restaurant, telling me what to order and making sure that neither of us doubled up on any of the courses. With his beard and his notebook on his knee he was, I would have thought, an instantly recognisable figure, but he was careful to preserve our anonymity, speaking in a low whisper and looking stealthily about the room before darting his fork into my dish and masticating his prey at some length, with a good deal of smacking and wiping of the lips. On one such occasion he took me to a short-lived African restaurant in Covent Garden: the proprietor was a stout Nigerian in a shirt decorated with palm trees, the menu was written out on a piece of cardboard tucked under his arm, we drained our drinks from hollowed-out coconut shells, and Christopher scribbled feverishly on the notebook on his knee as we compared the differing flavours of ground-nut stews.

At about this time we were invited to a fortieth birthday party by John Hopkins, the American novelist on whose behalf Jerry Epstein had advanced across Norah Smallwood's sitting-room on his knees. A former Princeton hockey-player and Tangiers resident, John and his family had recently abandoned Chelsea for Buscot Old Parsonage, an eighteenth-century rectory near Lechlade, which was owned by the National Trust and let only to Americans; and to celebrate his birthday they had taken over the basement of the Quat' Saisons – still, in those days, in its original Oxford home. The only people we expected to know there – apart from our host and his wife – were Jerry Epstein, and Clare and David Astor, at whose house in Sandwich we spent Arcadian weeks in summer; and the first person we sighted as we rounded the stairs was Jerry, busily moving from table to table and changing the cunningly worked-out *placements* so that the five of us could sit together. In this he partially succeeded before being discovered in mid-move, a card in each hand: although David was left in limbo, three of us were sharing a table, together with a white-haired woman in her sixties, whose elegance and rather washed-out beauty was sadly offset by an unhappy expression and the abstracted air of someone who would obviously prefer to be somewhere else, or was more suited to higher things. So abstracted did she seem, and so un-aware of what was going on, that Clare – eager to make her feel at home, and worried in case she was baffled by the menu – began, in the kindest of ways, to translate the various items on offer and explain, very slowly, what they tasted like. Far from showing gratitude for a helping hand, our dinner companion looked unhap-pier than ever; and when – unwisely, perhaps – I revealed that I was in publishing, she embarked on a tirade against the iniquities of publishers, and how shockingly she had been treated by a particular firm, better known for their mystery novels than for elegant, sophisticated cookery books of the kind she was best known for. By now three of us at least had realised that our companion was Elizabeth David, and Clare was busily trying to make amends – quite unnecessarily, I felt – for having tried to explain the menu: but Jerry, who had never heard of Elizabeth David, or any other English cookery writer, ploughed on undaunted, urging her to get a good agent who could make her *real* money and offering her warm-hearted, ebullient tips about how to write books and how to deal with publishers' editors. Miss David grew ever more restless as Jerry's Brooklyn accent swooped and whirled about her head; and no sooner had our host hoved to to suggest a change of places than she scurried gratefully away, and we saw her no more.

Elizabeth David seemed to me, on paper at least, entirely admir-able: but for as long as I could remember – since I first went to school at least – I had rather despised, and been irritated by, those squeamish souls who complained about tapioca looking like frogs' spawn and pulled faces at the mention of brains or prunes or sweetbreads; and over the years I had elaborated a theory – never tested, and almost certainly unfounded – that those who banged on most about food, in the most affected way, had been subjected when young to the handiwork of mothers who couldn't cook and, as a result, lacked that instinctive feeling for the stuff that marked the genuine gastronome. Brought up on a diet of game in a Glouces-tershire farm not far from Mollie Harris, my mother was a masterly practitioner, whose oxtail stew and bread-and-butter pudding and jugged hare with forced meatballs were infinitely superior to anything I had eaten in a restaurant, in England or elsewhere; Petra and her mother were quite as good, and so were many of our friends; what had these geometrical patterns of half-cooked vegetables and gelatinous dabs of sauce to do with food as we experts knew it? Much to my delight, all my prejudices seemed to be confirmed when, not long before we left Oxford, we were invited to lunch in his garden by one of the well-known foodies of the time. It was a warm, sunny day, and we arrived to find at least forty other guests – dons, writers, a hand-picked team of fellow-foodies – milling eagerly about the garden of our host's homely Cotswold farmhouse, drinks clutched in their hands and anticipatory smiles flickering about their faces. The meal, when it came, seemed harmless enough, but that evening both Petra and I were convulsed by diarrhoea, and our prim little town house in North Oxford swayed and juddered to the pulling of chains. Next morning, as I boarded the London train, I spotted an eminent economist, seconded to the Bank of England, clutching his stomach as his frame was racked with gripes: minutes later an assistant editor on the *TLS*, after agreeing what an enjoyable day it had been (as it had), confessed that he and his wife had been brought low by an attack of the 'squitters'; and as the train hurtled towards Paddington several other pallid-looking figures emerged with similar tales to tell. All this gave me much unworthy pleasure, so much so that I began to think that perhaps I had made it all up in support of my theory; but then, a fortnight later, a literary editor added a PS to a letter, asking me whether I'd felt at all queasy after that lunch, and I knew that all was well.

An author we never published at Chatto, but of whom I became extremely fond, was the pseudonymous Alan Judd: the pseudonym had been employed, or so he told me, in deference to his career at the Foreign Office, but since everyone appeared to know who he was, and his Christian name was shared by the writer and his *alter ego*, it seemed a slightly redundant piece of subterfuge. He was a lean, fit-looking man whose pale, boney, smooth-skinned face was unblemished by the broken veins, reddening noses, deepening lines and unwanted whiskers common to the rest of us – a disparity I relished since, unlike those fresh-faced Oxford dons whose faces seemed so oddly untouched by time, he had, one felt, seen far more of life than most. He had started out as a PT instructor before joining the army, with whom he had served in Northern Ireland – the subject of his first novel. He had then gone on to Oxford as a mature student, after which he had joined the Foreign Office and been posted to an African country – the subject of novel number two. Though a reluctant reader of modern novels, I relished his Waugh-like combination of comicality and sadness, of savagery and wit. He was now, I learned, at work on a life of Ford Madox Ford, and at the same time hoping to win a silver medal in the national ballroom-dancing championships.

Alan Ross knew of, and shared, my liking for Judd's two novels; and when, leafing through the *Bookseller*'s export number, he saw that a successor was imminent, he rang me up to suggest that I might like to combine a review of the new book with some kind of overall assessment of Judd's work. Why not give him a ring, he said, and see what he's like? Obedient as ever, I rang Judd up at the Foreign Office – taking care to use his real name when talking to the voices in between, but invoking his *nom de plume* when I eventually got through – and asked if we could possibly meet. He'd love to, he said: the only trouble was that he was off to Montevideo that morning, and wouldn't be back for several weeks. Why didn't we meet at Leicester Square in half an hour's time and travel down to Heathrow together on the Piccadilly line, when he could tell me all I needed to know? I liked the idea, and I liked his amused and genial tone, but, alas, that wouldn't be possible since I was about to go into a meeting, and would be in disgrace if I failed to turn up: I had to get my piece written within the next week or so, but we both agreed that we should meet all the same, and that he'd ring me at Chatto when he got back from his tour of South American capitals.

A copy of the new novel arrived while Judd was in Santiago or Buenos Aires, and I fell upon it eagerly. It was – and here my heart began to sink – an Oxford novel; it was also, very obviously, a first novel of the kind that should have been consigned to a bottom drawer but had been unwisely resurrected, no doubt at a publisher's persistence. I disliked having to write a rude review about someone I admired who had invited me to join him on the Piccadilly line, and I was tempted to suggest that we drop the whole thing; on the other hand, this seemed in some way a dereliction of duty and no service to the author, and even if I had harsh words to say about the new book I could at least urge readers of the *London Magazine* to try the other two. But as I posted off my piece, I felt, with a pang, that hopes of a blossoming friendship would have to be abandoned.

A month or so later, not long after my review had appeared, Judd rang me, as promised, from the Foreign Office. Far from bearing a grudge, he seemed to agree with everything I had said about his new novel – which was indeed a first attempt, rashly disinterred. He suggested that we should meet for a drink in the St Ermin's Hotel, that enormous, ornate Edwardian pile that lay between Birdcage Walk and Victoria Street and was much frequented (or so I liked to think) by men from MI6 and wedding parties from Caxton Hall. I liked him at once, and urged him to join Dennis Enright and me for drinks in the Marquis of Granby on Tuesdays; and when, a year or two later, his novel about diplomatic life in a South American capital came out, and was even funnier and blacker than volumes one and two, I was happy to praise it, without reservations, in the *London Magazine*.

An author we did publish, and whose novels were even funnier than Alan Judd's, was Howard Jacobson. When we first met, he was teaching at Wolverhampton Poly (the setting, tactfully renamed, of his first novel) while his Australian wife Ros, who dreamed of singing Brünhilde in a pair of Viking horns, and had the flaxen locks required for the part, was running a restaurant-cum-craft shop on the rocky, storm-lashed north coast of Cornwall. A bearded, irremediably urban figure whose loose-fitting cotton suits looked quite out of place between the hedgerows, Howard drove down to Cornwall at weekends to help in the restaurant-cum-craft shop, haggling with reps whose briefcases were crammed with fancy goods and chalking up the menu of the day, and his improbable presence in the seat of King Arthur formed the starting point for the second of the new novels we published at Chatto. Howard came from Manchester: his father, a taxi-driver, was a magician, and when, years later, he lay dying in hospital and was visited by fellow-members of the Magic Circle, who clustered round to show him their latest tricks, he insisted (or so Howard told us) on being temporarily unplugged from the drips and cables that festooned his bed in order to demonstrate some new turn of his own.

Every now and then Howard and Ros would appear in London and we would have lunch in an Australian wine bar off Leicester Square that specialised in coronary-inducing foods; invariably a very great deal was drunk, and on one occasion Ros changed colour from honey to putty and had to lie down on my office floor and wait for the ceiling to stop revolving about her head. Howard was, in his own eyes at least, a late arrival on the literary scene, and in *Coming from Behind* he wrote to great effect about the dodges and sleights-of-hand with which, as the years go by, we try, in vain, to console ourselves for the triumphs of friends or rivals, pretending to avert the gaze altogether, or feigning an other-worldly disdain for the ephemeral or second-rate. I thought him the funniest novelist I'd read in years, with a Connolly-like eye for weaknesses and failings familiar to us all, but not everyone in Chatto shared my admiration; and by the time he and Ros moved back to London, abandoning Wolverhampton Poly and the restaurant-cum-craft shop, Howard had moved on to a rival firm, and we were able to meet – as we often did – simply as friends, without any of those resentments and antagonisms that bedevil even the most amiable relationship between an author and his editor.

When I was young I had little time for heroes: timidly perched on the sidelines of life, I was imbued from an early age with a certain scepticism about the gulf that divided appearances from reality, and although I read and re-read the adventures of Captain Scott and hoped one day to emulate the suavity of Simon Templar, otherwise known as 'the Saint', I remained bereft of, and immune to, sporting or social heroes to idealise or pin my dreams upon. And yet, by some curious paradox or psychological freak, as I blundered reluctantly into my forties and beyond, into realms of abandoned dreams and narrowing choices, I shed some of the cynicism of my youth and became, for the first time in my life, an unexpected hero-worshipper.

Like many of those who combine self-indulgence, unfocused literary ambitions and no very strong sense of purpose or direction, I had dreamed, when young, of leading a carefree, vaguely bohemian existence, travelling the world and somehow scraping a living; but although my life as a publisher had been a good deal more agreeable and interesting than many (interesting, that is, for those who like that kind of thing; tedious to a degree to those who prefer, say, cars or the commodity markets to books and reading matter), I had always been far too fearful and law-abiding and, in the last resort, conventional to realise the fantasies of youth. Publishing was a seductively safe profession which combined a certain dash and vicarious literary endeavour with respectability and a regular if modest salary cheque; I dreamed of exotic places, but felt homesick in Dieppe, grew bad-tempered in the heat and ticked off the days till I could come home again; the idea of living out of London filled me with horror, for quite apart from my love of the place, which grew in inverse proportion to its descent into decrepitude and squalor, I had been brought up to believe that only in London was one 'in touch', though with what was seldom specified, and I would have reacted with a kind of baffled pity had anyone suggested that time spent teaching overseas or (like my old friend Weale) selling sticks of dynamite to dwarf kings in the Cameroons might have provided a useful ingredient for an interesting life – a subject by which I became narcissistically absorbed as middle age swallowed me up, listing in my mind the qualities required as I strode about Richmond Park, and ticking off those whom I knew in terms of work, friends, travel, achievements and the rest. Wearing baggy corduroys and taking long lunches and notching up publishing parties seemed in themselves acts of defiance, bows in the direction of bohemia: but as the girls grew older, and changing nappies and reading *Our Island Story* out loud and pasting up strips of Laura Ashley wallpaper and collecting balloon-toting toddlers from parties in small suburban houses took up less and less of our time, I became ever more aware of the gulf that lay between the day-to-day, directionless life I led, pleasant enough as it usually was, and the dreams, however absurd, of twenty-five years before. Passive as ever, always waiting to be acted upon rather than making things happen, I indulged instead in vicarious living, through the lives of those I admired.

My heroes tended, as such figures usually are, to be loners, men who had made their own lives and followed their own interests and inclinations in ways that the more dutifully good might well consider selfish and irresponsible. Enviably free spirits, unshackled by – or indifferent to – the more humdrum demands of domesticity, of mortgages and pension schemes and retirement plans, they had, or so it seemed, a heady, Peter Pan-like quality, defying or disavowing the pomposity and the tedium and the self-importance of conventional middle and old age. Endowed with a certain childishness, a delight in the absurdities and the misdeeds of their fellow-men, an eager embracing of experience, a tendency to travel light through life – the absence of emotional and physical blubber leaving them nimble beyond their years, but unprotected at times against the cold – they somehow seemed to suggest, however misleadingly, that time could be held at bay, and that it was still not too late to join their elusive company. They tended to be youthful in demeanour, raffish in behaviour, and stylish in matters of clothing and personal appearance, as though a particular combination of shirt and tie or a way of holding a cigarette was the outward equivalent and manifestation of a graceful turn of phrase or an unusual view of the world.

Most of my heroes, as it turned out, were writers of one kind or another, all of whom led enviably independent lives and managed, in a manner engagingly (if misleadingly) suggestive of old-fashioned amateurism, to suggest that their writing was merely one of a whole range of activities and interests in which they excelled. Naming my heroes would be an invidious exercise: enough to say that, like many timid and sedentary people, I had a particularly soft spot for writers who were also men of action; and for those – in my own profession of publishing – who had the energy and the courage and the determination to start their own businesses, and to keep them afloat without compromising the standards they had set themselves.

Heroes apart, many of the authors at Chatto I most admired and liked had a long association with the firm, and were well into their eighties or beyond: V. S. Pritchett, N. C. Chaudhuri, Frances Partridge and, my particular favourite, James Lees-Milne, whose autobiography, *Another Self*, may well be the funniest ever written, and whose combination of comical self-deprecation and punctilious professionalism I found entirely congenial ('I'm far too gaga and too far gone to write anything more,' he would tell us when we asked him what he was planning next or urged him to release another chunk of his diaries, cunningly concealing his tracks behind a rueful, hangdog smile). Those of an older generation, it seemed, wrote far better than those of my age or below; I much preferred autobiographies or memoirs to the tedium of so many modern novels, Howard Jacobson's first two and Antonia Byatt's *Still Life* proving exceptions to the rule; insofar as I took on any books at all, I plumped for elderly non-fiction – which produced some books of which I was extremely proud, but hardly had the life-bestowing side effect of bringing fresh young blood into the firm. An odd man out was Vikram Seth, whose first book – an account of his travels in China's Far West – I edited after Hugo had taken him on: every now and then he would appear in the office or the Marquis of Granby, a tiny, bright-eyed figure in a luminous anorak, a rucksack hitched over one shoulder, and tell us how his brother was getting on in his attempts – ultimately successful, if only for a night – to be arrested as a political agitator. And a series of books I thought up, each of which dealt with a threatened item of street furniture – red telephone boxes, pillar boxes, fanlights and the like – brought to the list a team of young fogeys in three-piece suits: but, like the items they described, the series was soon discontinued, and that particular source of new writers dried up.

Soldiers – as I soon discovered – often wrote far stronger and livelier prose than professional literary men, and none more so than that robust adventurer Denis Hills, who – after a lifetime spent teaching and travelling in Europe, Africa and the Middle East, including a spell in the death cell in Kampala, prompted by his having described Idi Amin as a 'village tyrant' – was now living near us as a p.g. in a semi-detached in Twickenham. A sturdy, well-built man with the head of a fit-looking Roman emperor and a disruptive glitter in his eye, Denis had been a hearty and a rugger player in his youth, keen on debagging and vigorous practical jokes; and he would, I felt sure, have written me off as the wettest of the wet had I been around in the 1930s when, after leaving Oxford, he had taken himself off to see Nazi Germany for himself, and then on to Poland and Romania. He had been at school in Birmingham with Enoch Powell, whom he remembered as a pallid recluse and something of a swot, and when, one year, Denis and I were among the first to arrive at the *Spectator*'s summer party, and he spotted his old school-fellow standing alone in the garden, Powell could be seen to flinch away as his erstwhile tormentor advanced upon him, a satanic smile lighting up his handsome features, and his hands making a sideways jerking motion, as if passing an imaginary rugger ball – a movement I remembered with dread from thirty years before.

As far as I knew, Denis had neither pension nor savings, and his worldly goods were contained within the four walls of his rented room: but he remained, as he always had been, the freest of spirits, and I admired and envied in him not only the things he had done and the places he had seen, but the sense – inherent in so many of my heroes – of his life as a continuum. Most lives, it seemed, were divided into three watertight compartments, with the dreams and ideals of youth and adolescence giving way to the glum reality of uncongenial labour, however well rewarded, and the sad oblivion of retirement; to have spent one's life doing what one wanted, following the same passion and interests through from childhood to the

grave, seemed a luxury worth any number of pension schemes, and
one which few were lucky or brave enough to indulge.

Dick West shared to the full my admiration for Denis Hills – and
for a fellow-adventurer and veteran of the war, Peter Kemp, who
had worked out a cunning compromise between the demands of
office life and his liking for danger and distant places. We never
published him at Chatto, though I always hoped that, somehow, I
might be able to smuggle him through; but every now and then
Digby Durrant, a long-standing pillar of the *London Magazine*, and
I would meet him for a drink in the Anglesea Arms in South Ken.
After leaving Cambridge, Kemp had fought for the Carlists in the
Spanish Civil War, wearing a beret and a scarlet cloak and taking
part in a cavalry charge on a flock of sheep; his having fought on the
'wrong' side in the war made him thereafter a somewhat suspect
figure in the eyes of right-thinking people. He had fought with the
Partisans in Albania and been imprisoned in Poland by the KGB;
since then he had kept himself as a freelance insurance salesman,
taking time off to visit Hungary in 1956 and Rhodesia at the time of
UDI and Vietnam while the war was going on, and wherever else
trouble was brewing. I once received a nine-inch long postcard
from Peter and Dick in Nicaragua – Peter's old enemy Enver
Hoxha had just died, and its opening line read 'Stoke well the fires
of hell' – and I like to think (inaccurately, perhaps) of his being
parachuted into Southern Rhodesia in his sixties, a walking-stick in
one hand, pipe in his breast pocket and hearing-aid at the ready.
Peter and Denis Hills admired each other greatly, but met only
once, when Digby Durrant and I took them for a drink in the
Anglesea Arms. Set beside Denis, Peter looked a frail, almost
ethereal figure: he was rather deaf, and one eye shot out at an angle
in the manner of Jean-Paul Sartre's, and as he moved about on his
stick it was hard to imagine him peering through the jungle in Laos
or taking cover behind a rock. Afterwards James Henry and Denis
and I went off to Daquise's Polish restaurant in South Ken for a
session of black sausage and Polish beer and vodka. Halfway
through the meal Denis recognised among our elderly fellow-
lunchers his commanding officer, under whom he had fought with

the Polish Division up the length of Italy; they hadn't met for over forty years, and greeted each other in a flurry of back-slapping and Polish salutations.

Nothing could have been further removed from the wartime heroics of men like these than my orderly suburban life, in which the greatest hazards I faced were a wigging at work or a cautionary note from the bank manager or missing the last train home from Waterloo after too convivial a party. It was at such a party that, years later, I met a younger, female equivalent of those free spirits whom I could never resemble. The party was almost exclusively populated by middle-aged men in grey suits, and whenever I caught her eye – which I did a good deal, since her butter-coloured dress and sunburnt skin provided the only dash of colour in the room – she grinned back in a conspiratorial manner from under the brim of a flat straw hat. Then in her early thirties, Sara Wheeler was a fit-looking woman with greying hair cut like a brush: her round, flat face, vivid colouring and shining black eyes gave her the look of an Uzbek or a Kazakh. Despite her exotic looks – made more exotic still by vermilion lips, enormous earrings like miniature chandeliers, a dolphin tattooed on her upper arm, and swathes of costume jewellery that clinked and shimmered as she moved – she came from a working-class background in Bristol, and her accent still had a touch of Mollie Harris about it, or my aquiline Gloucestershire grandfather. Single-minded, hard-working and fruitfully self-absorbed, Sara seemed to know exactly where she was going. After leaving school she had found a job in Paris for a year before taking up an exhibition at Brasenose, where she had begun by reading Classics and then switched to French and Modern Greek. She had then worked for a publisher in Athens for eighteen months before transferring her trade to London; always a loner, and badly bitten by the travel bug, she took time off to move about the world by herself, paddling a canoe up the Amazon (into which she inadvertently knocked a book from the London Library), taking a raft down the Zambezi, contemplating the verities in a Japanese monastery, popping up in Poland and Paraguay, Australia and Malaysia. A longish sabbatical on the Greek island of Evia had resulted in her first book, a likeable if uneven account of the time she had spent there; and when we met she had just come back from six months travelling alone down the length of Chile. Before long she would be off to Antarctica, the subject of Volume Three: she had been appointed writer-in-residence at the South Pole, and nominated me Patron of her expedition, fighting off keen competition from the Duke of Edinburgh and the makers of Kendal Mint Cake. Since – or so I read in the *Daily Telegraph* – Antarctica was becoming increasingly popular with tourists, I warned her, in my capacity as Patron, that she might well find a Travellers' bus pulled up at the Pole, disgorging elderly Americans in pastel-coloured babygrows, and the familiar contingent of white-haired ladies in lime-tinted trouser-suits clutching outsize handbags, and was sadly disappointed when she reported that this was not the case.

I enjoyed Sara's company a great deal, in a suitably avuncular way, but – unlike my more elderly heroes – she filled me, quite unintentionally, with a terrible sense of how much of my life I had frittered away, how purposeless and lacking in direction I had always been. She had done so many of the things that I – and so many others – had dreamed of doing in the far-off days of our youth; and whenever she left, as she often did, for India or Jamaica or New Zealand I was overcome by ignoble, panic-stricken waves of envy and self-pity, a sense of chances lost and the implacable passing of time.

CHAPTER NINE

Waiting for the End

THOSE OF US who are late developers, or feel we have frittered away too much of our lives in uncongenial offices, can take comfort of a kind from the career of Nirad C. Chaudhuri, the great Indian author, and far and away the most extraordinary writer I came across at Chatto – or anywhere else, come to that. Mr Chaudhuri – the 'Mr' seems obligatory; I have never heard him referred to in any other way, while 'Nirad', even behind his back, would seem an act of profanation – was fifty-four when his first book, *The Autobiography of an Unknown Indian*, was published in 1951, winning the Duff Cooper Prize. Four years later, he left India for the first time to visit a country with which he was intimately familiar through a life-long immersion in its history and literature; back in India after only five weeks away, he wrote *A Passage to England*, a shrewd, witty and alarmingly prophetic account of a country that, to Mr Chaudhuri's evident dismay, had lost both its way and its nerve. More books followed, including a biography of Clive of India, a life of Max Müller, the Victorian scholar of Sanskrit, and *The Continent of Circe*, which caused outrage in India and was the first of his books to be published at Chatto. Then, at the age of ninety, he produced *Thy Hand, Great Anarch!*, the long-awaited second volume of his autobiography – which, despite its enormous length, took him only from 1921 to 1952, and was written entirely from memory. Volume Three may well have to be delivered from celestial regions; be that as it may, the two books constitute one of the great autobiographies in the language, and one of the few contemporary works one can imagine people reading in two hundred years' time.

I first came across Mr Chaudhuri while I was still living in

Oxford and commuting up and down to Chatto. He had left Delhi for good in 1970, and was living in the suburb of Harefields, just beyond the ring road. One evening he asked Hugo Brunner and me to dinner, together with our wives. We made our way to a dark and gloomy housing estate, and knocked on the door of a modern semi-detached of the 'town house' variety, with the sitting-room on the first floor and an undifferentiated patch of grass in front doing duty as a garden. The door was opened, very briskly, by a tiny, elf-like Indian in his eighties, clad in an immaculate grey three-piece suit with lapels on the waistcoat and cuffs at the end of four-buttoned sleeves. He ushered us upstairs with repeated cries of 'Come in, come in, come in,' and introduced us to Mrs Chaudhuri – a benign, soothing presence, a good deal larger than her spouse, who referred to her, fondly, as 'my ballast'. 'Now,' said Mr Chaudhuri, after sitting us down in a row on the sofa – most of Mr Chaudhuri's sentences began with a 'Now', delivered with great emphasis and a nodding of the head – 'Now, we shall have some wine;' at which he produced an extremely expensive bottle of white wine – though perennially impoverished, Mr Chaudhuri saw no point in buying anything but the best – and, after explaining in some detail the label, the grapes and the part of France from which it came, he poured us each a glass before proceeding with the business of the evening. Making quite sure that he had our full attention – Mary Rose Brunner had once disgraced herself by producing some knitting from her bag – he strode up and down the room before us, speaking incessantly and very fast, pausing only to emit a high-pitched cackle of laughter or to lay a small brown hand on one's arm when seeking, albeit briefly, one's views on a subject. He reeled off the names of Napoleon's marshals and Jane Austen's heroines; he reproved Petra, firmly but kindly, for holding her glass of wine by the bowl rather than the stem, and showed us how it should be done, with a good many cries of 'Now'; he hurried away to fetch his dhoti in order to demonstrate how, as soon as he put on Indian clothes, his gait and demeanour became more markedly Indian. Mr Chaudhuri is a keen determinist, believing that such matters as climate, food and clothing have a profound effect on the way we think and behave. He claims it is impossible to write good English on a diet of Indian food, so when he is writing in English he sports his three-piece suit and Mrs Chaudhuri serves up the meat and two veg; when he is writing in Bengali, he wraps his dhoti around him and she gets to work on the curries. I don't know about the diet, but I share to the full Mr Chaudhuri's views on the importance of uniforms, whether formal, like a nun's habit or a judge's wig and gown, or informal, like a publisher's scruffy cords or the City man's much-lamented bowler hat. Quite apart from improving the colour and variety of life, uniforms make it far easier for those inside – and for those with whom they have to deal – to believe in the work they do and the parts they have to play.

A year or two later we received from Mr Chaudhuri the typescript of *Thy Hand, Great Anarch!* – well over a thousand pages of it, impeccably typed and bound in sections with strips of pink tape such as lawyers use. Written in a strong, sardonic Augustan prose, rollingly reminiscent of Gibbon, it described in gripping detail his life as an unhappy, poverty-stricken clerk with the Calcutta City Corporation, his work with the Bengali politician Subhas Chandra Bose, his passion for European culture – saving up to buy 78s of Mozart, reverently collecting and pasting up reproductions of Old Masters – and the mixture of admiration, resentment and despair with which he viewed the last years of British rule in India. Most touching of all was his account of his wedding night. His was an arranged marriage, and he had never met Mrs Chaudhuri before; they lay together, very shyly, on the bed, while Mr Chaudhuri – never at a loss for words – spoke tenderly to his bride about European composers and quizzed her about the spelling of Beethoven.

Publishing *Thy Hand* was a problem in terms of length and price; we began by turning it down, but – to her great credit – Carmen Callil, without having read a word of it but sensing its importance, insisted that we should go ahead. Editing it was a contradiction in terms, since there was no way in which it could be tinkered with or improved, and Mr Chaudhuri had anyhow forbidden us to cut a word. Once I had finished going through the typescript I put it into a large suitcase and caught the train to Oxford to raise my modest queries with the author. Since our last meeting the Chaudhuris had moved from the Harefields estate to a red-brick Edwardian house in Lathbury Road, conveniently placed between the Woodstock and the Banbury Roads and altogether more suitable for a man of his eminence. Within seconds of my pealing the bell the white-painted door was snapped open and Mr Chaudhuri stood before me, wearing the same impeccable three-piece suit and issuing the same cries of 'Come in, come in, come in.' Moving briskly about me like a nimble outside-right, he escorted me into the sitting-room, a large, light room with a three-sided bay window overlooking the front garden. On the walls and the bookshelves were the etchings by Daniell of Indian scenes and the leatherbound editions I remembered from the house in Harefields; and in the middle of the bay window was a gigantic music centre, like an enormous metallic crab, the legs of which were resting on pads of black rubber sponge. Noticing my interest in this, Mr Chaudhuri gave a gleeful, high-pitched cackle and, taking me by the shoulder – to do so, he had to reach well above the level of his own head – he steered me towards a black sofa on the opposite wall, and sat me down in the exact centre of it. Clasping his hands together, and cocking his head to one side, Mr Chaudhuri explained that money should be no constraint in life, and that whatever the state of one's finances one should only buy the best: that particular machine was not only the best that money could buy, but – working from the first principles of acoustics – he had positioned it so precisely that anyone sitting where I was now sitting could be assured of perfect reproduction. To clarify matters, he pointed at some geometrical-looking lines that had been ruled in pencil on the wall.

Gesturing to me with a downward motion of his hand to stay exactly where I was, Mr Chaudhuri then darted towards a dresser in which, it seemed, he kept his large collection of gramophone records, selected several, and then – once again clasping his hands together – announced that he was going to subject me to a musical quiz. 'So,' Mr Chaudhuri announced – 'So', it seemed, was as popular and as peremptory a prefix as 'Now', and much in use that

day – 'So, I am going to test you on music. I am going to
play you a familiar piece of music, and you will please tell me what
is different about this particular recording.' The music was familiar
enough – *Eine Kleine Nachtmusik* – but so befuddled was I by Mr
Chaudhuri's rhetorical flow, and so convinced that I would never
pass the test, that I quite failed to notice that an extra movement
had somehow been smuggled into Mr Chaudhuri's recording; and
when I confessed, in an agony of shame, that I had no idea how or
why it was any different from more conventional versions, my
tormentor dashed the record to the floor with a triumphant cry, and
moved on to question number two. As the morning wore on I failed
on Bellini arias, and Love Songs from the Auvergne, and Spanish
gypsy music; and with every failure Mr Chaudhuri let out a devilish
cry and danced on the spot like Quilp in *The Old Curiosity Shop*
and dashed yet another record to the ground. Every now and then
he interrupted his musical examination with a literary quiz, plucking *Jane Eyre* or *Pride and Prejudice* in their leather-bound editions
from the shelves above his head, making me read a selected passage
and then (in vain) inviting me to explain some point of etiquette
from the early nineteenth century; and book after book rained from
his hand to join the other discarded cultural artefacts on the floor.
All this, alas, provided shaming support for Mr Chaudhuri's loudly
proclaimed view – half gloating, half regretful – that even well-
educated modern Englishmen are shockingly ignorant of their
culture and history, and that this is all too indicative of a nation in
decline. From time to time I tried to stem the flow by hoisting the
typescript onto my knee like a neglected baby, but Mr Chaudhuri
brushed such diversions aside. Once only was Mr Chaudhuri
distracted, when Mrs Chaudhuri – who had recently come out of
hospital – hobbled in on a pair of sticks bearing cups of coffee on a
tray, and a brick-shaped chocolate cake and a mayoral silver trowel
with which to cut it into slices: Mr Chaudhuri moved restlessly on
the sofa beside me while the coffee was being poured and the
mayoral trowel sliced to and fro, and no sooner had the door closed
behind his ballast than the interrogation resumed once more.

Over lunch – three courses, English-style – Mr Chaudhuri once again explained the label on the wine bottle before moving on to naval armaments and Hitler as a military strategist; and while Mrs Chaudhuri cleared away, we moved back to the front room – the floor still littered with books and gramophone records – and the quizzing resumed once more. Lunch and a couple of glasses of wine had done nothing for my powers, and I continued to fail every test; but Mr Chaudhuri seemed in mellower and more merciful mood, pausing every now and then to lay his hand on my arm and offer a word or two of paternal advice. At four o'clock I made my excuses and left: I had, rather to my surprise, become extremely fond of my host during the day we had spent together, but my brain – which had given a predictably poor showing – could take no more. Mr Chaudhuri showed me to the door, still talking and making his points with a cautionary finger raised, while his wife beamed indulgently behind him; and they were still there when I turned at the garden gate and made my way towards the Banbury Road and a restorative tea with the Brunners.

Some six weeks later Petra and I drove down to Oxford with the same suitcase to pick up the proofs of *Thy Hand*. It was a bright spring morning when we drew up in Lathbury Road, and Mr Chaudhuri – clad in a dhoti this time – was standing in the front garden with a spade in his hand and a deep hole at his feet. He had, he explained – his words interrupted by a gleeful, high-pitched cackle – been digging a hole two spits deep in which to plant a rose, and had dug with such force that he had sliced through a telephone cable, plunging half Lathbury Road into silence. We stood for some moments around the hole, admiring Mr Chaudhuri's handi-work, after which he led us into the house, chuckling to himself in a gratified way.

I found myself, once again, in the bright front-sitting-room, seated side by side with Petra on the same black sofa; but – much to my relief – there was no question of a quiz today. Mrs Chaudhuri made her way very slowly in the direction of the kitchen, whence came a pleasing whiff of curry. She reappeared some twenty min-utes later with coffee and an identical brick-shaped chocolate cake on a doily, the mayoral trowel gleaming alongside. While we talked to Mrs Chaudhuri, her husband, as agile as a ten-year-old, lay on his stomach on the floor before us, one leg cocked in the air above him, making last-minute corrections to nine hundred pages of proofs, and occasionally springing to his feet to consult a reference book.

Since then I have met Mr Chaudhuri three times – once in a dream, twice in the flesh – and my liking as well as my admiration have grown with each encounter. On holiday in Cornwall, I dreamed that Mr Chaudhuri was living in a shoebox with a snail and an octopus, and that when I scattered some grain he sprang out of the box in his dhoti and – elbowing aside the snail and the octopus – began eagerly pecking about my feet. Not long before I left Chatto he came round to Bedford Square: *Thy Hand* was a finalist in a literary prize-giving, and we were to escort him to the party and its subsequent beauty competition. The invitation had carried the words 'Black Tie' in its bottom left-hand corner, and Mr Chaudhuri – looking tinier than ever – had risen to the occasion, sporting a plum-coloured velvet jacket, a lace-fronted shirt and a mauve velvet bow tie. Emerging from the lavatory on the landing, he denounced us for hanging reproductions of paintings in such a place, which he saw as a form of sacrilege; in the taxi he spoke, at some length, about the Hohenzollerns' family tree; at the reception, dwarfed by the throng about him, he stuck to me like a twin, occasionally plucking at my sleeve to find out what was going on, and who was there whom he might like to meet. The reception was followed by dinner, the finalists and their entourages all seated at separate tables, agents and literary editors and publishers and journalists nodding and winking all about; and then, when the last mouthful of pudding had been scooped inside, and lips were being wiped and smacked, the lights were dimmed save for a single spotlight, which followed the figure of a trim-looking fifty-year-old – a television personality with an interest in 'books' – as he made his smiling way down the centre of the room, leapt nimbly onto the platform at the end, and turned to greet his admirers with a boyish, charming smile and one hand diffidently raised, as if imploring silence. He then read out the names of the finalists, saying a word or two about each of them; as he did so the spotlight veered round and picked out the writer concerned where he or she was sitting, and a great round of applause went up. When Mr Chaudhuri rose to his feet, looking lost and out of place, and dazzled by the light, I felt both touched and protective – and still more so when, quite rightly, he was announced as the winner, and picked his way through the tables to say his few words of thanks.

A month or two later we met again when Oxford – somewhat belatedly – gave him an honorary doctorate. Togged out in his three-piece suit, highly-polished black brogues and a child-sized doctoral gown, he seemed both nervous and delighted. After much banging of gavels and thumping of staves, the great doors of the Sheldonian swung open, the recipients of honorary degrees processed into the hall, and – when Mr Chaudhuri's citation came round – the Public Orator began to boom in Latin about Delhi and Calcutta. Mr Chaudhuri was standing next to a huge, bearded academic; his head was at about the level of the other man's elbow, and every now and then he would look up at him for reassurance, like a small child adrift among the adults. Later, over tea in Lathbury Road, I suggested to Mr Chaudhuri that, given his belief in the influence of clothing, he should try wearing his doctoral gown while seated behind his desk. But since Mr Chaudhuri is far wiser and better informed than almost any Oxford don it may not, after all, have very much effect.

Publishing – like journalism, or politics, or the law, or the City (at least in the days of bowler hats), or, indeed, almost any other business one can think of – is, by tradition at least, a bibulous affair, the best-known manifestation of which is the publisher's lunch. During the 1980s this noble institution was driven almost to the point of extinction, partly by Perrier culture, the adherents of which would toy with a lettuce leaf and a glass of water before hurrying back to the office on the dot of two, and partly because publishing became increasingly bureaucratic, so that in even the most old-fashioned-seeming firms editors were expected to waste far more of their time attending meetings and sifting through bumph than would have been the case some twenty years before. Neither the Perrier nor the paperwork made publishers any more profitable or efficient – quite the reverse – but by the end of my time at Chatto I had become, as far as lunches were concerned, a kind of coelacanth, a relic of a world that had long ago passed away.

In its ideal form – one's fellow-luncher a friend, his company paying the bill – the publishing lunch is one of the perks of a poorly-paid profession, and something eagerly awaited as the editor munches his sandwiches behind his desk, a copy of the *Bookseller* spread open before him, or restlessly stirs in his seat while a voice at a meeting drones steadily on in the background. When the great day arrives at last, the sensible luncher will clear his desk and cover his tracks as much as he can, just in case the lunch runs on a little longer than anticipated, or takes an unexpected turn, and at a quarter to one he will thrust his head – guiltily, and over-brightly – round the door of his secretary's office to say he'll be back around three and could she very kindly guard the fort, before tumbling into the street below, where other eager lunchers can be spotted striding purposefully out in the direction of Soho or Covent Garden. Like a sonnet or a blurb, the lunch itself falls into a formal pattern, with publishing gossip taking us through to the pudding stage, while any business is crammed in over the coffee; and after a flurry of ritual disclaimers ('Are you sure you can chalk this up? Well, next time it's on me') and expressions of mutual regard, the two parties will stagger back to their various offices, doing their best to creep up the stairs unnoticed by the Perrier-drinkers.

Enjoyable as they almost always were – blighted only by the claiming of expenses, something to be endlessly postponed and exciting terrible spasms of guilt – one lunch was much like another, and only a few stand out: a lunch with Dennis Enright in the Grigsonian dining-rooms at OUP which went on so long that the cleaning ladies hoovered about our feet and, still later in the afternoon, a puzzled-sounding colleague with a beard from the Educational Division rang me to say that Dennis had been found asleep on his floor and couldn't be roused; a disgraceful incident at the Gay Hussar, when Dick West and I got carried away and washed down the cold cherry soup and the hortobagyi with four large carafes of wine, so that, on regaining my office, it took me two hours to type a memo six lines long on the subject of Mr Chaudhuri, striking a key and applying the Tippex, striking it once again and re-applying the Tippex; and an unusual lunch at the Greek restaurant opposite Centre Point to which I had recently been introduced by James Michie, a cigar-puffing colleague at the Bodley Head who devoted part of the working morning to the crossword and was a much-underrated poet as well as the trans-lator of Martial and Catullus. One of Hugo's many good deeds was to persuade Richard Cobb to come to Chatto, where we published two volumes of autobiography, *Still Life* and *A Classical Education*, the typescripts of which consisted of sheets of blue Basildon Bond paper, typed across rather than up and down the page. Although I had no formal dealings with Cobb, we seemed to like the same sort of books, and I would send him forthcoming publications – Marie Vassiltchikov's *Berlin Diaries*, or *The Captain's Lady*, the book about C.B. Fry's sadistic wife – in the hope, often gratified, that he would review them or include them among his seasonal books of the year. We had arranged to have lunch, and when I asked Cobb whether he minded going to a Greek restaurant he simply asked 'Do they serve wine?' and seemed perfectly happy about it when I told him that they did.

At a quarter to one I came down to reception to find Cobb turning the pages of the latest catalogue. His face was pink and scrubbed-looking, and he was wearing a Bellocian black serge suit with the red flash of the Légion d'Honneur in the buttonhole of his jacket. We strolled round to the restaurant together; I ordered a bottle of wine, which we drank with our first course, and sum-moned up another; we chatted agreeably about books we both admired, and mutual friends like Norman Stone, and how, in a halfway reasonable world, Hugo would have been made the master of an Oxford college. I had forgotten, in the excitement of it all, to call in at the lavatory on the landing on my way down to reception, so while we were waiting for the main course I made my way behind the scenes, carefully stepping over the restaurant cat, which lay asleep in the middle of the floor. When I got back I found that my guest had emulated the cat, his head bowed on his chest and a low, contented drone emitting from his lips. He looked so peaceful that it seemed a crime to wake him; but his food would be getting cold and the new bottle had been uncorked, so I leaned across the table and shook him gently by the shoulder. He gave a juddering, startled gasp, like a rep at a sales conference suddenly woken from slumber, and began to gaze distractedly about him. 'Where am I?' he asked; and when I told him that he was near the Tottenham Court Road, he said, 'But I thought I was in Oxford – I really must get back to Oxford,' and began to struggle to his feet, as if making for the door. Eventually I persuaded him to finish his meal before hurrying away to catch his train and, with that agreed, he went back to sleep – the steam from the main course playing about his nose and misting up his glasses – while I finished the meal and polished off the second bottle of wine. After I'd paid the bill I once again shook him by the shoulder, and once again he woke with a start and asked me where he was. We made our way, very slowly, towards the door, and out into the windy street, Centre Point looming above us. A particularly ferocious tornado gusted round the corner, carrying sheets of cardboard and polythene bags before it, and, quite suddenly, ramrod stiff and with no bending of the knees, Cobb toppled over backwards. His head was only inches from the pavement when I caught him, like Nureyev catching Fonteyn, and brought him up to the vertical once again. That done, we made our way to the Tube station, for he was muttering once more about hurrying home to Oxford. I offered to go with him as far as Paddington, but he would have none of it, stepping sharply onto the moving staircase at Tottenham Court Road and gliding down to the depths; and I plodded back to the office, half relieved, since it was well after half-past three, and I dreaded the familiar palimpsest of stickers, and half guilty, in case the Professor of Modern History fell asleep on the Tube and ended up in Uxbridge or West Ruislip. I dreaded a phone call from Mrs Cobb saying what *have* you done with my husband; in the end, unable to stand the strain, and convinced that Cobb had boarded a train but woken to find himself

in Truro, I rang up Hugo in Oxford. Yes, Hugo told me, Richard
was fine, having tea in the garden and in splendid form; at which he
handed me over to my lunchtime companion, who sounded as
sprightly as ever.

Sometimes, in summer, we spent a week in Sandwich Bay in a
house which – in itself, if not in its surroundings – provided an
intimation of Arcadia, an elusive, ever-present promise that somewhere, in one of its dazzling, Delft-tiled, white-painted rooms the
passing of time would no longer apply and all manner of things
would somehow be revealed. Set at a right angle to the jade-green
sea and a steep and shingly beach, its gravel drive and long white
garden wall hemmed in by the scrubby, salty detritus of the shore,
the house had been built in the early years of the century by our
host's grandmother, a well-known lady politician of American
ancestry, who combined her political activities with a passion for
golf and sea-water bathing: golf courses and whizzing white balls
were all about us, the taps on the huge Edwardian baths offered hot
and cold sea-water as well as the more usual kind, and we shared a
double bed with the ghost of Ribbentrop. A cross between an
outsize golf club and a prep school catering for at least three
hundred boys, the house itself was an elegant and very English
confusion of gables and dormers and bow-shaped balconies and
white-painted mullioned windows and pebbledash and brick-
coloured hanging tiles and twisting fire-escapes, down which one
expected to see tweed-jacketed assistant masters chivvying boys to
safety while flames leaped from the dormitory windows and Matron
wrung her hands in the garden below. On the garden side of the
house was a long gravelled terrace, bordered by flowerbeds and
pink-flowered urns, and set out in fine weather with white-painted,
slatted reclining seats with handles and wheels, like long, be-
cushioned wheelbarrows; and beyond was a square, rather scrubby
lawn with sandy bunkers in one corner, on which golfers could
practise their strokes and children ride bicycles round and round.
Behind a red-brick wall, with a door in its middle and espaliered
fruit trees touching hands like paper cut-out men, were a kitchen

garden, a tennis court and a squash court. On the landward side of the house, like the tail of a high-backed dinosaur, were the former servants' quarters, occupying a miniature version of the main house and forming an integral part of it.

But the great quality of the house – apart from the hospitality of its owners and the promise of one's fellow-guests – had to do with its lightness and its whiteness, combining the nautical with the institutional, New England high-mindedness with raffish elegance. Even on the dullest, most windswept day, when the sea drummed against the seven-foot wall and the windows were smeared with salt, the house was ablaze with light, streaming in through the huge mullioned windows with their window-seats below, bouncing off the white-painted walls and the gleaming white floorboards, each one of which was eighteen inches wide, glistening off glass and highly polished furniture, fading the covers of the books that lined the walls. Most of the furniture was painted blue and white, and the armchairs and sofas were blue and white as well, though the sand-coloured drugget in the corridors bore a border of maroon along its edge. All this enhanced the nautical, blustery, windblown flavour of the place, as did the ornate red-and-gold painted windvane in the centre of the hall ceiling which, connected by a huge brass rod to a windvane on the roof, twitched over our heads with every slight change in the wind as we helped ourselves to a pre-lunch bloody Mary from a Jacobean-looking sideboard groaning with bottles, or leafed through the magazines on a glass-covered table, or drifted out onto the terrace to discuss the burning issues of the day – who was having an affair with whom, who was suffering from alcoholic poisoning, who had written what about whom, and where . . .

Creatures of darkness, of evasion and duplicity, we spent our days there in an unfamiliar blaze of light: working up an appetite for yet another enormous meal by walking into Deal, with its bosomy Regency houses and narrow piratical lanes, or up the beach towards Pegwell Bay, a vase-shaped power station looming above us, to watch frozen-looking nudists playing cricket on the sand or squatting uncomfortably among the prickles of marram grass; plunging into the jade-coloured sea, and finding ourselves being swept away in the direction of Cap Gris Nez, visible on a clear day from our bedroom window; sampling pints of Shepherd & Neame, or bicycling into Deal for a supply of charcoal biscuits to counteract the mayonnaise; reading in a wheelbarrow on the terrace, or in a blue-and-white armchair when the rain was drumming on the windowpanes; snoozing on our beds all afternoon; running a bath at half-past six, a large gin and tonic glinting through the clouds of steam; reassembling for yet another enormous meal, where new arrivals are introduced who will linger on after we have left, exciting stabs of envy as we drive away. Of all the company, our host and hostess were – as they should be – the two fixed points: both fair, irradiating light themselves, convivial, kindly, amusing and amused; both exuding that patrician ease and confidence that comes so unnaturally, if ever, to anxious, suburban souls, for whom the great house and its inmates represented, for a week or a long weekend, an escape from the struggles of everyday, a chance to pretend, among the billowing white and blue, that the *lacrimae rerum* – a hopeless love or infatuation, physical decay, the fright and tedium of work, hurtling into middle age and beyond – will somehow pass away, and that we will inhabit once again a world of prelapsarian ease.

In matters of conventional religion I remained as frivolous and uncommitted as I always had been when it came to the graver aspects of life. I loved the ancient rites, whether Catholic or C of E, and regarded their demotion as a form of vandalism worse – since more pervasive – than setting fire to the contents of the Tate or the National Gallery; I liked nothing better than to hover in some damp, crepuscular church and sniff the aromatic air and watch the candles flickering before resuming my endless perambulations round the streets of London; I disliked thin-blooded rationalists quite as much as the priggishly pious; and although, for all my numinous yearnings, I found it impossible to believe in a god, benign or not, or in any kind of organised religion, I had no objections whatsoever to my daughters being brought up as Catholics, if only because children who were brought up without any kind of religion – like those who were deprived of cats or hamsters

– somehow seemed to be missing out. For some years after our return to London we attended the local Catholic church, where the priest – whom I greatly admired – conducted the service in a curious nasal drone, preached incomprehensible sermons which drew extensively on the suffering of the saints at the hands of assorted demons (pliers and tongs were much in evidence) and on his own childhood experiences in Argentina, and, having spotted me smiling appreciatively at the back of the church, bullied me into reading the lesson on a distressingly regular basis. One evening he turned up unannounced on our doorstep carrying in his arms a lifesize statue of the Virgin Mary, clad in the familiar robes of blue and white, swathed in rosaries and wearing a beatific smile on her pallid, careworn face (had my mother come across her she would have recommended a dose of sea air, a brisk walk across the Downs, and a week at least of early nights). She was doing some kind of tour of the parish, he told us, and we were to be honoured with her presence for the next ten days; and, after parking her at the bottom of the stairs and bestowing a blessing upon us, he hurried away on other parochial business. I enjoyed the looks of surprise and indignation she excited during the time she spent among us, and although my daughters felt otherwise I was sad to say farewell.

Quite apart from a weakness for the memoirs of SOE men and journalists in macks, one of the many ways in which I was out of sympathy with the spirit of the eighties was in the matter of book design. Fondly remembering the small-format Penguins of my youth, with their plain lettered jackets and horizontal bands of orange and white, and much taken by the austerity and elegance of German publications, I loved books that could be carried about in one's overcoat pocket and, being printed on the lightest possible paper, could be read on one's back in bed without their boards gouging deep trenches in the sides of one's fingers: but we lived in an age of gigantism and hype, when publishers fought for space and attention in the bright new bookselling chains, with the result that each new production was made to look larger and more lurid than the last. Skimpy novels looked skimpier still in a format more suitable to a road atlas, like five-year-olds swamped in their mothers' clothes; solid works of reference that, twenty years before, would have had the self-confidence to wrap themselves in sombre lettering, sought to ingratiate themselves and deflect accusations of exclusivity or elitism by featuring on their covers pop stars or TV comedians, like clergymen or Radio 3 announcers struggling to be 'relevant'. I pined for the airy, heavily leaded pages that had once been the hallmark of the CUP, and for the dazzling patterns of Albertus lettering that Berthold Wolpe provided for the jackets of Faber books of poetry – legible gems of abstract art, far bolder and more beautiful than the pallid pastiches with which they were replaced. Of current book designers there was none I admired more than John Ryder at the Bodley Head. With their jacket lettering by Michael Harvey, and David Gentleman's title-page colophon of a beruffed and bearded Elizabethan, and a paper that had enough cream in it so as not to dazzle the eye, and a page that was instantly recognisable by its combination of generous margins, narrow type area and a typeface that was unobtrusively appropriate to the subject matter, his books stood out like elegant, streamlined whippets in a crowd of cross-eyed mongrels.

Two or three times a year I would be roused from my torpor by a quiet, nameless voice suggesting lunch, to which I eagerly agreed. I knew at once whose voice it was; I knew, too, that we would never meet in any other place than the Pizza Express in Coptic Street, near the British Museum, and that since he liked to eat early and was a man of regular habits, we would do so at half- or even a quarter-past twelve. (Another friend whom I met only in that particular Pizza Express, eating an identical meal each time, was a jovial, apple-cheeked academic called I.F. Clarke. Clarke, who had ended his days as the Professor of English at Strathclyde University, was an authority on the ways in which writers had envisaged the wars of the future, the sky over London darkened with gigantic, heavily armed airships and Oxford invested by regiments of mounted Uhlans with pennants fluttering from their lances: his great work on the subject, *Voices Prophesying War*, seemed to me to be one of the finest and most original slices of literary history I had ever read, but because its author bent his mind to what were considered the marginalia of literature, neither he nor his book was as well known as they deserved to be.) John Ryder was the most punctual and punctilious of men, the neatness of whose dress and habits was reflected in the grace and discretion of his books: I hated to keep him waiting, but almost every time I agreed to have lunch I was detained by a peremptory phone call or an unexpected summons just as I was hurrying from my room, with the result that I ended up running to the Pizza Express, and arrived with steamed-up specs and sweat-lashed brow. John in the meantime had secured a marble-topped metal table and ordered up a bottle of Italian red, and looked as calm and as orderly as ever, a quizzical smile playing about his trim, rather hawk-like features; and once I'd finished puffing my apologies ('Oh Christ, I'm so sorry, yet again – will you ever forgive me?') and mopping my brow and demisting my specs with a handkerchief that looked a good deal greyer than I might have wished – all of which John received with a deprecating grin, and a reassuring hand on my arm – it was time for the meal to proceed.

Ordering lunch was no problem, and not simply because John was well known to the red-shirted regiment of waiters and waitresses: he invariably ordered a Fiorentina, and since I had never tried anything except an American Hot, I was equally easy to please. As the meal advanced towards the pudding stage (cassata ice cream) we indulged in what was, after gossip, the most enjoyable of all forms of conversation – the gloomy, almost apocalyptic survey of the state of the world, with special reference to the publishing trade, accompanied by much shaking of the head and drawing in of the breath and quite inappropriate laughter. (In this the greatest practitioner was that most astute and underrated of publishers, David Burnett, whose underground bunker at Victor Gollancz was crammed with crates of wine and fishing tackle, as though he was anticipating flight or the imminent end of the world, and who was, with Miles Huddleston of Constable and Euan Cameron of the Bodley Head, one of the publishers whose company I most enjoyed.) Sad to say, not all our moans were of an agreeably self-indulgent kind: for John – who had started in publishing after the war – embodied an attitude towards the book as an object combining (ideally) utility and beauty, and towards the interdependence of literacy and typography, that was becoming increasingly rare and wretchedly undervalued. Hemmed in by hideous, ever-changing company 'logos' and childlike ideograms, we lived in an age of grammatical and typographical illiteracy, in which the graceful typefaces and intelligible prose favoured by Victorian city fathers or London Transport in its heyday had given way to the kind of gibberish offered up by the London Borough of Richmond on Thames, with its random capitals and out-of-place full stops ('Please help to protect our Borough's Parks and open spaces. *KEEP* Richmond upon Thames. TIDY'). And when one looked at the dismal standards of layout and design in books produced by well-known publishers – some of whom had, in their zeal to seem 'dynamic', abandoned their graceful 'literary' colophons in favour of ideograms more appropriate to earth-moving machinery – one realised how few seemed to share John's belief that the designer is there to assist the reader, and to present the writer's work in the most appropriate and unobtrusive way he can. Despite the tycoons and the takeovers and the million-pound advances, publishers seemed to have become timid, imitative folk, for ever changing their minds about how their books should look and glancing worriedly over their shoulders to see what their rivals were up to, and imbued with the defeatist notion that even the most literary or academic books should look like CD covers or glossy magazines. And yet, dazzled by overblown full-colour jackets or etiolated pastiche, literate book-buyers fell with cries of relief and gratitude upon a perfectly proportioned lettered jacket of the kind the Germans prefer, and which John masterminded for Graham Greene and others in his years at the Bodley Head. John and a few others – among them Ron Costley, who redesigned the *London Magazine* in the early 1960s, and worked for some years at Chatto – carried forward the classic rules of book design, like recusant priests in a hostile world. In the last few years the elegant, small-format book and even the lettering jacket have made welcome reappearances: evidence, one hopes, that their work has not been in vain.

One of Carmen's most engaging traits – shared with other lively and entertaining figures such as Barbara Skelton – was her love of animals in general, and cats in particular. She visibly stiffened whenever unwary or badly briefed subordinates waxed glutinous about children and half-terms and homework, and despite my detached, half-in, half-out approach to office life I shared her sense of outrage, partly on the grounds that (my own daughters excepted) toddlers were bad enough on the home stretch without intruding on the office, and partly because colleagues who were rash enough to raise the subject tended to do so in the sanctimonious, self-satisfied tones reserved for those whose eyes glaze over at the mention of childhood, and were keen (as I was in other ways) to bolster their sagging morale at work by contrasting the eternal verities of parenthood with the transitory frenzies of meetings and memoranda: but cats were a different matter altogether, and her face would soften and her eyes grow moist at the merest mention of a catnip mouse.

Quite early in our working life together I found myself plunged into a disgrace so deep that Carmen could only address me at meetings through gritted teeth, her gaze fixed firmly on a point a yard or so above my head, while everyday communications were restricted to formal memos and messages from her secretary. Far too much of a coward to march manfully into her office and have it out there and then ('Now what is all this nonsense?'), I cowered in my cell, grateful for the way in which sympathetic colleagues raised their eyes to heaven, and wondering for how much longer I would remain a pariah. About three weeks into my disgrace our old cat, Raymond, died in Petra's arms and, after a formal ceremony, was buried in the garden before I climbed on my bike and pedalled off in the direction of Oxford station and the London train. I must have mentioned our loss to someone in the office – perhaps my eyes were still red with tears – but after I'd been at my desk for an hour or so, hardly daring to venture out in case I ran face-to-face into my leader, the internal phone pealed out a cry and I found myself talking to Carmen. 'Darling,' the voice said, charming and seductive as its owner could easily be, 'I'm *so* sorry to hear about your cat. How *awful* for you. Are you sure you wouldn't like to take the rest of the day off?' I was touched by her solicitude but told her that, sad as I was, I would soldier on in the office. 'Well, feel free to do what you like,' she said, and I stretched back in my chair, warmed by the same glow of gratitude and affection that had formerly swelled through me after Norah had enquired tenderly after dear Petra and those nice little girls of yours, or lain her sad, misshapen hand on my desk. An hour or two later Carmen rang again. 'Jeremy, are you *sure* you're all right?' she asked, and once again urged me to leave early if I felt too overcome to struggle on. Next day, alas, I was back in disgrace, and remained so until, a fortnight or so later, we finally had it out in an exchange of views worthy of our sophisticated and articulate profession ('You're far worse than I am, and nobody likes you!' 'I'm not!' 'Yes you are!' 'No, I'm not! *You* are!' and so on for half an hour at least, while the production department on the floor above crammed their ears to the boards). Things got better after that, and – on my part at least – a certain wary fondness set in; and when, years later, one of Carmen's cats died, and she was almost distraught with misery, I remembered the kindness she had shown, and wished I could have somehow reciprocated.

And so the weeks and the months and the years rushed by, until one day I realised with a sudden stab that, far from being a new arrival, I had been with the firm for over ten years, and was nearer fifty than forty. The age of the put-upon spinster and the devoted old retainer was over; in the years since Carmen's arrival wave after wave of eager young graduates had arrived, learned what they could and left, and were now running well-known publishing houses while still in their late twenties, or writing books of their own, or making their names on *The Times* or the *Independent*. Lumbering heavily after my sprightlier, younger colleagues, I wrote a book of my own, which – apart from a couple of stinkers – got more and better reviews than it deserved. The publishers asked me, as publishers will, if I could somehow come up with a sequel, and I produced an ingenious outline using Claude's paintings, and my undergraduate memories of Greece, as a starting point. At Chatto, my face no longer fitted, and somewhere Arcadia awaited; it was time to be moving on.

CHAPTER TEN

Taking the Plunge

BANISHED FOR EVER – or so it would seem – from the painful delights of office life, my name removed from where it had hovered (rather fraudulently, I had always felt) on the Chatto & Windus notepaper, I happily resumed the habits of the freelance hack – brewing myself endless cups of coffee, watching an elderly lady over the road brushing her hair in her petticoat and inching her car out of the garage amidst Wagnerian clouds of smoke, waiting for the phone to ring, laughing at my own jokes, striding keenly across Richmond Park when I felt I'd earned myself a break, creeping guiltily up to bed after lunch and waking up to find that half the afternoon had gone. Apart from worrying about money – and even then I saw no reason why I should be paid more than a booking clerk on British Rail for sitting at home doing work I enjoyed – it was, and still is, a way of life that suited me far better than any other. I found no difficulties in settling down to work as soon as Petra had left for work between half-past seven and eight, and – much as I hated to see her go – I would shunt and nudge her to the front door, like an old-fashioned housewife in a pinny and a flower-patterned turban, eager to get her husband out from under her feet so that she could get on with the duties of the day; as a creature of habit, I soon established familiar routines from which I was loath to depart, in much the same way as London was criss-crossed with intricate private routes from which I seldom strayed. I relished being responsible only to myself and my family, and de-lighted at being shot of memos and meetings and the wearisome charade of having to feign enthusiasm or rage or delight or in-dignation about matters which, more often than not, I felt neither here nor there; I loved being by myself all day, still more so if I had the occasional lunch or trip to the London Library or publishing party to look forward to, as well as my Tuesday lunch with Dennis Enright and Ron Cortie, which provided, and still provides, the one fixed point in my week.

For a time, though, I missed the gossip and the company of office life and, in particular, drinking pints of stout with the sullen-looking girl with the pasty face and the purple hat, for whom I felt a fondness inappropriate in a middle-aged family man; and to exorcise that particular demon I took myself off to Arcadia on the grounds (bogus and unrealised, as it turned out) that by wandering about those gigantic, green-clad hills with a copy of Pausanias in one hand and a *Teach Yourself Greek* in the other, I would somehow provide the book I had been commissioned to write with a focus and a starting-point. No sooner had I bought my ticket on a bucket-shop flight to Athens and laid out my socks and underpants ready for Petra to pack than I realised that I was not the stuff of which travel writers are made. As an admirer of (in particular) Leigh Fermor and Thesiger and both varieties of Durrell, I had, years earlier, contributed to the revival of interest in travel writing. In between carousing with the chief accountant and his nautical first mate, I had sold – for a tenth of the amount that would have been extracted by a competent literary agent – Paul Theroux's *The Great Railway Bazaar* to Hamish Hamilton, and while at OUP I had commissioned Eric Newby to edit an anthology of Travellers' Tales, which he delivered to Walton Street in several tea-chests a week before I left to go to Chatto, removing them to Collins a year or two later after my successor, daunted by the scale of the undertaking, had managed no more than to riffle through a handful of pages before sinking back exhausted: but faced by the possibility of travelling as far as Calais or the Isle of Wight, I was overcome by unmanly terror. I had no desire to go anywhere by myself. I was far too timid and law-abiding to stray from the beaten track, or to enjoy the kind of adventures that genuine travel writers gathered hungrily about them and wrote up with enviable ease; I fell asleep over Pausanias, and my efforts to teach myself Greek proved even more ineffectual than earlier stabs at French and Italian; quite apart from being unable to understand a word they were saying, I was much too stiff and English to nudge mustachioed peasants in the ribs or drink interminable toasts under a trellis of vines before joining the locals in a frenzy of Balkan dancing, our arms linked like the members of a rugger scrum. Very much to my relief, my friend Jane, the co-owner of Sparrows Hanger, with whom we had spent so many rainswept holidays on the Isle of Wight, asked if she could possibly come with me, since she needed to do some paintings for an exhibition. Quite apart from enjoying her company a good deal – both of us preferring long lunches and a snooze in the afternoon to plodding round sites with a guidebook to hand – I knew that she was just as fearful and unresourceful as I was; nothing could be nicer, I assured her, and within twenty-four hours we had not only boarded a midnight flight and spent the early hours dozing on a bench in Athens railway station – itself no larger than Bishopstone Halt, halfway between Seaford and Newhaven – but were trundling through the peaks and gorges of Arcadia on a train two carriages long, moving at speeds of up to twenty miles an hour. Already suffering from intense suppressed diarrhoea, I kept falling asleep as the land of nymphs and shepherds wound its way, very slowly, past the windows of the train, looking a good deal sterner and rockier than the languid Claudian scenes amongst which I had whiled away the occasional lunch hour across the road from William IV Street. In the seat behind me was a gaggle of middle-aged Greeks, bent low in conspiratorial conversation, whose voices sounded, to my comatose ear, so surprisingly English that I became convinced that we were travelling with a party of aldermen from the Midlands. Every now and then, during a waking moment, I would stagger to the end of the compartment with the intention of assuaging my incipient diarrhoea and its accompanying gripes; but at the sight of the train's lavatory I fell back, gasping for air, and returned cross-legged to my seat, preferring to writhe and sweat and clamp my buttocks together like a fist than to add to the mounds and khaki-coloured streaks that lay behind that harmless-looking wooden door.

Kalamata, our destination, was the place in which – as I knew from my reading and re-reading of *Mani* – Leigh Fermor and Xan Fielding, overcome by the heat, had moved their restaurant table into the sea, the waiter dancing attendance behind them, recharging their glasses of retsina and bearing their fried fish to them through the waves. Since then it had been partially destroyed in an earthquake, and rebuilt in raw-looking concrete, with rusty nails sticking out of the top in the customary Greek fashion: the vertical mountains behind, the sea before us, the custard-coloured sand, the jagged purple backbone of the Mani striding into the distance were as bright and shimmering as the scenes I remembered from trudging round Greece thirty years before, sweating heavily into my Aertex shirt and casting hopeless, lovelorn glances in the direction of ffenella, but in other respects this seemed a very different place from the idyll I'd imagined. I had arranged to pay Leigh Fermor a visit; and while a team of vociferous workmen, looking like extras from a Passion Play, were banging more rusty nails into planks of wood in the marble-lined entrance hall of our hotel, I struggled to get through to my hero's household on a cowpat-shaped Bakelite telephone, one finger jammed into my left ear and the receiver screwed against the other. Eventually, piercing crisply through the whirrs and hisses on the line and the bangs and cries of the carpenters, an English voice, both authoritative and friendly, could be made out inviting us to lunch next day. All gripes and intestinal disorders long behind us, we picked up our bags – Jane's unnaturally leaden since, for some curious reason, she had insisted on bringing with her an ankle-length black overcoat, a woollen scarf, a felt hat, a pair of leather boots and a full supply of winter underwear, as well as brushes and paints, several books in hardback editions, and a more sensible selection of summer clothes – and set off through the sunshine towards the Kalamata bus station and the first of a succession of olive-green buses, their windscreens crammed with beads and icons and doilies, the air loud with bouzouki music and the cries of the passengers, in which Jane and I, and then Petra and I, inched and jolted our way round the Peloponnese over the next five weeks or so.

After winding our way through a green vertiginous landscape of ravines and pinnacles and teetering Frankish castles, we booked into a small hotel which, together with the sea slapping on the rocks below, and the Neapolitan sweep of the bay, and the dusty ochre-coloured paths, and the spring flowers, and the thyme-scented air, so reminiscent of a roasting leg of lamb, and the tortoise-like Byzantine churches perched on spurs of the hills behind, and the pervasive whiff of orange blossom, and the pitchers of pinkish retsina, and the statue of a whiskered national hero which looked as though it had been carved out of molten lard, suggested at last a Claudian paradise; it proved to be one of the kindest and most congenial places in which I have ever stayed, so that – far from exploring the bare green mountains of Arcadia as intended, Pausanias in hand – all three of us found ourselves drawn back there again and again to eat long lunches and even longer suppers, and doze on our beds in the afternoon and stroll about the ochre-coloured paths while the sun went down over the Neapolitan bay and the great bulk of Mount Taygetus, still with a dab of snow on its peak, faded into blackness. On the ground floor of the taverna was a dark, shuttered dining-room and bar, with a fire crackling in one corner and the kitchen behind; a marble staircase led upstairs to five clean, Scandinavian-looking bedrooms, with lavatories very different from those we had encountered on the slow-moving train or at Kalamata bus station, and wide, wooden-slatted balconies round which the swallows swooped and swirled, and from which one could look out through the trees on the terrace, lit up at night by flickering candles placed in gourds, to the blue-black sea and a distant coastline beyond. The terrace itself was wide enough to hold seven or eight wooden kitchen tables, each surrounded by four straw-seated wooden chairs – bent forward as if in prayer when not in use – and covered by pink-and-white gingham table-cloths, held in place by snapping plastic clothes pegs; two large, dusty-looking trees stood in the middle of the terrace, while additional vegetation was provided by pink oleanders planted in blue-painted olive-oil drums, by the familiar lattice of vine and trellis covering a corner much favoured by elderly Austrians in socks and shorts, and by a great burst of bougainvillaea along one end of the building. To one side of the taverna stood the ruins of an olive-oil factory, the chimney of which – more evocative of Witney and blanket-making than of the southernmost tip of Greece – was the first thing that caught one's eye from a great height as the olive-green bus, freighted down with black-clad crones with faces as seamed as scenes of soil erosion and flat-capped elderly men in collarless shirts, brown pinstripe jackets and grey flannel trousers, wound its way down from the foothills of Taygetus in a series of hairpin bends; on the other was a tiny jetty where the fishing boats tied up, off which Jane could sometimes be spotted swimming slowly up and down, her head held upright out of the water like that of a paddling dog. On the seaward side of the terrace, beyond a bulbous-jointed, blue-painted railing such as I remembered from the wind-lashed front at Seaford, were the rocks on which a solemn-looking German with a towel round his waist was sighted at dawn worshipping the sun – balanced on one leg, eyes closed, hands clasped before him, a sound like the drone of a bagpipe competing with the lap of the waves – and from which an occasional white-bodied Englishman would dive or (in my case) lower himself into the deep green waters, whatever the time of year. When Jane went home and Petra took her place – meeting this beaming, Tartar-faced figure off the train from Munich at Athens station was one of the most touching moments of my life – I worried that our motherly landlady would look at me askance, or even show me the door; but not an eyebrow was raised – quite rightly – and within minutes of her arrival Petra was as enthusiastic and as welcome an inhabitant as Jane had been before her.

Although the Leigh Fermors' house was only twenty minutes' walk away, our landlady's son insisted on driving us there in his open-backed pick-up van, Jane sitting beside him in the cab while I perched on a sideboard in the back, feeling doggy and pleased with myself, and very far from the world, so recently abandoned, of office Christmas parties and bibulous speeches of farewell. Perched in a green and shady inlet, with the dizzying mountains behind, a rocky, secluded bay below, cypress and olive trees scattered all about and only the occasional concrete monster with its crown of rusty nails peering over the brow of the hill like a demon about to spring or the outrider of a loud barbarian army, the Leigh Fermors' house – designed and built by them – was a long, low, elegant building, with a pantiled roof and large, cool rooms and a loggia and stone floors and an abundance of greenery and flowers. We approached the house via a heavy gate in a wall with a tiny barred window like that in a prison door, beyond which a patterned black-and-white pavement made from upended pebbles led to a cavernous front door; we were met there by a maid, who led us through the shadowy cool of the loggia to the room in which the Leigh Fermors were sitting. Our host at once sprang up to greet us and hurried to where we stood blinking in the sudden darkness, one hand outstretched and an eager smile lighting up his features.

Although we had corresponded while I was at Chatto, I had only met Patrick Leigh Fermor once before, at the publishing party Charles Sprawson had crashed. There I had found myself addressing a stocky, square-cut, ruddy-featured man in a neat, charcoal-coloured suit and a spotted silk tie and highly polished shoes; with his wavy, cleanly-parted hair and bright eyes and firm jaw and even firmer handshake, he had the look of an old-fashioned naval officer who was now running a training ship, or acting as bursar in one of the more congenial and raffish Oxford colleges: a far cry, it seemed, from the conventional literary man (yet a far better writer than all but a handful) or from the scruffy, tweeded, shock-haired figures who jostled and wavered about him, clutching and re-charging half-empty wine glasses and looking anxiously over each other's shoulders at the new arrivals pouring into the room. He appeared to be the kind of Englishman – familiar from the films of the forties, or from the memoirs of retired members of SOE – who had become almost extinct since the 1960s and for whom I had come to feel such a mixture of nostalgia and admiration: and I was pleased and reassured to see that, out here in his adopted country, he looked and sounded as English as ever. Despite the heat, he was wearing a fiery tweed jacket with a ferocious check of the kind preferred by Lord Scamperdale in *Mr Sponge's Sporting Tour* or by

Evelyn Waugh when working in his library, grey flannel trousers, a blue-and-white spotted silk tie, and well-polished brogues. His wife, Joan, was a tall, elegant, agreeably diffident figure in dark glasses, clad in a cotton smock with kangaroo pouches in front, dark blue cotton trousers and espadrilles. They had been sitting in a square, Turkish-looking bay window overlooking the garden, and they urged us to join them there and help ourselves to several glasses of ouzo and a large plate of taramasalata which stood on the table before us since – or so Mrs Leigh Fermor warned us, in the kindest possible way – this might well be all the lunch there was. (Were Mediterranean vagaries and volatility involved? Would a sudden cry of rage from behind the scenes, followed by the dashing of crockery to the ground, a muffled sob and the patter of footsteps hurrying from the room announce that lunch was no longer a possibility?) As Paddy poured us our opening glass of ouzo, I peered unashamedly about me. We were sitting in a large, book-lined room lit by tall, mullioned windows with pale grey shutters matching the paint on the walls. The floor was of stone, and a padded bench ran round the edge of the room, in the middle of which were sofas and comfortable, low-slung chairs and tables covered with flowers and books and an old-fashioned leather-topped desk. The bookshelves stretched up between the mullioned windows to the room's crowning feature – a coved wooden ceiling, which looked like a giant waffle iron painted in dark green. Cool, bright, elegant and unashamedly civilised, it was – like the house itself – a magical spot, and one in which any reasonable soul might be tempted to linger for ever.

After several ouzos and much dipping into the taramasalata – which had since been joined by olives and squares of cheese and peppery slices of sausage – the maid reappeared in the door to say that, despite our hostess's worst fears, lunch was now ready; and we moved out into the shadowy loggia and down a flight of steps onto a patio paved with a mosaic of pebbles where a table had been laid under a tree. Paddy equipped us all with large straw hats – large enough even for me – and the first of several red metal jugs of retsina was placed on the table. As the meal progressed and the jug was replenished and the conversation stormed to and fro – embracing literary gossip, publishers, mutual friends, SOE, the meaning of 'rupestral', Surtees, Smollett and the horrors of modern Romania, from where our host had recently returned – Paddy, overcome perhaps by heat and the excitement of the moment and the vigour with which he hurled himself into each new anecdote, discarded first his fiery tweed jacket, then his blue-and-white spotted silk tie, and finally, though it was hard to see what cooling effect this might have, a pair of royal blue velvet braces, pleasing variants on the more familiar clubman's scarlet. For some reason I found myself in charge of the retsina, earning a mild reproof for filling the glasses too full – one should never fill them more than half-full, I was told, since that way one ended up drinking more; and so the afternoon wore agreeably away.

Like all sensible people – my mother, snoozing away each afternoon on her bed, my Gloucestershire grandfather tilted back in his chair, a red-and-white spotted handkerchief draped from his Wellingtonian beak, whole armies of matrons and prep school masters – the Leigh Fermors were firm believers in the afternoon rest, the absence of which (and of let-down beds specially installed for that purpose) seemed so obvious a flaw in conventional office life; and instead of sending us on our way after we had risen from the table – pushing back our chairs to a rumble of appreciation, rising unsteadily to our feet while at the same time dabbing our lips with our napkins and taking a last, long swig from the wine glasses before us – they insisted that Jane and I stretch out on the padded seats in the library for a couple of hours of well-deserved slumber. Towards evening our host reappeared, bearing with him a pot of tea and tea-cups on one of those oriental-looking trays that is suspended from above rather than carried from below, along with a towel and bathing-costumes in case we wanted a swim in the bay below the house, which was reached by a steep set of steps. He explained that, alas, he would have to desert us for a while since the plumber was about to descend on a long-awaited visit, so we insisted that we must stay not a moment longer, clogging up the house while men in boilersuits bustled to and fro with plungers and rods at the ready.

Mrs Leigh Fermor said she would walk part of the way back with us, through a landscape of dappled olive trees and lizards sunning on dry-stone walls; and as we moved away in single file I caught a last glimpse of Paddy's face, like that of the Cheshire Cat, grinning through a cactus bush and crying out in a voice of concern 'Joan, Joan, is there anything the plumber needs to do in your part of the house...?'

A day or two later we encountered our host once again. We had been bathing off the shingle in the bay, and as we clambered away from the beach we surprised a spruce, briskly-stepping figure striding purposefully out along the dust track that ran parallel to the sea, walking-stick in hand, a two-day-old copy of the *Telegraph* tucked under his arm; with his English-looking chestnut-coloured cords and his dark blue sweater, he looked more like a senior naval man than ever. He reeled slightly as I engaged him at once in yet more literary gossip, backing nervously down the path as I advanced upon him, bathing-costume dangling from one hand and Boswell's *Life of Johnson* clutched firmly in the other; but he was as charming and as courteous as ever, expressing polite hopes that we would meet again soon, most probably in London, before setting briskly out in a westerly direction. Since then we have met from time to time, and my admiration for the ways in which he evokes places and pleasures and vanished worlds and the dreams and expectations of youth grows greater with every re-reading.

In the weeks that followed I made no real effort to get to grips with my elusive subject-matter, but happily trundled about in olive-green buses and a rented silver-grey car, like any other middle-aged tourist suddenly freed from the restraints of office life. Several weeks after the author of *Mani* had stepped smartly into the sunset, his walking-stick flickering to and fro, Petra and I took the Bari ferry from Corfu – the Arcadia I remembered from thirty years before still recognisable, just, between the naked, ham-coloured lager bellies and buttock cleavages peeping out from below waists that seemed, in contradiction to all natural laws, to be wider than the parts above and below. At Bari we jumped on the overnight train to Rome. I wanted –

or I thought I wanted – to take a look at Tivoli, where Claude had painted some of his Arcadian scenes; Petra had to leave me there and return to office life, but Charles Sprawson had decided to come out to Italy to research his book about literary swimmers, and we had agreed to travel round together for a week or two in pursuit of sacred pools and glowing Claudian scenes.

At Rome station there was no sign of the Swimmer – as Alan Ross and I liked to refer to our friend – and we paced anxiously up and down, peering in ticket halls and left-luggage offices and wondering what we should do if he never turned up. And then, quite suddenly, he had loomed up behind us, leaning against a pillar in much the same way as he had leant against my office door so many times in the past, materialising silently out of the darkness in his familiar uniform of open-necked shirt, V-necked sleeveless pullover, corduroy trousers and brand-new gym shoes, his face as rubicund as ever and a Mephistophelean smile lighting up his Cranachian features and his unwavering bright blue eyes. Some months earlier he had published in the *London Magazine* an odd, obsessive piece about swimming, in which unusual lore about Byron and Rupert Brooke and Leni Riefenstahl had been inter-woven with Charles's own experiences – apart from swimming the Hellespont with his eldest daughter, pausing in mid-stream to allow a Russian tanker past, he had spent much of his time on his trips to America swimming vigorously up and down legendary Hollywood pools into which he had somehow insinuated himself. Charles's piece had excited an admiring postcard from Simon Raven, an equally enthusiastic letter from an Anglican bishop, an expert on knitting, who revealed that he was writing a history of bathing-costumes, and – most importantly of all – the suggestion from Jonathan Cape that he should write a full-length book on the subject; which was why he was now in Rome, ringing up a puzzled-sounding soda-water company to find out the whereabouts of the Egarian Spring, the first of many such spots that we would be visiting over the next two weeks.

Charles had brought with him as a mentor a book which, it turned out, had inflamed us both with visions of Arcadia when we had read it as schoolboys in the late 1950s: Gilbert Highet's *Figures in a Landscape*, in which he set the lives and works of six Roman poets against the apparently idyllic pastoral scenes among which they had grown up. With Highet at the ready – the soda-water company had proved surprisingly unhelpful, baffled perhaps by Charles's refusal to attempt any language other than English, or to adapt his rumbling, staccato manner of speech in any way when addressing foreigners – we set out in search of the Egarian Spring, jolting south along the Appian Way into a scruffy, suburban landscape which Claude had once painted, the dome of St Peter's gleaming like an egg in a fold in the hills, and pushed our way downhill through brambles to where the sacred waters flowed out from a cleft in the rock, the Roman basin still intact but the spring itself littered with rubbish and strewn with brightly-coloured rags. We visited Horace's villa, where I dozed among the ruins while Charles followed the course of a stream uphill in search of the Bandusian Spring, returning two hours later with his only pair of trousers plastered in mud to his thighs. The view from Tivoli looked like Slough, the waterfalls of the Villa Gregoriana smelt of sewage, and the fountains had been turned off in the Villa D'Este, where empty Coke tins rattled along the gravel paths and black polythene rubbish bags flapped in their cages in the wind, and the dried-up Renaissance basins carried notices in three languages warning visitors not to touch, let alone drink, the celebrated waters. Clitumnus, the most sacred spring of all, had a motorway running along one side, yet despite the howling traffic smartly-dressed Italian families were moving sedately along its gravel paths, like Edwardians round the lake in St James's Park. The spring itself appeared to bubble out from under the motorway, spreading into a clear, pebble-bottomed pond before trickling away through meadows to the west. Like a proprietorial dog lifting its leg, Charles felt it his duty to somehow immerse himself in any waters with literary or mythological associations, yet Clitumnus on a Sunday afternoon with its families sunning themselves on benches and its uniformed attendants strutting importantly up and down with their chests stuck out and their hands behind their back, was clearly forbidden ground. As he scowled at the happy throngs milling about us, Charles's brow grew darker and more misanthropic, and he lashed at the shingle with his foot in anger, like a denizen of Olympus watching a nymph escape his clutches. Unable, in the end, to bear it any longer, he undressed behind a tree – the trunk of which was a third the width of his chest – and eased himself into six inches of water, overlooked by a cow on the other side of the pool and a puzzled-looking fisherman, while I kept guard; and honour was satisfied at last.

I had no interest in plunging into ankle-deep pools or contorting myself into a mossy crevice from which, or so I was assured, some sacred water sprang, nor did Charles expect such antics of me; but it was a very different matter when it came to the more strenuous kind of swim. Within hours of strolling about the Baths of Caracalla with my hands in my pockets I found myself looking down from a circular, saucepan-shaped rim on the black, bottomless waters of Lake Nemi, the volcanic lake in the Alban Hills where – according to Sir James Frazer – the Fisher King was slain by his successor in the Sacred Grove; and as we made our way down a side as steep as a pudding bowl's – a boat inching its way across the metallic surface of the lake below like a water-beetle in a pond – it became apparent that we were expected to swim not only across it, but back again from the other side to where we would leave our car, our clothes and (most importantly of all) my specs. Suggestions of postponement or even cancellation were brushed aside with a brusque 'Don't be so wet'; nor were my protestations more than half-hearted, for although I dreaded the embarrassment of being struck down by cramp or a seizure halfway across and dragging us both to the bottom as Charles fought, in vain, to rescue me, I welcomed any opportunity to assuage, however absurdly, my lifelong feelings of physical inadequacy and ineptitude, provided it didn't involve diving off a ninety-foot cliff or taking part in any form of organised game. We parked our tiny rented car on one side of a small, crescent-shaped beach; on the far side of the lake – shimmering in the heat, and reduced to a fuzzy-edged blur as soon as I removed my specs – was a large white house which Charles told me we should aim for in case we ended up slicing across one side of the circle instead of heading through the middle. We picked our way down the beach, through mud and stones and the spiky grass and lace-like foam at the water's edge, and struck out for the opposite shore. So metallic and smooth from above, the surface of the lake had been whipped by the wind into a flurry of miniature waves; after the salt of the Aegean, the water tasted oddly dry and sulphurous and lacking in savour. For the first half hour or so we talked as we swam, much as we would were we walking on dry land, interrupted only by spluttering when one of us swallowed a wave; but before long we lapsed into silence, while the white house in the distance, far from getting any nearer, appeared to have been mounted on casters and to be trundling ever further out of reach. Whereas Charles, an expert in these matters, employed a powerful crawl for much of the time, churning ahead like a motor-boat in a flurry of foam and flailing limbs and then waiting for me to catch up, I edged my way along in a dull suburban breast-stroke, occasionally rolling over onto my back when boredom or exhaustion set in. An hour and a half after setting out we dragged ourselves onto a log from which some rather surprised-looking boys were diving; behind some reeds the white house was shimmering still, looking not a great deal larger than it had from the opposite shore. We sat among the divers while the sun edged its way down towards the black volcanic rim of the hills; and then, reluctantly – since there was no other way to get back to our clothes and the car – we plunged back into the water and struck out for our tiny beach. As we swam it grew steadily darker, and the wind whipped at the miniature waves, tearing at their crests and lashing the spray in our eyes. The return journey seemed to go on for ever, but eventually we dragged ourselves up the beach and changed into our clothes behind a bush and I was able to see again; and that evening, though aching in every joint and hobbling from place to place like the bent-up inhabitant of a very old people's home, I had an intimation at least of what it might feel like to have scaled some stupendous peak or made one's first parachute jump.

Although Charles went down with a fever a few days later –

groaning horribly and lashing sweat in the middle of the night in a huge, deserted farmhouse we had been lent in the Campagna – I knew it would not be long before I was expected to climb into my bathing-costume once again in pursuit of further heroics. Swimming across the bay at La Spezia was, to my relief, ruled out by bad weather, and though I enjoyed the idea of Charles cleaving his way through what looked to be the entire Italian navy, I worried that he might be run down by an aircraft carrier, and that I would be left not only in charge of our rented car, but having to explain matters to his grieving wife and daughters; but that evening in a bay near Porto Venere – the waves thundering on the rocks below us, clouds scudding over the face of the moon, a solitary fishing boat pitching up and down like something in a maritime painting by Turner or a seventeenth-century Dutchman – his eye was caught by a reference to Byron and swimming and the words 'Vietato di Bagnare' on a notice-board pinned to an arch, and I knew that my fate was sealed. Next morning we made our way past the floating gin palaces in the harbour – aboard which tax exiles could be spotted lighting large cigars and turning the pages of the *Financial Times* while their wives patted the cushions and mounds of golden candy-floss impersonating hair, and white-clad crew members in knee-length shorts and knee-high socks bustled about the deck – and threaded our way through the arch and on to the black, forbidden rocks: Charles leading the way, towel and bathing-costume dangling from one hand, while I trailed unhappily behind, my accessories tucked invisibly under my arm so that if, as seemed very likely, my nerve cracked and I remained on dry land it would appear to any Italian who happened to be watching that I had never had any intention of swimming in the first place. The wind was howling as fiercely as it had the night before, the clouds were still racing over the sky, and boiling white horses were crashing over ragged, gleaming rocks. Not pausing for a moment, Charles climbed down onto a flat, horizontal rock over which the waves were running rather than pounding, and which seemed to offer the only feasible way of lowering oneself into the cauldron; and within a matter of seconds he was bobbing about among the jade-green waters like a plastic duck in a bath, his face the colour of a poppy, his hair streaming in the wind, and his voice, as intermittent as an elusive radio signal, urging me to join him. I shook my head and made semaphoring motions with my arms and, perched primly on a rock, waited for him to drag himself from the inferno. By now Charles was being watched by five or six Italians in overcoats, leaning against a railing on the rocks above; and then, overcome by curiosity and embar-rassment – for Charles was still issuing instructions from the deep – I suddenly clambered into my togs, hobbled short-sightedly to the edge of the flattish rock, the water washing in and out over my feet, and allowed myself to be carried out to sea on an outgoing wave. Tossing up and down among apparently mountainous seas, cliffs on three sides of us and the open sea beyond, I felt for a moment that I had wandered into the world of Shelley and Tre-lawney, a Dickensian clerk let loose among Regency swells; it was, in fact, a far less alarming swim than it looked from the shore, though I felt suitably heroic as we picked our way past the men in overcoats and back to where we had left the car – noticing as we passed that the menfolk aboard the gin palaces had abandoned the *Financial Times* for the telephone, while their wives were hard at work on their nails.

By now I had quite forgotten about Claude and Arcadia in the pursuit of literary swims. In the hills to the west of Bagna di Lucca a river, to the bottom of which Shelley had once sunk, was green with chemical dye, and the air was noxious with fumes; at Lerici, where he had drowned, our ankles were enmeshed in skeins of drifting lavatory paper; at Portofino, the home of Yeats Brown, of *Bengal Lancer* fame, the harbour was clogged with yet more gin palaces and the air was loud with the rustle of financial pages being turned, but we poked our way about the deserted oriental chambers of Castello Brown and swam off his tiny private beach at the foot of the cliff; and on our penultimate evening we found ourselves, for no good reason, swimming in the chill black waters of Lake Como, with the Alps looming icily above us and the chink of tables being laid for supper drifting over the water from the terrace of the old-fashioned, ochre-coloured hotel into which we had booked for the night. That evening over dinner – in between listening in to the conversation of a domineering Englishwoman in her seventies and her hen-pecked only son, an awkward figure of our age with trousers that reached up under his armpits and sticking-out ears, who carried his mother's bag to the table and trailed out after her when the meal was over, two dutiful paces behind – Charles asked me, with a sideways nod in the direction of the lake, whether I would be interested in swimming across it and back next morning. This, I felt, would be going too far, and bracing myself against a withering stare from those bright blue eyes and accusations of wetness, I told him I really couldn't face it. Rather to my surprise, he made no effort to convince me. Next morning, at about six, I heard a creaking sound as he got out of bed, followed by a splash as he dived from the terrace, and a moment later I had turned over and gone back to sleep. I got up at half-past eight, shaved, went down to the terrace, put off having my breakfast since I felt I should wait until Charles had come back, paced up and down and looked at my watch, put off breakfast once again, peered out across the lake through narrowed eyes like a retired admiral at Seaview, failed to see even a ripple in the distance, read my book in a chair, looked at my watch again and finally decided to go ahead and eat breakfast on my own, if only to kill the time. Ten o'clock passed, and then eleven, and still no sign of Charles. Once again I began to worry about how I would break the news to his sorrowing widow and daughters; and the domineering English-woman and her son, in whom I had confided my concern, shook their heads gravely as they gazed out across vast wastes of untroubled water to where a castle on the opposite shore jutted out a millimetre high. By now the terrace was crowded with people, clad in their Sunday best and forgathering for drinks in a stately, decorous manner: and then, quite suddenly, as if summoned to the fire escape, they all rushed to the edge of the terrace and peered down into the water. Seconds later a vast, juddering figure, mauve and blue with the cold, dragged itself dripping up the iron ladder and staggered to where I was sitting. He had made it to the other side and back, but only just, and for the next two or three hours he shivered and chattered with cold; and next day, after he had warmed up a bit, we took the overnight train to Paris, and our watery adventures were over.

CHAPTER ELEVEN

Scenes from a Garden Shed

SAFELY BACK in the suburbs, I resumed the lonely, agreeable routines of freelance life. By now my momentary repudiation of half-timbered semis and whirring lawn-mowers and the companionable cleaning of cars, and my ignoble fantasy of somehow combining the delights of domesticity with life in a South Ken broom cupboard and a rackety social life had faded into oblivion; but I retained to the full my long-standing fascination – half loving, half loathing – with the world of clerks and commuters, and the perils and pleasures of office life. Most of us spent the better part of our lives in these curious, airless places, and – however reluctant we might be to admit it – the office often provides us with the greater part of our gossip and social life, with romance and intrigue and adventure as well as with boredom, humiliation and misery; and yet, unlike their nineteenth-century and Edwardian forebears, contemporary novelists in particular seemed, all too often, to despise or ignore the office as a subject worthy of their attention, in much the same way as Oxford dons disdained the trappings of commerce while eagerly angling for Japanese subventions. Anxious to do what little I could to set the record straight, I put together an anthology on the subject, trawling through Sinclair Lewis and Roy Fuller and P.G. Wodehouse as well as through Dickens and Trollope for scenes from office life that were familiar to us all, from the first day in the new job to the sad oblivion of retirement.

Some years earlier Dennis Enright had asked me to write an essay about offices in a book he was editing for OUP about euphemisms and their deployment in everyday life. Exploring the dainty circumlocutions with which we sugar the pill of life between nine and five – 'He's a bit tied up at the moment', meaning 'He's completely paralytic, and there's no way he can come to the phone', or 'I'm afraid we're going to have to let you go' meaning 'You're fired!' – I described in some detail the forceful and often alarming figure of the human dynamo. My particular dynamo was based, to a large extent, on Carmen, with supporting evidence from the Chairman and André Deutsch and Norah Smallwood; and when, much to my alarm, she read my piece ('Darling it *is* all about me, isn't it?), far from resenting my ungentlemanly behaviour she made me promise that, if I ever did a book on office life, I would give it to her to publish – which I very happily did.

Every Tuesday I abandoned suburbia for the Marquis of Granby, where Dennis Enright held court, his hair still shooting from his head like the flame in an Olympic torch, a twisted, rueful smile and a raising of eyebrows illuminating his features as he picked his way through the baying, black-suited office escapees, his pipe in his hand and a canvas satchel of books on his shoulder. Les, alas, was seen no more, but his place had been taken by Ron Cortie, who entertained the company with lurid accounts of how he had hurled defiance at Mrs Smallwood, accompanied by much banging of the table and spilling of beer: occasional visitors included my old friend Weale, who joined Dennis in the rodding and tamping of pipes, laying out the tools of their trade on the table before us and taking appreciative sniffs at the other's baccy pouch; Jane, my travelling companion from Greece; Ian Whitcomb, on flying visits from California to see his mother in Wildcroft Manor, where life seemed exactly as it had been thirty years before, the fridge well stocked with Dring's frankfurters, the larder with Dring's steak and kidney pies, and the sideboard with the gin-and-its which Mrs Whitcomb so liberally dispensed; the novelists David Hughes and Alan Judd; Christopher Hawtree and Charles Sprawson; and – most welcome of all – Petra, who made it once a year on the boat from Chelsea Harbour until the service was discontinued. Every now and then some heretic – myself among them, in the early days – would suggest transferring the Tuesday lunch to The Lamb and Flag off Garrick Street, where the food was better and the lunchtime clerks less given to whinnying shrieks of mirth so loud that conversation in the tables around was sometimes brought to a halt and where I had, in my frenzied final days at Chatto, downed pint after pint of stout with the putty-faced girl in the purple hat, but Dennis argued that it would be folly to move since people knew where to find us. Hardly were the words out of his mouth than Vikram Seth, unexpectedly arrived from Delhi, materialised before us with an enormous orange rucksack on his back. Dennis turned to us with a triumphant smile, his forefinger slicing the air, and after that no more was heard about moving to The Lamb and Flag. Next week, in the Marquis, Dennis and I spotted three men with girths like Mr Pickwick trying – in vain – to have a whispered conversation in the middle of the bar, thwarted not by a baying clerk but by the hugeness of their bellies, which made it impossible for them to stand sufficiently close; another good reason, it seemed, for staying where we were.

Early on in my second year as a freelance my week acquired another fixed point, and one that gave me more pleasure than anything in my career so far. I had first come across Alan Ross of the *London Magazine* while practising my skills as London's most ineffectual literary agent, submitting the occasional story to the magazine, and noting on its return the editor's unusual promptness and the way in which, far from using a printed rejection slip, he would write some kindly, encouraging comment on the author's covering letter, or the back of an invitation to a publisher's party, or on a label pasted down on the back of someone else's postcard to him, the original writing often clearly visible underneath; but I didn't meet him until I was at the OUP, when I commissioned him to edit a volume on The Turf in my series of miniature anthologies. I went to see him one day in his office on the top floor of a white-stuccoed building in South Kensington, next door to a hair-dresser's shop. A debonair, raven-haired figure, with only a trace of badgerish grey, he looked far fitter and trimmer than many men half his age – not surprisingly, perhaps, since he had just come back from playing tennis in a nearby square, and was dressed in a white shirt and shorts rather than the literary man's more familiar uniform of corduroy and suede. He had the enthusiasm and the lack of pomposity and the refusal to seem serious, in company at least, of a comical and sophisticated undergraduate; with his darting, hesitant manner, his slight stammer and his large brown eyes, he was oddly reminiscent of some tropical night animal – a humorous and unusually articulate lemur, perhaps – while the pointed black beard of nautical cut which he was wearing at the time made him look surprisingly like one of the brighter members of the Russian royal family.

By the time The Turf had been delivered – bang on time, no doubt, for Ross is the most punctual and professional of writers – I had been lured away to Chatto in the bottom of Hugo's briefcase; but a year or two later I was in touch with him again when I found myself writing an account of how I had first sighted ffenella and her exciting-looking bosom on the storm-lashed deck of the Holyhead–Dun Laoghaire ferry. I knew that the *London Magazine* had a soft spot for slices of autobiography, however unimportant; and hardly had I put my 4000-odd words in the post before I received a saucy seaside postcard featuring a middle-aged golfer in plus fours and a blonde with breasts like barrage balloons, on the back of which the editor had written to say that he liked ffenella a good deal, and was eager to learn what happened next. Two further instalments followed – plus an invitation to the first of an innumerable series of lunches in the Italian restaurant over the road, each as agreeable as the last, in which Negronis were followed by a bottle of Lambrusco and the conversation flitted lightly over the follies of publishers and editors, and the peccadilloes of friends we had in common.

By now the *London Magazine* had moved from the top floor in 30 Thurloe Place to a garden shed at the back of the house; and, taking care not to arrive a minute before 1.15 – impatient lunchers who turned up early were sent away to walk round the block or cool their heels in the pub next door – I paid my first visit to a place of which, in the years to come, I was to become extremely fond, and would spend an agreeably large amount of time. To reach the garden shed one went straight through the main building, out through a glass-panelled door at the back, and down a flight of steps on which, in hard winters, unwary visitors would skid and tumble on the ice. From the top of the steps one looked out over grey garden walls and towering London plane trees to the vertiginous backs of shops and houses; in several windows elderly South Ken ladies could be spotted leaning uncomfortably back in grey mock-leather chairs while men in mauve shirts lowered egg-shaped driers over their heads or screwed their locks into plastic rollers. To the right of the shed, which filled up most of the garden, was a small, brightly-coloured border, which the editor tended while taking a break from his battles with the roll of Sellotape with which he pasted scissored-up chunks of galley on sheets of blue-lined layout paper; and immediately opposite the door of the shed grew an alarmingly fecund fig tree, the branches of which blotted out the sunlight within months of being hacked back once again. The shed itself was shaped like a cave, in that, apart from a narrow, cobweb-strewn strip of window at the back, all the windows were on the side facing the border and the garden wall, on the far side of which lady hairdressers could be sighted hurriedly dragging on cigarettes on the steps next door, casting nervous glances over their shoulders in case they were caught in the act.

The door to the garden shed was in the corner nearest to the steps; under the window, to the right of the door, were two functional teak desks, set back to back and divided from one another by a wall of reference books, topped up by a stapler, a book with blotting-paper pages interleaved with sheets of stamps in various denominations, a large blue address book and the troublesome roll of Sellotape, the saw-toothed cutter of which had been angrily abandoned and hurled into one of the three brimming waste-paper baskets that stood like sentinels alongside the desks. The desk nearest to the door was reserved for visitors, of whom there were many; that beyond belonged to the editor, who could keep an eye out for visitors as they picked – or stumbled – their way down the garden steps, while at the same time monitoring the progress of the cigarette-puffers next door. To the editor's left, along the window-ledge, stood a small wooden Indian, smartly clad in saffron, and an aerosol can of Pledge which the editor would, when the spirit moved him, spray about the surface of the desks, producing a duster from a drawer containing photographs of a naked lady hoovering in her small suburban home. Behind his chair, bulging fan-like from a cardboard box, were hundreds of used envelopes and jiffy bags, waiting to be pressed into service once again. Moving away from the window, into the blackness at the back of the cave, I made out three chairs and two tables, both covered with review copies of new books, a few of which would be sent to regular reviewers or, from time to time, to people who had written in asking if they could try their hand at reviewing a particular title or subject. In the far corner stood a red-fronted wardrobe, the top shelf of which was reserved for contributions which had been accepted but not yet sent to the typesetter, and were piled up in three wooden trays, one for stories, one for poems, and one – the most intriguing of all – for those miscellaneous oddities which gave the magazine its stylish, unpredictable flavour; and about its foot were randomly piled boxes containing current and recent issues of the magazine, headed notepaper and the brown envelopes in which copies of the magazine were sent to contributors or new sub-scribers. To the left of the doorway was a table covered with galleys, some of which were waiting to be cut up and pasted down, some corrected by their authors and on their way back to the typesetters; and, in the corner behind the door, beneath some unfamiliar photographs of Hitler taking tea on a terrace and late-Victorian nudes, was a filing cabinet weighed down by a teetering mound of unwanted review copies, waiting to be removed by the 'flogger'. The filing cabinet itself contained all the letters received by the firm over the past six months or so, filed away alphabetically: since Ross's replies were always hand-written on the back of whatever came to hand, and no copies were kept, this was, inevitably, a rather one-sided archive, but none of this prevented the librarian from the Brotherton Library at Leeds University from turning up in the garden shed every now and then with a cheque-book in his pocket and a large suitcase at the ready, in which he carried away the accumulated correspondence to be filed and catalogued for the use of literary scholars.

The back wall of the shed, where the darkness was most stygian, was covered by bookshelves containing file copies and back numbers of the magazine, their brightly-coloured spines glowing through the darkness, as well as the remaining stock of the books Ross had published under the imprint of London Magazine Editions. Every now and then a bookseller would order one of these, and an invoice would be written out in triplicate on a Ryman's invoice pad – deducting 35 per cent from the cover price as the bookseller's discount – and popped, with a copy of the book, into a brown envelope; it would then be placed on a chair with the rest of the day's post – rejected typescripts for the most part, sent back within a day or two of their arrival with a kindly note attached – which the editor would drop off at the local post office on his way home later in the afternoon. And pinned to the walls of the garden shed were photographs and drawings and posters which, like the magazine itself, reflected its editor's taste and interests: a photograph of Barbara Skelton and Cyril Connolly, side by side and in profile, gazing sternly out to sea; his dog Boppa brooding on which horse to back in the 2.15 at York; a Bardot-like blonde leaning over an altar rail in what looked like the Brompton Oratory, her miniskirt so brief that one bare buttock bulged below its hem; an erotic Indian painting in which an expressionless, almond-eyed couple were about to be linked together by an object the size of a giant marrow; photo-finishes of his horses, nose to nose on the line; and the familiar faces of his friends, Betjeman and Spender and Anthony Powell. As for the editor himself, he remained as I remembered him, an elegant, youthful, pleasingly stylish figure, though he had shaved off his pointed beard, and traded in his tennis shirt and shorts for a pink open-necked shirt, a cricketing sweater, a battered suede jacket and mustard-coloured cords.

Over the next few years I saw a good deal of Alan Ross and the garden shed. I became a regular reviewer for the magazine, contributing to which gave me far more pleasure than writing for anybody else, despite the modest cheques scrupulously sent out with a copy of the magazine on the day of publication; at Chatto I commissioned and edited an anthology, culled from back numbers,

to celebrate Ross's twenty-fifth year as editor; and for the *Spectator*
I wrote an anonymous profile of Alan, inspired by a missionary
feeling that neither he nor his magazine was as widely appreciated
as they deserved to be. Ross had edited the *London Magazine* since
1961, when he had taken it over from its founder, John Lehmann.
Whereas rival magazines like *Encounter* had employed secretaries
and switchboard operators and circulation managers and space
salesmen (work done, in the case of *Encounter,* by an elegant,
diffident poet named J. C. Hall, who was Keith Douglas's literary
executor, and made a welcome change, in my earliest days at
Collins, from the bottle-nosed men with ginger moustaches in
RAF blazers with whom I more usually consorted), Ross had run
the magazine single-handed, choosing and editing contributions,
dealing with the printer and the distributor, drumming up a tenuous trickle of advertisements, choosing the cover and pasting up the
pages. Occasional assistants and deputy editors came and went –
Charles Osborne, Hugo Williams, Christopher Hawtree and, most
important of all perhaps, his bearded collie Boppa, who also advised
him, with rather less success, in his daily battle with the bookies –
but the magazine was, and remains, the creation of one man, and a
reflection of his tastes and interests. Over the years Ross had
established himself as the last great magazine editor in the tradition
of John Lehmann or his friend and Sussex neighbour, Cyril Connolly, to whose much shorter-lived *Horizon* he had contributed as a
young writer recently demobbed, just as he had contributed poems
about the war at sea to Lehmann's *Penguin New Writing:* no one
had done more for writers, and for young writers in particular, than
this most modest and self-effacing of men, who had combined his
editorial work with a busy literary life of his own, writing poetry
(much under-rated), two vivid and often extremely funny volumes
of autobiography, cricketing lives and memoirs, children's books
and a long stint as the *Observer*'s much-admired cricket correspondent, doubling up as a foreign correspondent when his friend John
Gale began to suffer from persecution mania during the Algerian
War. The magazine had its team of regular contributors like Roy
Fuller, Gavin Ewart, Stephen Spender, Julian Symons, Peter Van-

sittart, Frank Tuohy, John Mellors and Digby Durrant, all of whom would, from time to time, join the editor for lunch in the Italian restaurant on the other side of the road: but although Ross was happy enough to publish the occasional famous name, what he really relished was discovering new and unpublished writers, and his enthusiasm for unearthing new talent was as sharp in his seventies as it had been when he started out. Not all his geese proved to be swans, but no other editor had a comparable gift as a talent scout. Paul Theroux, Jonathan Raban, William Boyd, Graham Swift, Derek Walcott, Peter Carey, Tony Harrison, Hilary Mantel and Ben Okri were among those who had been first published in the *London Magazine;* and although too many of its readers tended to be middle-aged or older, young writers eager to find their way into print continued to send in their work, so that the magazine retained its freshness and that essential mixture of the new and unexpected with the familiar and the dependable. What its readers enjoyed above all – apart from the stories and the poems and the book and art reviews – was Ross's eye for the unusual, for Charles Sprawson on von Cramm or James Kirkup on Japanese lavatories, and for stylish and suitably louche photographs and drawings; and whereas many writers and editors are puritanically narrow in their range of interests, the magazine – like the photographs pinned to the office wall – reflected not only Ross's dislike of lit. crit., his lack of interest in politics or abstract sociology, and his suspicion of the fashionable and modish, but his enviably wide enthusiasms: for racing and sport of almost every kind (he had played cricket and squash for Oxford before joining the Navy during the war); for India, where he grew up; for modern painting (at times he had funded the magazine, as well as the occasional racehorse, from the sale of Nolans and Drysdales picked up while covering cricketing tours of Australia in the fifties); for the female form, preferably unclothed, which he viewed with an expert eye; for that sexy seductive terrain – inhabited by the likes of Lucian Freud and Stephen Spender and Patrick Leigh Fermor and the pantherine Barbara Skelton – where bohemia and high society intersect. Nor was that the end of it, for, outdoing professional publishers at their own game – in terms of the look and the contents at least – he had simultaneously published a complementary list of books, including such autobiographical masterpieces as Julian Maclaren-Ross's *Memoirs of the Forties,* John Mellors' unjustly neglected and highly comical *Memoirs of an Advertising Man,* and T. C. Worsley's *Flannelled Fool,* as well as a series of tiny, slim-format books which looked as though they had been bound in old-fashioned grocer's brown paper, and had been modelled by Ron Costley on a successful series published in Paris.

Three or four times a year Alan and Charles Sprawson and I would meet for lunch, alternating between South Ken and somewhere closer to William IV Street. Not long after this had settled into a regular occurrence, Alan issued us both with salmon-and chocolate-coloured ties, with firm instructions that we were to wear them at our lunches. The ties, he told us, were leftovers from a cricket team he had captained in Sussex; they may well have originated in some disbanded prep school, since however ingeniously I tied the knot the longest end would never stretch below the third shirt button from the top, producing an inelegant, Bunterish effect, while the broad salmon and chocolate stripes were unusually repellent to the eye. Unwilling to be spotted in the office wearing this unusual clubman's tie, I put it on in the Chatto lavatory before hurrying away to an Italian restaurant at the bottom of St Martin's Lane, one hand clutching my shirt collar in case passers-by were dazzled by the stripes, and fainted away in the street. Rather to my disappointment, neither of my fellow-lunchers was wearing his club tie, and they flinched back in their seats as I advanced towards them, as though blinded by a headlight; while Alan was ordering the Negronis I unknotted the tie and stuffed it in my pocket, and no mention was made of it again. As for the lunches themselves, I was perfectly happy to remain an observer, chipping in with the occasional item of publishing gossip while the conversation moved from public school racquets players and Indian cricket teams to blue movies and sex shows in Hamburg or Barcelona – all subjects of mutual fascination to my fellow-lunchers about which I knew next to nothing. When it came to matters closer to home – who was publishing what, or who had been sacked by whom, or who was having an affair with whom – I relished, and shared, Ross's love of gossip, his sense of the absurd, his powers of exaggeration, and his clipped, conspiratorial summaries (more often than not amused and affectionate) of the follies of mutual friends, like the contributor who had, allegedly, been arrested in a public lavatory for 'cottaging', clad – or so the editor assured us – in a rubber frogman's suit and flippers, and brandishing a trident (the trident was, in fact, a flourish on my part). But Ross had, as I soon discovered, a low threshold of boredom, so that over-long anecdotes would be greeted by a glazing of the eyes and the impatient shuffling of cutlery, unnervingly reminiscent of Norah Smallwood in a rage; and nothing could be more damning than his staccato, undertone dismissal of those he considered fraudulent or over-rated ('He's no good, is he?').

Exactly a year after I left Chatto, Alan fell ill, and he asked me if I would 'mind the shop' while he was in hospital. Apart from opening the post and sending back most of each day's offerings and dealing with new subscribers and marking up copy for the printers and sending out proofs – none of which was too alarming – minding the shop also involved pasting up the next issue, work of a kind I'd never done before. Alan had chosen what was to go into that issue: the problem was to fit the material – some of it set full out on the page, some of it double-column, some of it in the form of photographs and drawings – into 160 pages without too many loose ends and aching white spaces. Help was at hand in the convivial form of the novelist David Hughes, an old friend of Alan's whose first job after leaving Oxford had been as John Lehmann's assistant on the old *London Magazine*. Armed with some layout paper, a pair of scissors, the roll of Sellotape and an armful of galleys, I set out for David's house in Kennington, where he cleared a space on the kitchen table and opened the first of several bottles of wine designed, he assured me, to help matters along and clarify our every thought. Casting his mind back to the middle-1950s, David came up with the curious idea that we should start at the back – where the complicated, double-column setting was found – and work our way slowly towards the front, where the problem-free stories and poems and longer articles held sway; and so, helped on by generous draughts of wine, we began to snip out and paste up the book reviews, starting with the last paragraph of the 'Special Notices' and, almost imperceptibly, inching our way towards the front. Every now and then a column or – more dangerous still – a tiny snippet of scissored-up galley would be spotted, with a terrible cry of agony, lying under the table, and we would have to unpick the work of the last half hour; but in the end the job was done, and we set off through the darkness, like two triumphant children, to show the editor our handiwork and receive his approbation. Propped up in bed, he seemed less impressed than we had hoped: 'You *are* a couple of chumps,' was his only comment when we explained how we had – quite unnecessarily, it seemed – pasted up the whole thing back to front.

For the next few weeks I had the garden shed to myself; and for a year or two after Alan's return I would come in once or twice a week, and hold the fort when he was on holiday. His routine was unvarying and – or so it seemed to me – entirely agreeable. Every morning he walked to the garden shed from his tiny mews house in Elm Park Lane, sometimes stopping off at the post office in the Old Brompton Road if the supply of stamps was running low, arriving in the office between half past eleven and twelve. The post was dealt with before lunch, interrupted only by telephone calls from the printer or from friends and contributors, and – if I happened to be in the office, facing him across our two desks with the barricade of books between – by an occasional flurry of gossip, his voice a low and comical mutter, his eyes bulging in their sockets at moments of particular excitement or hyperbole. After lunch in the Italian restaurant over the way he strolled back to the office sometime after three, a large cigar between his lips, and put in another couple of hours before gathering up the post and setting off home again. Despite a languid, self-deprecating manner, he was – and still is – formidably quick and efficient, knowing at once what he wanted and what would or wouldn't work: high technology in the garden shed was restricted to a dusty portable typewriter (Ross himself had never learned to type), a pair of scales, a pair of scissors, a Bakelite telephone with a KEN prefix and the snarled-up role of Sellotape, and I relished the ease with which, single-handed, he produced the most elegant and punctual and handsomely produced of literary magazines in an alien world of VDUs and fax machines and desktop publishing. After twenty-five years bemoaning my lot and chafing against the tedium and the strain and the restraints of office life and ever-inflating bureaucacy, my association with the *London Magazine* and its editor seemed, in publishing terms, like a glimpse of Paradise; and there was nothing in my working life of which I was prouder, or in which I had more pleasure.

The only other branch of publishing in which I was still involved, and which gave me a similar if more sporadic start of pleasure, occupied a very different segment of the literary firmament while sharing its engaging mixture of amateurism and efficiency. I had first become aware of R. S. Surtees, the mid-Victorian hunting novelist, in Bumpus's bookshop in Baker Street, where I was filling in an odd half hour playing truant from the office up the road where I was employed as a trainee advertising man. Desperate to escape from the boredom of office life into the world of Victorian novels, I had worked my way through the whole of Dickens and a good deal of Thackeray: Trollope seemed thin gruel to an eighteen-year-old – since then I have come much to prefer his subtler shades of grey and his handling of women and love to Dickens's flamboyant monsters and angelic china dolls – but I was drawn at once to Leech's gloomy, cross-hatched line engravings in the tiny World's Classics edition *of Mr Sponge's Sporting Tour*, in which whip-waving huntsmen dragged their recalcitrant steeds out of ditches while the rain sheeted down and the rest of the hunt streamed away in the distance, and dubious 'theatrical' ladies from the demi-monde in ringlets and low-cut dresses puffed small cigars and swigged glasses of champagne in draughty baronial halls; and when I read the book itself I liked it equally well. Surtees was neither an elegant stylist nor a subtle moralist: but he was brutally funny about the humbuggery and the double-dealing of horse-copers and hard-drinking, bottle-nosed, tight-fisted country squires and tuft-hunting mamas in search of suitable sons-in-law; and although I remained as ignorant and as over-awed as ever by hooves and fetlocks and grooms and stirrups, and tended to skip or skim the hunting scenes, I delighted in the similarity between Surtees's bleak, hard-bitten world and my grandfather's gaunt Gloucestershire farmhouse with its fox's head pinned in the hall and neatly-laid-out lines of highly polished boots and salty whiff of saddle soap. Partly from missionary zeal and partly from an ineffectual urge to irritate those of my friends who were reading English at university – many of whom seemed never to have read anything beyond their set books, dutifully parroting what passed as conventional wisdom – I urged my hero's claims as one of the greatest novelists in the language: few of my friends were convinced, but I went on pressing his case all the same, half angry that so vigorous and so vivid a writer should be neglected or disdained, half-dreading – as lone voices always do – that my cause would be taken up at last, and its prophet brushed aside in the rush to acclaim its merits.

Unlike those of Dickens and Trollope, Surtees's novels – and *Mr Sponge's Sporting Tour* and *Mr Facey Romford's Hounds* in particular – seemed neither to improve nor deteriorate as I aged around them, and I remained as faithful to them as ever. Eager to advance his cause, I commissioned a new biography while I was at OUP (an unnecessary act of piety, since there was little to say or add) and wrote about him in the *Spectator* and in an introduction to a World's Classics reissue of *Facey Romford,* defiantly quoting Virginia Woolf as well as Siegfried Sassoon in unexpected support of my views.

A year or two after these excitements, I was sitting quietly in my office in William IV Street, gazing absent-mindedly at the silver globe slowly revolving on top of the Coliseum, when George rang to say that a gentleman called Sir Charles Pickthorn was seated downstairs: he hadn't an appointment, but would be very grateful if I could spare him a moment or two. Although I had never heard of Sir Charles, anything seemed preferable to bending my mind to the small print in a contract, so I asked George if he'd like to send him up. That done, I fell back in my chair and gazed once more at the revolving ball, for I knew it would take Sir Charles at least five minutes to grapple with the lunging lift gates and inch his way up to the second floor; after which I made my way along the winding prep school corridor to find my visitor, looking dishevelled after his struggle with the lift.

Sir Charles was a lean, brick-faced man in his late fifties who could well have stepped from the pages of Surtees were it not for his wearing, in place of a wasp-waisted hacking jacket and hunting boots, a dusty-looking black pinstripe suit, a white shirt and a sombre-looking tie. He had a nut-crackerish kind of face, very Victorian in its cast of feature, white hair and Sprawsonian blue eyes, permanently narrowed against the smoke from a succession of cigarettes that dangled from his bottom lip, each lit from the remains of the last, the ash of which had settled in a fine drizzle on his jacket lapels and waistcoat; a fawn gaberdine mackintosh was hooked over one arm. He was, he explained – settling himself down into the white wickerwork chair on the far side of my desk – the founder and chairman of the Surtees Society, which had been set up to republish the complete works of Surtees in facsimile form: it was, as I probably knew, extremely hard to find complete sets in second-hand bookshops, and the Society, sensibly emulating an eighteenth-century bookseller rather than a modern speculative publisher, was issuing the novels on a subscription basis, soliciting advance orders from members of the Society but not pressing ahead with printing and binding until they had amassed a sufficient number to cover the production costs. Auberon Waugh, Lord Blake, Rebecca West, Michael Wharton and Enoch Powell were among those who had agreed to write appropriate introductions. He had heard of my interest in Surtees; would Chatto be interested in selling copies through the trade – through bookshops, in other words – leaving Sir Charles and the Society to deal with members' orders from his home in Somerset, where the books were stored in a waterproof barn?

Nothing came of our possible collaboration – Sir Charles's sumptuous reprints, with ornate gold blocking on the front cover as well as the spine, and a list of subscribers, many of them fellow-baronets or rustic peers, printed in the back, were far removed from Chatto in its new and most recent incarnation – but a year or two later, when I was freelance once again, Sir Charles wrote to ask if I would be interested in joining the committee of the Surtees Society. Shortly after his visit to William IV Street I had joined the Society, receiving a numbered cloakroom ticket and regular news of forth-coming publications in exchange for a modest lifetime's subscrip-tion; but apart from writing in from time to time to suggest a party for members, or an outing to Surtees's home in County Durham, I had done nothing to mark myself out. A generous, impulsive character, Sir Charles brushed aside my modest disclaimers – my knowledge of publishing would be of great benefit to the Society, he assured me – and ordered me to report for duty at the Garrick Club the following Tuesday evening, where a committee meeting would be followed by a dinner of pheasant and claret. A day later some minutes arrived through the post – handwritten, with a good deal of proposing and seconding and committee members putting one another up for re-election, plus familiar details of stock levels and rates of sale and costs of reprinting another 500 of *Jorrocks* or binding up the remaining stock of *Ask Mama,* all set out with a clarity, commonsense and occasional comicality that made a conventional publisher's paperwork look dull and obscure by comparison. From the names at the bottom of the paper I learned that my fellow committee members – about ten of us in all – included a peer, a Tory MP, a lady Master of Fox Hounds who had written the life of Beryl Markham, my old friend Michael Wharton, an architectural historian, a member of the Surtees family, and the owner of a well-known bookshop-cum-publishing house in Victoria, specialising in books about horses, a roly-poly figure in his eighties, clad in a black serge suit and black boots, wonderfully redolent of the shrewd and dusty world of pre-war publishing. From the minutes themselves I learned that an attempted coup by a Somerset major and a lady committee member had been beaten off by Sir Charles, and that the two plotters had been banished from the committee: I was replacing one of the rebels, and a retired naval officer the other.

All this sounded promising enough, and though I dreaded the moment when the lady MFH quizzed me about fetlocks or the Quorn, exposing me at once as a townie and an impostor, I felt sure that Michael Wharton knew even less about such matters than I did, and that we would be able to shelter one another like orphans in a storm. Punctual as ever, I arrived at the Garrick on the dot of half-past six, and was directed by the porter to the green dining-room at the back, opposite the lavatories. The room had been cleared, the dining-tables placed end to end and covered with well-ironed white tablecloths to form an enormous bar, loaded down with bottles of champagne, behind which two white-coated barmen were busily polishing glasses and laying them out in lines. Life was improving by the minute, and my anxieties about snaffles and the Vale of White Horse drained away as I watched the barmen's wrists rotate among the glasses, though I was momentarily puzzled by the numbers of glasses and the quantity of drink that the committee members were expected to consume before moving on to the pheasant and the claret. Sir Charles was, I felt sure, brisk and punctual in his dealings, and I would have expected us, by now, to be grappling with the balance sheet or brooding over how many copies to print of *Plain or Ringlets:* yet the room was empty of weatherbeaten, bandy-legged men in mustard-coloured tweeds and hacking jackets, let alone of a lady MFH with a fox's head pin at her collar or Sir Charles with his eager lope and a cigarette glued to his lower lip. I asked one of the barmen whether I had come to the right place: he seemed never to have heard of Surtees or his Society – unsurprising in an Englishman, let alone an Italian – but suggested I fill in the time with a glass or two of champagne. One glass was followed by another, after which the genial barman suggested I should try a third; suddenly fearful that I had got the wrong day or the wrong club, I scrabbled through the minutes Sir Charles had sent me in search of the final clause giving details of the next meeting, only to find that all was as it should be. Eager to impress my new colleagues with my rural qualities, I had climbed into the same wasp-waisted, tubular-trousered bramble-bush tweed suit that I had worn, years earlier, to tea with John Sparrow, and a combination of heat, panic and champagne caused me to break out in a tropical sweat, misting up my specs and pasting my shirt to my chest in unseemly transparent swathes. I was halfway through my fourth glass of champagne when – much to my relief – a suitably red-faced man in a chalk-stripe suit strolled into the room and was helped to a glass of champagne. This was undoubtedly another committee member, most probably the peer or the Tory MP, so I strolled over to him, looking as debonair as I could with steamed-up specs and a shirt like a sodden sail, and introduced myself as a fellow-Surteesian. At this he looked quite blank, and when I repeated my enquiry he asked, 'What in heaven's name is a Surteesian?' Utterly unnerved by now, I unburdened all my problems to him, explaining how I had recently been appointed to the committee, how I had arrived not a moment too early or too late, how I had been directed to the green room by an authoritative-looking porter, and how I had – for the past quarter of an hour or so – found myself drinking glass after glass of champagne with two men in white coats in an otherwise empty room. 'Ah, you want the pink room,' he said, as if talking to an imbecile child; and taking me by the upper arm of my bramble-bush suit he steered me to the door and pointed me in the direction of a room that lay between the green room and the lavatories, from which I could hear, like the distant baying of hounds, Sir Charles's voice from the head of the table, and an occasional rumble as a committee member raised a point of order. My guide returned to the green room, where other red-faced men were beginning to gather, leaving me standing outside the pink room door like a schoolboy awaiting a summons. I must have remained there for at least half a minute, pretending to examine the Spy prints on the wall whenever another red-faced man sauntered by and wondering whether I mightn't do better to make a run for it and write a grovelling apology next day invoking a sudden bereavement or a breakdown on British Rail; but eventually Sir Charles's peroration died away, followed by a rustling of papers as the committee prepared to move on to the next item on the agenda, and I screwed up my courage and knocked. 'COME IN!' cried Sir Charles in unusually forceful tones; and feeling far more like Uriah Heep than Jack Spraggon or Lord Scamperdale, I oozed round the door in a fluster of apologies, and prepared to be introduced.

The committee members were seated round a long and highly polished table, with books and papers spread before them: Sir Charles – who, as I soon gathered, did most of the talking – was standing at the head of the table, peering at papers over a pair of gold-rimmed half-moon specs, his eyes screwed up against the smoke. He introduced me with merciful brevity as I peered down on a ring of unknown faces, and suggested that perhaps the time had come for a drink. Some ten minutes later, with my specs demisted and my shirt dried out and a glass or two of claret coursing through my veins, I began to enjoy myself, and even, at times, to chip in; and after the papers had been cleared away, the table laid, and the meal brought in, and the faces of my colleagues were no longer a baffling blur, life as a committee member seemed quite as agreeable as I had hoped it would when I clambered into my bramble-bush suit and made my way to Mortlake Station earlier in the evening.

As was made immediately and mercifully apparent, all the important decisions were made by Sir Charles, who proved himself an eccentric but highly efficient publisher, reissuing facsimile works by Thackeray and Kipling and the Brer Rabbit books as well as the works of Surtees, and making a modest profit as well. Twice a year we gathered in his house in Chelsea for a meeting followed by dinner. Sir Charles moved among us with a bottle, cigarette dangling from his lower lip and sprinkling its ash down his shirt-front, as we discussed the cost of reprinting *Mr Sponge* and whether we should publish the life of Jack Mytton, the Shropshire squire who set fire to his nightshirt to cure the hiccups, or where we should hold our Christmas dinner; and afterwards we trooped down to the basement, where Sir Charles opened bottle after bottle of vintage claret with the abandon of an undergraduate, a lock of white hair falling down across his forehead as he wrestled with the cork between his knees. Surplus diners were seated at an ironing-board adjacent to the dining-room table, and Lady Pickthorn served up delicious if unusual meals of, on one occasion, Irish stew with croissants. Facey Romford and Soapy Sponge would certainly have approved; and for those of us who relished the tangential and the marginal – in approach, if not in content – the kind of publishing practised in Hobury Street, like that in the garden shed, was infinitely congenial.

A perk of the freelance life is that one can up sticks at short notice, and when Jonathan Barker – an occasional visitor to the Marquis of Granby – rang from the British Council to ask if I would like to spend two days in a castle near Munich, I hurriedly agreed. The Council was running a two-day conference for Bavarian civil servants, during the course of which a team of high-powered experts on subjects ranging from sewage disposal to the siting of airports was to be flown across from Britain to take part in a series of seminars. Would I be prepared to wind up the proceedings on what my graver, more responsible fellow-citizens referred to as a 'lighter note'? I could talk about whatever I liked, and when I suggested national stereotypes, and the ways in which fogs and bowler hats and mustachioed Frenchmen in matelot shirts lingered on in the minds of foreigners and cartoonists a whole generation after they had vanished off the face of the earth, both Jonathan and his equivalent in Munich seemed to think that a good enough idea; and a day or two later I found myself peering out on a grey and black landscape of snow and pine trees as the plane inched its way down to Munich airport.

The castle in question was a square-cut, mediaeval affair, with a drawbridge and blue-and-white chequerboard flags fluttering above the portcullis. Inside – rather to my disappointment – was a series of up-to-date conference rooms, complete with fitted carpets and spotlights let into the ceiling and tubular chairs set out in rows; and as I joined my fellow-delegates for our opening seminar at nine o'clock next morning ('Whither the Nation State?') I found myself confronted by an army of benign-looking Bavarian civil servants, each of them wearing a carefully trimmed and sculpted beard, a raspberry- or chocolate-coloured tweed jacket and shoes with tractor soles, and clutching in one hand a mug of milky coffee and in the other the programme of events for the next two days, with my forty-minute paper bringing up the rear. I had given little thought to what I was going to say, on the grounds that I could surely bluff my way through cold baths and watery veg without much difficulty; but brought face to face with these kindly, anxious-looking men, I felt a sudden spasm of guilt, and as the opening speaker clambered onto the podium and began to address the conference in a low, important drone, I sat scribbling at the back, putting my thoughts in order.

The proceedings were all in English, and although the civil servants put their British equivalents to shame when it came to the mastery of foreign tongues, we soon found ourselves inhabiting the airless, over-bright world of Euro-good will and the community of nations, in which language is reduced to semaphoric simplicity, with an abundance of boisterous good humour and not much room for innuendo or ambiguity. Eager to prove myself a serious citizen, I spoke up boldly during the more intelligible debates, chairing the odd discussion group and unravelling syntax when the civil servants tied themselves up in linguistic knots, only playing truant when the sun on the snow was too bright to resist or a paper was pending on 'The Future of Waste Disposal', a subject on which I had shamingly little to add.

Towards the end of the opening day we were addressed on the theme of economic integration by the long-serving Brussels correspondent of a leading London newspaper. An incompetent linguist myself, I have always admired those seemingly diffident souls who speak languages fluently but in such a way that they sound as though they are still speaking English, and held in deep suspicion show-offs who, whenever they stumble on a foreign word, even when speaking English, insist on pronouncing it as a foreigner would, the 'r's accompanied by guttural rasping sounds and much clearing of the throat and the 'u's impeccably fluted. The bearded Brussels correspondent was very much of this school, seizing every opportunity to introduce a French or Italian word and taking particular care with his German pronunciation, given the company we were keeping; and when the seminar was over and it was time to circulate, I approached him with the trepidation the monoglot Englishman always feels when faced by a polyglot man of the world. He seemed a friendly soul, and since he was staying in the same hall of residence, but had no idea where it was, I offered to escort him there. As we strolled across the drawbridge I told him that although the rooms were comfortable enough, no soap had been provided, and that he should ask the woman in reception for a bar of soap before she went off duty for the night. At this the Brussels correspondent stopped hard in his tracks, and – peering through the gloaming – I saw that he had turned quite pale. 'But,' he asked me, visibly shaken, 'how do I ask for soap?' Overcome by pity for his plight, I took him to reception, and after a brief display of mime – rubbing my face with the palms of my hands, and making stirring movements under the armpits – I extracted a bar of soap and presented it to my new friend, who hurried nervously away in the direction of his room.

After such excitements, my end-of-term address seemed sadly anti-climactic. Fogs and bowler hats got a mention, but the tone of my address was, perhaps, more melancholy than the Council might have wished. I remembered how, as children, we had been brought up to think of the English as a clean and orderly people, superior in such ways to the Latins in particular, whose lavatories and drinking water had to be treated with the gravest caution; and yet, when I thought of England, for all my fondness for it, I conjured up a dispiriting vision of brimming-over waste-paper bins, and screwed-up crisp packets perched on unemptied ashtrays, and overweight families in shiny black shell suits hatched with chevrons of lime and purple tucking into cardboard trays of chips, and 'out of order' notices sellotaped to finger-marked sheets of plate glass at the counters of post offices or railway stations. My catalogue of woes appeared to delight the Bavarian civil servants, who clustered keenly about me after it was over, clucking sympathetically and patting me on the back; after which it was time to return to the land of litter, and the company of friends.

* * *

And so life ebbed away, almost imperceptibly, from one day to the next. Every morning I watched the old woman in the house opposite edge her car, very slowly, out of the garage, with a good deal of revving and clouds of smoke; every Tuesday I met Dennis and Ron in the pub, with whomever else chanced along; every weekday I made Petra her packed lunch to take to the office, and longed for her voice on the phone. Jemima grew ever more languid, peering out through a haze of smoke and a loop of hair like Lauren Bacall's, whiling away the hours at St Paul's playing snooker in the pub and her time at university cooking salmon and asparagus, taking baths in the middle of the day and slinking about the house in a tiny dressing-gown and a towel on her head, a cigarette in her cocked hand and her face encrusted with lime-green mud; Hatty, a more Amazonian figure, strode purposefully from room to room in hob-nailed boots, slicing up cloves of garlic and prefacing every word with a ' flaming' ('Why does no one wear any clothes in this flaming house?' was a familiar cry after an outburst of mass tribal dancing); and once a week at least Petra sprang out from behind the kitchen door with a coronary-inducing cry, causing me to stagger back like one electrocuted. Work came in, as it always does, in fits and starts; Petra kept us afloat, and my bank statements – held at arm's length, like an explosive device or food that has gone off – were stuffed unread in a drawer after lying for weeks, unopened, on the dresser in the hall. Our life remained, in material terms, as precarious and as hand-to-mouth as it had been when we started out together twenty-five years before, but we told ourselves – quite rightly – that we were luckier than many in having a roof above our heads, and in the company of our friends.

All this time my book remained unwritten. My delivery date flashed by, like a station glimpsed from a hurrying train, and two anniversaries were upon me with little written other than the occasional memoir in the *London Magazine*; ever more racked by guilt, I took to dodging behind pillars whenever I sighted my editor, the most patient and tolerant of men, advancing through the throng at a party. And then, to make matters worse, I was commissioned – unexpectedly and at relatively short notice – to write the authorised life of Cyril Connolly. Six months after signing the contract I found myself, far from the suburbs and my familiar, soothing routines, in the library at the University of Tulsa. I had long admired Connolly for his wit and his romanticism, for the accuracy with which he evoked feelings and states of mind common to us all, and his terrible honesty about his own, all too familiar, weaknesses and failings. After his death, his widow had sold his library and his papers to Tulsa University; which was why I found myself, lonely and homesick, crunching through the snow from my monk-like cell on campus to a neo-Gothic library where Connolly's papers were housed. For six weeks I barely left the campus, filling notebook after notebook in a pencilled scribble so frenzied that my second finger came up in a blister, immersing myself in Etonian love affairs and London literary life in the 1940s while the snow melted from the roofs of the clapboard houses and the sky turned from grey to blue and the first fuzz of blossom appeared on the trees. I had reached the age of fifty, yet I had never been alone for so long before; and although the Tulsans I met were hospitality incarnate, time weighed heavily once the Special Collections Library had closed at five, and I was banished from Balliol and Bedford Square, and the company of Desmond MacCarthy and Sligger Urquhart, Patrick Kinross and Logan Pearsall Smith. Every evening I swam twenty lengths before eating supper in the university canteen, which closed its doors at seven; I traded in my television set for an ironing board, preferring a well-pressed shirt to an evening skipping channels; from time to time a culture-loving Tulsan would invite me to dinner or to listen to a visiting string quartet, but so early that I found myself back in my cell at half-past eight, with the evening still stretching ahead. Most evenings, though, I made my way back to the main library, which remained open till two in the morning, saluting as I passed an oil painting of a former President of the university, a shiny, smiling, salesmanlike figure in rimless glasses and fluorescent academic robes, looking much as I imagined my hero, George F. Babbitt, and more redolent of *Horse Feathers* than of dons on high table; and there I settled down to do some background reading among Connolly's friends and contemporaries: Maclaren-Ross, and Denton Welch, and Barbara Skelton's hilarious first novel, *A Young Girl's Touch*, and, best of all, T. C. Worsley's *Behind the Battle*, an account – half comical, half tragic – of his exploits as an ambulance driver and amateur sleuth during the Spanish Civil War.

But although I was devouring a book a day, quite apart from the letters and journals in the Connolly collection, I had to find other ways of filling in long, dark winter evenings on the prairie. I was thousands of miles from home, yet all about me were the footprints of my friends, and traces of my past. I spent my days reading postcards to Palinurus from Alan Ross at the *London Magazine*, or letters from Leigh Fermor, written from his house in Kardamyli; Connolly's letters from Eastbourne were redolent with the scenes of my childhood, with Hope Gap and Birling Gap and Seaford shopkeepers like Mary Ranger, the second-hand bookseller, or Mr Rolph the fishmonger, whose wares he recommended to Baron Philippe de Rothschild; Tulsa had bought all André Deutsch's papers, and somewhere in the stacks were memos and letters I had written or received over twenty years before. The omens were propitious; of time there seemed no end; I had no excuses for delay. One evening, after supper, I exiled myself among the scientific reference books in an under-populated wing of the library, opened a brand-new lined notebook with the university's crest emblazoned in gold on the front, took my pen from my jacket pocket and leaned portentously back in my chair. 'One day is much like another for the desk-bound office worker', I wrote; and as I edged my way, very slowly, towards the bottom of the page, Oklahoma dropped away and I found myself back in my little grey room in William IV Street, listening to the cries from the floor below, watching the Post Office workers opposite gazing back across the street, wondering how soon I could decently slip away; dreaming of home, dreaming of Arcadia.

Envoi

SUMMER RAIN: 1975

It rained all afternoon, drumming in waves
Upon the windowpane. The garden was
    underwater green,
Our room a dark and yellow cave.
My father stood, said nothing, looking out.
I thought: he's suddenly turning grey;
    it's time we spoke,
Threading what stayed unsaid together,
Spelling out love before it's too late:
But I stood there as stiff as a stranger,
And the words that I wished I could say
Twisted and died in my throat.
And then it was raining no more:
The room was a shimmer of light,
The garden steamed in the sun,
And the birds burst out in a scatter of song.
Why don't we walk, my father said;
And silent still, we wandered out.

Lightning Source UK Ltd.
Milton Keynes UK
UKOW05f2350280617
304254UK00001B/76/P